'As citizens become more individualis
neighbourhood ties are weakened. This book shows how the
weakening of communities is related to the weakening of respect.'
Bob Holman

'This book will make you think again about the subtleties and
complexities of community life. It offers cogent and well-evidenced
explanations of how informal interactions at local level affect
people's relationships and quality of life. The authors' thoughtful,
yet practical approach supplies the reader with plenty of ideas for
actions and policies that could make a real difference for
generations to come.'
Alison Gilchrist, Community Development Foundation

'At a time when the debate about 'Respect' is becoming ever more
esoteric on the one hand and politically loaded on the other, here is
a book which not only offers an astute analysis of the nature and
effects of 'respect', as it is lived out in the day to day lives of
ordinary people, but also points to ways in which it might be
sustained and, even more ambitiously, restored.'
Professor John Pitts, Editor of the Community Safety Journal

Respect in the Neighbourhood

Why Neighbourliness Matters

Edited by Kevin Harris

Russell House Publishing

First published in 2006 by:
Russell House Publishing Ltd.
4 St. George's House
Uplyme Road
Lyme Regis
Dorset DT7 3LS

Tel: 01297-443948
Fax: 01297-442722
e-mail: help@russellhouse.co.uk
www.russellhouse.co.uk

© Kevin Harris and the various contributors

British Library Cataloguing-in-publication Data:
A catalogue record for this book is available from the British Library.

ISBN: 978-1-905541-02-7

Typeset by TW Typesetting, Plymouth, Devon
Photographs: page 53 and cover – Kevin Harris; page 47 – Jan Steyaert
Printed by Bell & Bain, Glasgow

About Russell House Publishing

RHP is a group of social work, probation, education and youth and community work practitioners and academics working in collaboration with a professional publishing team.

Our aim is to work closely with the field to produce innovative and valuable materials to help managers, trainers, practitioners and students.

We are keen to receive feedback on publications and new ideas for future projects.

For details of our other publications please visit our website or ask us for a catalogue. Contact details are on this page.

Contents

'The organic life of a neighborhood, created by the persons who live in a particular geographic area, is always a fragile reality. A neighborhood's character is determined by a host of factors, but most significantly by the kinds of relationships that neighbors have with each other. A neighborhood is not a sovereign power – it can rarely write its own agenda. Although neighborhoods differ in a host of ways, a healthy neighborhood has some sort of cultural and institutional network which manifests itself in pride in the neighborhood, care of homes, security for children, and respect for each other.'

(Kromkowski, 1976)

'Once you leave behind such class concerns as how to balance the peas on the back of a fork, all the important rules surely boil down to one: *remember you are with other people; show some consideration.*'

(Truss, 2005)

About the Authors

Aydin Mehmet Ali was born in Cyprus and came to the UK to seek refuge from war in the 1960s. She is an international education consultant, project manager and award-winning writer, specialising in multiculturalism, bilingualism and anti-racist work with the Turkish speaking communities in London. She has worked as an assistant director of education and advisor to numerous Local Education Authorities and voluntary and statutory organisations, advisor to Ken Livingstone, London Mayor, and Chair of Hackney Action for Racial Equality. Aydin has set up numerous empowering projects as an intellectual activist over the last 30 years targeting young people and women. Recent projects include *The Way we Are*, a photographic project for Cypriot young people across the divided island, *Talking About Barriers* a film project between African-Caribbean and Turkish speaking young people in London, arts summer schools for Turkish speaking young people at London Metropolitan University and *Let's go to University*, a project between four LEAs and three universities to raise aspirations amongst Turkish speaking young people. Her articles and literary work have appeared in numerous journals and anthologies. Publications include *Turkish Speaking Communities and Education: No Delight* and *Pink Butterflies/Bize Dair,* a collection of bilingual short stories and poems.

Jacqueline Barnes is Professor of Psychology at Birkbeck, University of London, based at the Institute for the Study of Children, Families and Social Issues. After a BSc in Psychology from University College London and a Master's degree at the University of Wisconsin she gained a PhD in Psychology from London University in 1983. Research in London on young children's behaviour problems was followed by research at Harvard in the USA concerned with the influence of communities, returning then to London University. Her current research interests are: evaluation of early intervention programmes related to children's health and development and parenting; community characteristics and the environment as they relate to family functioning and children; and the use of child care in the early years. Professor Barnes is one of the directors of the national evaluation of the UK government's Sure Start local programmes initiative.

Philip Connolly is the former Campaigns and Communications Manager for a national charity promoting walking and an improved walking environment. He has written two reports *Liveable London* based upon the experiences of older and disabled Londoners and *Safer School Journeys: A DIY Guide for the School Community*. He is one of the UK's leading experts on walking and specialises in ease of movement for the disabled, recreational and cultural uses of public space, crime in or arising from public space and road safety. He is a Director of *Heelgood Factors* a consultancy working to deliver streets and public spaces that are supportive of outdoor community life.

Kevin Harris is a community development consultant who focuses on the ways in which people communicate and interact in neighbourhoods. Previously with Community Development Foundation, Kevin has contributed extensively towards the understanding of local residents' experience, having worked in various neighbourhoods and been an advisor to several government departments. As the author of numerous reports and articles he has contributed to the literature of community development, social inclusion and community cohesion. Kevin runs the *Local Level* consultancy and is the author of the Neighbourhoods weblog, which he established in 2003.

Liz Richardson went into practically applied research in LSE Housing in 1994, where she co-ordinated the research programme between 1998 and 2006. She currently works in the Institute for Political and Economic Governance at the University of Manchester. Her work has focused on understanding the efforts of residents and practitioners to tackle problems in disadvantaged neighbourhoods. She has been involved in policy development on neighbourhood renewal, housing market renewal and sustainable housing growth, neighbourhood management, and community engagement. Her work includes co-directing a national experimental project trying to stimulate and facilitate community self-help in low-income neighbourhoods.

Jan Steyaert is professor of Social Infrastructure and Technology at the Fontys University of Professional Education in Eindhoven, Netherlands and visiting research fellow at University of Bath, UK. Research interests are technology and quality of life (digital divide, internet and loneliness, assistive technology, accessibility) information management in social services and active citizenship. He has published widely on the application of technology in human services as well as on the dynamics between technology and social quality of society. His work focuses on research and development projects for local agencies, local and national government (e.g. city of Eindhoven, Dutch Ministry of Welfare) and international work for the European Commission. An overview of publications is available at http://www.steyaert.org/Jan/. All publications can be downloaded full-text.

Acknowledgements

Thank you Tony Amaechi; Simon Bastow; Helen Beck; Bev Carter; Will Davies; Patrick Dunleavy; Dennis Guiney; Mark Harris; Tom Hostler; John Pitts; Margaret, Mary and Lauren Robson; Danielle Sanderson; David Wilcox, and all the residents of The Woods who gave their time to be interviewed.

Introduction

Kevin Harris

A resident complains

Here's a tiny problem for a whole civilisation. On a housing estate, a resident completes a complaint form like this (reproduced here as written):

> Some teenagers boys play football or other ball games and keep kicking the balls across the Alleyway (street) resulting the breaking in windows of house on the ground floor.

> They keep throwing, rubbish, bottles, broken furniture, planks of wood or small stones in the alleyway, results not only leave the street dirty, but also saftey hazards. Few times I was injured because some one throw broken pieces of chair which landed on my head and shoulder, and I ended up in Hospital. If we try to tell these teenager boys they gang against us, swear at us and throw stone and kicking on our front door. Few times they dented & scratched our cars, but unable to point out that which boys did the actual damage. We requested the Authorities to erract a wire net fence on the wall which is facing the Alleyway, which might save us from the Harrasement and also if they send letter to these above householder to respect other people's property and abstain from Harrasing other people.

(Housing association complaint form, West London, May 2006)

There are themes in this testimony that ought to attract our attention. The resident's sense of disempowerment and injustice; the difficulty of engaging with the boys; the inappropriateness of the space in which the boys are playing; perceptions of disorder; the struggle to get an effective response from an authority; the paucity of options for the complainant. In this book these themes recur, and our reflections suggest two fundamental questions to help us put these issues into context for practitioners and policy makers. First, is there some commonly understood notion of *consideration and respect for others* that is essential if people are to live together on reasonably good terms? And secondly, is the government's attempt to package this notion into its Respect Agenda (Respect Task Force, 2006) adequate to nurture or re-invigorate such norms? This book suggests that the lack of an understanding of neighbouring is a key weakness in this agenda.

Promoting respect in the neighbourhood doesn't mean that we can all expect to live together harmoniously. We mislead ourselves if we imagine that by government edict we are all suddenly going to start behaving with saintly selflessness towards each other and living side-by-side in perfect harmony. Nor should we expect necessarily to revert to old norms that evolved for other contexts. But how do we re-establish *organically* a new code of norms and values to which a higher proportion of people feel an affiliation? How do we ensure the growth of a set of assumptions about mutual responsibility and considerate behaviour which serves to stabilise the social ecology?

Civility in freefall?

It is possible to live without interaction with one's neighbours, and theoretically it's possible to live without respect for any other people. But it would not be possible to establish a society or a civilisation on that basis. A society could sustain a few misanthropes, but it cannot be based on misanthropy. Society *implies* civil relations – relationships which by their degree of respect, the informality of their exchanges, and the generation of trust and co-operation, make other things possible.

So if we were to pay less attention to the impact that our presence or behaviours have on those around us, it would put a great deal of pressure on all sorts of other social structures and resources – the family, the health system, trade and local economies, public space, public and private transport and so on. Anti-social behaviour and physical disorder would increase, probably stimulating crime and increased fear. We would gradually become less inclined to venture out unless armed and protected, we would move in fear of others because actions of disrespect would be acceptable and expected. In time, civilisation – the complexities of co-existing cultures – could not exist. There are claims that the very principle of civility in our society is already in freefall: in Chapter 1 we consider the implications, and some of the nuances, of this perception.

What constitutes respect?

It seems surprising, given the high profile of the government agenda, that there has been so little public debate about what constitutes respect. Is it something that has to be earned or is it a neutral value which you hold until you are deemed unworthy of it? For example, should prisoners be treated with respect, as the Home Office currently seeks to ensure?[1] (And how does this policy square with the Respect Task Force definition which we discuss in Chapter 1?) Or is respect something that can be confiscated along with liberty? Perhaps a prisoner has failed to show respect for others by committing a crime: many people would argue that they have therefore forfeited respect themselves. Does society expect the prisoner to have learned – to have been taught – respect? If so: where and how? At home, in the neighbourhood, in school and the workplace? With this book we offer a much needed exploration of respect in the local context, in an effort to broaden the debate beyond the current media-stoked frenzy focused on anti-social behaviour.

Structure of the book

Beginning with a general introduction to respect, the book goes on to consider various aspects of social relationships at local level. Two chapters offer findings from recent research, and these are followed by an assessment of the contemporary context of neighbouring. Two further chapters attempt to set respect and neighbouring in their spatial context, first through examining general principles of design and the environment, and then through a case study. Another pair of chapters then considers ethnic and cultural differences in understandings of respect. The final chapter offers reflections for policy.

The book raises and seeks to answer a number of questions about this under-examined topic. What do we know about how residents jointly manage the behaviour of young people in the

---

[1] HM Inspectorate of Prisons includes among its four basic tests the requirement that 'prisoners are treated with respect for their human dignity'. See http://inspectorates.homeoffice.gov.uk/hmprisons/our-work/

neighbourhood? Is it practical to reward residents for neighbourly behaviour? How can authorities work with residents in promoting positive neighbouring relationships, generating energy for community involvement and stimulating social capital? How might the built and green environment be managed to help us re-establish social ties in neighbourhoods? What difference does the design of the street make to interactions between neighbours? How do young people respond to confused cultural messages about respect, and how do they reconcile the understanding within their own ethnic groupings with those broadcast around them? How does the UK approach compare with neighbouring European countries?

A measure of being civilised?

In Chapter 1 respect is presented as a fundamental criterion of civil relations. It is not the same as deference or admiration: as a default human value it should be a measure of being civilised. The chapter goes on to discuss the genesis of the government's Respect agenda. It argues that it is mistaken and misleading to imply that a dearth of respect in society is concentrated in low-income areas: this simply reflects a partial and inadequate definition of the concept. The system of rampant individualistic consumption, condoned by policy, generates disrespect far beyond these areas on a scale that is at least comparable, if not far more problematic. Policy that reinforces this misconception betrays an arrogant insensitivity that is likely to be divisive.

Norms of parenting

In Chapter 2, Jacqueline Barnes reports on a detailed study based in four localities in England. Her research explored parents' perceptions of their neighbourhood and the implications for supporting children. The study sought to explain differences in informal control, and shows that the higher the level of social disorganisation, the lower the likelihood of informal social control. In particular, the research clarifies the relationship between anticipated retaliation and lack of informal social control of children and young people. If norms of parenting are regarded as consistent in the neighbourhood, there is a greater likelihood of informal social control. The detail of the study allowed the researchers to conclude that the two key factors that predict more informal control of children by neighbours are low expectation of retaliation and more non-family local social networks. However, perhaps the most worrying conclusion of this chapter, a message that sends a challenge to practitioners, is about widely differing understandings of parenting. There is growing concern that when neighbours, who are themselves parents, make efforts to constrain inappropriate behaviour of local children, the children's parents are more likely to react with anger and outrage, rather than support such interventions. Policy and practice needs to respond to this. Parenting has become an aspect of our identity such that it is seen as a personal insult if one's child is disciplined by others. It's hard to understand this other than as an outcome of an age of individualism in which notions of collective responsibility have been allowed to wither.

Encouraging good neighbouring

So is it possible to encourage people to become better neighbours? The research reported by Liz Richardson in Chapter 3 explored three incentive schemes for neighbourliness, and compared them together with one local authority area where there were no schemes but area-wide strategic initiatives against anti-social behaviour. The scheme offering cash incentives was most able to change behaviour, the others less so, but overall the concept of incentives was not seen by residents as a priority. Richardson notes that even where people have a commitment to the neighbourhood and friendly contact with neighbours, these are not enough in themselves to change their behaviour to protect that neighbourhood. Her comments need to be taken into consideration especially by those who promote 'the contractualisation of social relations with regard to neighbourliness' (Flint and Nixon, 2006: 950).

Contemporary neighbouring

These two research chapters are followed by a more detailed review of literature in Chapter 4 to assess what contemporary neighbouring amounts to, and whether it still has a role. The chapter emphasises the significance of the diminished *need* to be neighbourly as a feature of contemporary local life, which has the effect of people disregarding their neighbourhoods and retreating from them. It also considers the benefits of neighbourliness, the importance of neighbourhood stability, and some aspects of informal social control. The chapter stresses the role of informal social ties in maintaining viable neighbourhoods, as a resource to be drawn on in time of need, and ensuring that there is still a context in which respect is practised.

Street level

In Chapter 5, Philip Connolly's focus is the street – as abandoned rat run and as a potential space of social connections. He details the reasons why our streets have been allowed to fail in their role of sustaining local life: submission to the car, poor lighting, flawed design, inadequate maintenance. An important theme in Connolly's analysis is the question of who gets left using the street, and who is missing. One interpretation of the way streets were surrendered as public spaces in the second half of the last century is that it amounted to an expression of social disrespect for older people and younger people in particular. Hence his argument that a quality street environment is one that has been designed and is maintained around the principle of the social inclusivity of public space for pedestrians. Respect in the neighbourhood depends heavily upon removing the barriers that discourage people from walking their local streets.

Contact in the cul-de-sac

What's it like then, when something goes wrong in a neighbourhood and people have to get together to sort it out? In Chapter 6 we zoom in on a tiny cul-de-sac and find out how residents got together when one of their neighbours was victimised. This case study illustrates the significance of spatial design in facilitating informal contact between residents, and argues that the gradual accretion of collective familiarity is what makes a coherent response to anti-social behaviour by neighbours possible.

Black and bilingual communities

Understandings of respect are hard enough to pin down in such a stable and attractive environment. When we consider the added dimension of diverse ethnic groupings, where people from black and bilingual communities are facing multiple disadvantage in urban areas, there are complexities that need careful exploration. Aydin Mehmet Ali begins this process for us in Chapter 7, showing how global events and the changed socio-political context have brought particular pressures on the behaviours of Turkish speaking young people. The gravitational pull of the gang culture, the confusion of messages from Islam and a macho history of armed struggle, long-standing educational under-achievement, and new trends in self-harm, all make the establishment of self-respect and the experience of being respected problematic and elusive for many of these young people.

Respect viewed internationally

The problem of incivilities and anti-social behaviour is not peculiar to the UK, nor are issues of cultural comparisons and assumptions. In Chapter 8 Jan Steyaert guides us round the Netherlands and Flanders, picking up some curious comparisons and lessons to relate to the UK approach. The similarities seem more significant than the differences, and what's available in terms of data suggests not so much that there has been an increase in incivility, but rather that our societies are less tolerant of *diversity of behaviour*.

What role for policy?

None of this means that measures are required to formalise respect. The final chapter argues that, on the contrary, government should be cautious about formalising informal processes and instead should give such processes greater recognition and support. This book shows that there are crucial aspects of life in neighbourhoods – such as the design and use of streets, levels of transience, the fundamental value of informal social interactions – which merit closer policy attention. If such features of local life are nurtured and allowed to flourish, respect will look after itself.

Informal behaviour at local level

So this book is about understanding how people relate to one another and influence each others' behaviour at local level. Throughout the book we have sought to avoid an emphasis on crime, which dominates much of the literature and drives much of the thinking in this field, with anti-social behaviour orders (ASBOs) in particular dominating the debate. The government has promoted respect primarily as the missing ingredient in the long term reduction of crime, and its approach – involving a barrage of press releases about anti-social behaviour, the hectoring of local authorities for under-performance in the ASBO league, and establishing a central 'mission squad' – has been described as 'the reduction of policy to pest control.'[2] We have tried not to reinforce any of this emphasis, instead stressing the impact of incivility and the importance of informal civility in local social relations. It may be, as the Respect Task Force insists, that there is 'no excuse for anti-social behaviour,' but in our view there is plenty of room for explanation and understanding.

Reducing the emphasis on crime reveals informal behaviour in the local context as a complex subject, packed with little nuances and riddled with potential misunderstandings. Take a small space on the edge of a housing estate for instance. At first sight it might seem to me like public space, but to you it might be community space, your territory: if I understand that, my behaviour will be

---

[2] The remark appeared in a post by Will Davies on the Potlatch weblog, http://potlatch.typepad.com, 5 July 2006.

modified. Community space is not quite the same as public space, and civilities and incivilities have to be understood in their spatial context (Dixon et al., 2006).

A crisis of difference

Apparent incivilities and challenges to norms can be vague and undirected – from the irresponsible abandonment of a supermarket trolley by someone who wears a tie to go shopping, to a gawping group of lads, who have just learned to spit that very morning, blocking the pavement and intimidating others. Directed or not, such behaviours show a lack of respect. As Jan Steyaert argues in Chapter 8, we need to develop new skills that allow us to build respect and exercise informal control without reinstating hierarchy in the public sphere. The challenge is to replenish society's depleted stock of skills in engaging and recognising the legitimate interests of others, of learning to challenge behaviour within a shared understanding; to hone our readiness to show consideration to others, whether we know them or not. It's not that we don't do this: it's just that we tend to avoid doing it with those with whom we have little in common. It's as if – conditioned to the taciturnity of the supermarket checkout rather than the inevitable greetings of the corner shop – we have abandoned the practice of conducting trivial interactions, because they don't matter to us. But they do matter, and we need somehow to rediscover the vernacular of mundane encounters.

Above all, the insight we should take into this debate is that if there is a crisis, it is a crisis of difference. Respect and disrespect are experienced very unequally, as Aydin Mehmet Ali's chapter demonstrates. But as Jane Jacobs wrote, 'it is possible to be on excellent sidewalk terms with people who are very different from oneself' (Jacobs, 1961: 73). Her point is that if we do not occupy our public spaces, and expose ourselves to the chance of encounter with others, much of what we value will be in jeopardy. What we need to be talking about more is respect for differences, and finding ways of recognising commonalities among such differences in order to establish firm bases for social relationships: in other words, community cohesion. The mistake that we must not make is to assume that this is an exercise in establishing model harmonious communities. As Alison Gilchrist (Gilchrist, 2004a: 6) has highlighted, community cohesion is not the absence of conflict, but the ability to manage differences and deal with conflict when it arises.

Levels of incivility are probably not close to a tipping point, but if they are declining then that is a serious issue. We cannot expect to rebalance these levels without focusing on social relations at the neighbourhood level. The neighbourhood is an essential context for the practice of respect. The values of human relationships are not concrete, they have constantly to be reviewed and reasserted; understandings have to be compared and reconciled. It's critical that some of this process takes place with the people who live around us.

Chapter 1

To Doff my Cap: Talking About Respect

Kevin Harris

We should build a culture of respect for the modern age, based on values of mutuality and shared responsibility rather than deference and hierarchy.

(Respect Task Force, 2006: 5)

The practice of everyday respect

When I was a kid I was expected to doff my cap at the sight of any passing funeral car, as a mark of 'respect'. In those days (the early 1960s) such social norms were of course seldom practised by schoolboys but they represented a binding power. Behaviour in public places was either correct or it was not. Those who knew the codes and carried them out, belonged to some vague dormant unifying cause. Those who did not, apparently belonged elsewhere.

Nowadays we might justifiably question the doffing of one's cap to an unknown cortege as artificial. We could readily offer an argument to show how class, power and status maintain themselves through such norms. This is the kind of action sometimes mistaken for civility and criticised for its excluding power. In this case, there may well be links to ancient customs of hospitality, peaceful purpose, or reverence; but the practice has lost its link to the cause. We might point out that such an action in itself does not necessarily demonstrate respect but more likely acquiescence and complicity, submission to norms that are dominant and unexamined. And if I failed to raise my cap on a given occasion, was I showing disrespect?

Norms like this will have evolved partly as a way of instructing young people, as they grow up, in civil relations. By insisting consistently on various details, a broad unwritten code of acceptable behaviour becomes established. Some behaviours are more proactive and less encoded – holding a door open for someone, stooping to pick up an item that someone has dropped, helping lift a buggy on the steps, or proactively asking a bewildered stranger if you can give them directions – actions that we might wish to see widely practised. This is not to imply of course that taught behaviour is necessarily inauthentic. What it does suggest is that showing deference – or indeed standing in awe of someone – doesn't necessarily involve authentic respect: the doffing of the cap could be meaningful or it could be an empty gesture. By contrast, an action like helping to lift a buggy up steps on the underground, whatever the motivations, is unlikely to be empty of respect.

This line of thinking leads us to ask if in late twentieth century Britain we could detect a general weakening of inauthentic, stylised norms of unrequited respect – the doffing of caps, pupils standing when a teacher came into the room, audiences standing to attention at the playing of the national anthem and so on; and whether this decline put exceptional pressure on more authentic, more equal, perhaps less formal norms, as hierarchies fell into disarray. The giving up of seats on public transport provides an illustration: I was taught to offer my seat to any female, and I recall childhood arguments about that. Within a few decades, that custom has been challenged and abandoned, but at the risk of losing sensitivity to the needs of more specific categories of user who might have need of the seat. ('Give up your seat to a pregnant woman, and she will thank you. Give up your seat to a woman who *looks* pregnant and she may punch you on the nose') (Truss, 2005: 163). And so today, we have signs on buses and trains *instructing* us in this very public act of consideration.

Over the same period, we could note the growth of self service in shopping and entertainment. You don't need someone to serve you when you go to get cash or petrol or a train ticket any more. You can rent videos and buy your groceries without exchanging words with anyone. When you communicate with others, you can do so remotely and asynchronously, in touch but out of reach.

And where does life take place? Increasingly, valued enclaves in urban areas are juxtaposed with areas populated by poorer groups, the former distinguished by fortress images of gated residential spaces or commercial complexes in which design, surveillance and network infrastructures establish a subtle but formidable separation (Graham and Marvin, 2001). Elsewhere, less affluent neighbourhoods are characterised by fractured transport links, poorly maintained amenities and commercial connections which are inadequate for the provision of basic services and utilities in a privatised context. The significance of this emerging spatial divide lies in the incremental effect of 'cocooning' and 'ghettoising', whereby those with the power and connections need never encounter a population which inhabits those separated spaces.

In a context where an increasing proportion of human relationships are maintained remotely through 'anytime, anyplace, always-on' connections, a higher proportion of people's connections are likely to be to those with whom they have much in common, and to be mainly about what they have in common. This phenomenon of 'homophily' (McPherson et al., 2001) combined with reduced serendipity in the public sphere, in theory changes the volume and quality of weak ties at local level (Van Alstyne and Brynjolfsson, 1997). It could account in part for assumptions about the decline of civility.

These trends don't necessarily mean that we communicate less or care less about others (Harris, 2003). The answerphone hasn't replaced conversation; we are not becoming what Locke calls an 'autistic society' (Locke, 1998: Ch. 7). Formal instruments of a punitive nature have *not* replaced informal social control (Burney, 2005: 3). But we may be communicating less than in the past with people who do not inhabit our immediate spheres of interest. Our lifestyles enable us to eliminate a proportion of unwanted contact (Bauman, 2000). It follows that we may be failing to practice the verbal and physical language of respect for others in the public realm – politeness, consideration, tolerance. This we might call the desuetude of mansuetude. Does it matter?

If a society experiences a decline of the inauthentic respectful gesture – epitomised by the sense that doffing a cap to a funeral car would now seem eccentric – it doesn't necessarily imply a decline in authentic respect also. But other factors might; and media and government alike have hardly been hesitant in fanning the embers of popular concern about a *general decline* in civility and respect, leaving us apparently morally impoverished and our neighbourhoods at risk of tipping into a dismal fractured anarchy. Some commentators – notably politicians who speak of the volume of complaints from their constituents, a wholly valid democratic medium – suggest that there is genuinely a crisis of civil relations. While this is debatable, it's clear that a sensible debate is overdue, given that numerous questions have arisen about the quality of relations between strangers, and those between acquaintances such as family, in contemporary society. Not all the questions will get answered in this book of course, but we set out to offer a framework and examples for thinking about these moral issues, most of which are both personal and social.

In a consultation on a 'respect standard for housing management' in April 2006, the government defined respect as a value:

. . . it is about all of us being considerate to the needs of others around us, being decent, honest and caring about the community as well as our own individual concerns. It is essential in creating sustainable communities where people feel safe, secure and happy to live.

(ODPM, 2006: 5)

One feature of this credo that recurs is the degree to which it mixes a neutral notion of social relations ('live and let live') with positive, pro-social notions like caring. It could be argued that many citizens are more comfortable with a requirement of 'neutral citizenship' by which they do not have to be proactive in relations with others, so long as they are not anti-social in their actions. A citizen might claim the right to live peacefully without being expected to 'care' about their community or their neighbours – 'keeping themselves to themselves' and adhering to traditional conservative values of self-regulation and minimal state dependency. We will come across this notion again when we explore understandings of neighbouring in Chapter 4. For the time being, we need to recognise that policy has a purchase on this argument because it is government that provides the citizen with a guarantee of a peaceful environment, with an organised economy and with a range of organised facilities to help maintain that way of life. In the final chapter we will consider the extent to which it makes sense for policy to try to formalise respect.

Everyday respect is practised in our routine correspondence with authorities and agencies of all kinds, in the quotidian niceties of trade and consumption, in our nodding acquaintance with fellow residents, in unrehearsed subtle movements adjusting to other public passengers or road users, in all sorts of encounters with other citizens known and unknown. Much of the practice of respect in the neighbourhood is unconscious or invisible. That woman coming towards you on the pavement now, pushing the buggy, it's obvious she has not space to pass alongside you beside the lamp-post, you have already slowed slightly, you smile neutrally as she takes the gap before you. Contemporary policy that focuses on respect needs to be based on an understanding of the extent to which such behaviour as this is habitual, is learned, is culturally conditioned, is culturally consistent or varied.

Respect and disrespect

My intention in this section is to contextualise respect and disrespect by considering them as everyday concepts in relation to other characteristics of interpersonal relations.

To begin with, we can consider a simple spectrum of civil/uncivil behaviour along the following lines (Fig. 1.1).

Thus we might say that at one extreme of civil relations we have cold-blooded murder, which is about as uncivil as you can get; and at the other, at least in theory, some form of unconditional

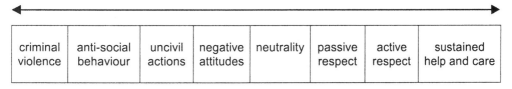

criminal violence	anti-social behaviour	uncivil actions	negative attitudes	neutrality	passive respect	active respect	sustained help and care

Figure 1.1   A simple spectrum of civil/uncivil behaviour

devotion. In between, we find respect and disrespect as features of the central parts of the spectrum, and here our behaviour is often fluidly varied. We might come to a given local context with a negative attitude – such as an exchange with a neighbour about where they park their car – but still behave in a wholly respectful manner towards them.

We can also consider incivilities in terms of the perpetrator's *acquaintance* with their victim. How is it different being the subject of an incivility from someone you recognise in the stable context of your neighbourhood, as against a situation where a complete stranger is abusive towards you in a fluid, ephemeral urban setting? Assuming hypothetically that the specific act of incivility was identical, can we suppose that you are likely to find it easier to recover mentally from the *anonymous contact*? It seems fair to say that overt disrespect from a known individual will have a more lasting effect, given the greater likelihood of repetition of the behaviour.[1] It certainly seems to be recognised that repeated and unrelenting anti-social behaviour – repeat victimisation – is deeply damaging, and much of the momentum of the government's anti-social behaviour policy has built on this (Burney, 2005).

We should beware implying a simple dichotomy here. Many complaints of anti-social behaviour seem to concern people who are recognised by but barely 'known' to the victim, and it is here – just around the boundaries of social networks and often at the boundaries of people's perceived neighbourhoods (Atkinson and Flint, 2004) – that people most seem to need the support of formal services. Martin Wood's analysis of the crime survey figures found that 'Local people themselves were not widely felt to be responsible for reducing problems except in cases where there was a personal relationship between the parties' (Wood, 2004: 3).

Acquaintance with the perpetrator is often likely to compound uncertainties over reprimanding them and/or reporting the incident. If the individual is known to you – and you to them – you may well fear their response to your reaction, whether that be their immediate response or a more deliberate organised act taken subsequently. Likewise, any witnesses to the incident may also feel intimidated or may even be threatened. This area is the dark end of overt disrespect, where anti-social behaviour fringes on criminal behaviour. The question of intervention was addressed in the research reported by Jacqueline Barnes in the next chapter, and is further discussed in Chapter 4.

Not all incivilities are directed at an individual or group of people. Some behaviour is more diffused and undirected – for example if someone smokes on a bus, or throws a bottle from a speeding truck, it suggests a generalised disrespect for fellow citizens without being targeted at any one person or group. Thus Phillips and Smith (2003) note that incivility can involve either direct and confronting encounters between individuals, or be less targeted, for instance something that is accidentally seen or overheard.

We can also note how uncivil actions that *are* targeted may be aimed at a specific individual, or aimed generally at a social group. Someone may seek opportunities to abuse a particular gay man, or someone with a foreign accent; but equally it may be all gay men, or all foreigners who are the targets of their disrespect.

Finally, it is appropriate here to comment on cultural differences in interpretations of 'respect'. These differences can emerge in all sorts of ways. For instance, on urban roads in Brazil, it's hard to make the use of the car horn sound reprimanding: tooting is all part of the ceaseless, lively urban conversation that Brazilians have with one another. Similar use of the horn on a British road would be likely to be regarded as uncivil and provocative. Richard Sennett offers another example, referring

---

[1] Research into the distress caused by acquaintance rape compared with rape by a stranger shows contradictory findings, and is thus inconclusive at this stage (M Harris, Victim Support, personal communication) but in any case we should be cautious about comparing the experience of intimate violence with incivility.

to the understanding of adult dependency among strangers in Japanese culture. A sense of helplessness made overt creates an immediate connection between people who don't know one another. 'In Japan surrender is not a loss of face; shame comes to the person who fails to respond, shame comes to the indifferent individual' (Sennett, 2003: 11–115).

More sinister contrasts abound. I interviewed a young white girl who grew up in a neighbourhood where Asian boys had a significant presence on the street, in a town in the north of England. She spoke about the unrelenting disrespect – mostly sexually provocative verbal abuse – that she experienced over several years. As the only white teenage girl in the street and one of very few in the neighbourhood, she knew full-well the peculiarly challenging nature of her situation. For Pakistani boys, the presence of a girl on the street – especially one who did not cover herself with particular thoroughness – could be seen as something of a challenge to their cultural understanding of respect for women. 'All the blokes hassle you. They'll make comments about you. Even the older men, they've got that undertone of disrespect.' As she got to know some of the boys, mainly through forays to buy cigarettes at the row of shops they frequented, she feels she became partially accepted as 'an honorary lad'. This brought with it contempt from her white acquaintances, who at various times called her a 'paki-shagger'.

The social construction of belonging to a given ethnic community is often produced through a transnational network of social and technological linkages (ceremonies, telephone conversations, broadcast media, videos, music etc.). Locally clustered groups such as Italians or Turkish-speaking communities employ this network all the time. It is therefore part of their perception of their 'community' and may have an impact on connections with neighbours who are not part of that network. (See also Aydin Mehmet Ali's observations in Chapter 7. I discuss issues of diversity and cohesion at the end of Chapter 4). It's not just that people may have attenuated affiliation with the communities with which, increasingly, they are being asked to 'become involved': the sense of everyday local identity in a transnational context (Smith, 2001) is necessarily viewed through these murky flows so that the 'mean definition' of the community – the common understanding of local identity – is increasingly difficult to establish. 'How *we* do things here' may not be the same as 'How we do things *here*' – nothwithstanding the publication of the Dutch handbook described by Jan Steyaert in Chapter 8 (see page 107). What comes into focus for one person may be indistinguishable for their neighbour. Within that cultural context, different understandings of civil behaviour have to be learned and practised.

The practice of respect also has to undergo revision as new cultural contexts emerge. The etiquette of using the lift in a tower block, for instance – ('It's considered good manners to hold the lift open for anyone entering the building, even if they look like mass murderers . . . and they invariably do' (Ward, 2006)) – is a particular twentieth century refinement of urban civility. In Chapter 8 Steyaert points to other forms such as 'netiquette' and notes how values and norms are a 'moving target', so it's unsurprising that as a society we have to carry out routine 'maintenance'.

Respect is a moral issue

To talk meaningfully about respect we have to explore it as a moral issue. One young person I spoke to suggested that in some circumstances if people are scared of you, that's a form of respect. Because she went to school in an area more affluent than where she lived, she found that some of her peers were in respectful awe because her neighbourhood had a bad reputation. This would seem to be a defensive and negative conferring of respect out of a degree of fear.

Respect can be presented more positively as the notion of deference for unusual virtue or status. In this meaning, presumably most of us would reserve our respect until we felt we had cause to confer it on another, although in some readings it can be associated in particular with office and/or uniform. On the spectrum of regard for others, this sense of respect as deference comes close to admiration. Hence any policy implication that we should all show respect for another comes across as absurd to some. Michael Neumann, for instance, argues that:

> *It flies in the face of reality to hold that all persons, cultures or religions are worthy of respect . . . You needn't go . . . far to arrive at the surely reasonable idea that some people really haven't done or been anything of which you should stand in awe.*

(Neumann, 2006)

This argument simply conflates the notion of respect with 'standing in awe': I shall argue below in direct opposition to the first assertion. But it helps us in considering the sense in which the UK government argues, or rather claims (in capital letters 1.5 cm high) that:

RESPECT
CANNOT BE
LEARNED,
PURCHASED
OR ACQUIRED
IT CAN ONLY **BE EARNED.**

(Respect Task Force, 2006: 30)

If this is to be the basis for an influential policy, there has to be concern about it as a theoretically disempowering premise, which raises questions which have so far been ignored. For example, who accords the status of being respected, who deems respect to have been earned, and by what criteria? What opportunities do we have to gain respect, and how are these opportunities distributed through society? Like democracy, respect is not experienced equally. Why does it seem that some people apparently are able to inherit such opportunities, or (as in the case of so many prominent politicians) have privileges that appear to allow them quickly to recover lost respect? It is as if, in putting forward this particular definition, the government is attempting to redirect the moral conversation of society.

We might also ask, reflecting on the notion of respect as deference, what sort of relationship is left for those on whom we have not yet had the chance to confer respect? What is neutral, in this context? Suppose you are reading these words at a table in a café. You will stop at the end of this paragraph, but as you get up to leave, I happen to brush against you as I move, cup in hand, to find a seat. Never having met, two strangers in an urban context, what is the basis of our encounter, however brief it be? It's unlikely to be deferential, but hopefully it will be not be inimical, neither of us should feel threatened or intimidated. Hopefully it will be civil.

Civil relations matter because they represent a default for all social relations beyond the most intimate, beyond the level of the household. They lubricate most kinds of social transaction. The origin of the concept is not trivial: it refers to people ('city-zens') who, because of the scale of their social environment, live in proximity but are not likely to know one another. (For a review of the meaning of civility, see Misztal, 2000: 71–9. See also Sennett, 1978.) Their relations are in this respect to be distinguished from those of villagers. Since it is not certain that they will have dealings with one another, but they may seek to repeat any dealings they have and may come to depend on each other for some reason, citizens have evolved ways of behaving towards one another, in a 'civil' way, making social co-operation possible without the need always for 'deep moral agreements' (Boyd, 2006). Misztal's analysis is more negative:

> *To protect themselves from unknown others, while preserving some illusion of fraternity and communal experience, people need a mask of civility.*

(Misztal, 2000: 74)

Either way, in terms of everyday life, this means that when we get on a bus or go into the street or a public venue, we take account of others around us and thus our behaviour is influenced by that context.

So 'respect' could mean little more than unregistered recognition – a latent civility and passive acknowledgement of another's legitimate presence, described by Goffman as 'civil inattention' (Goffman, 1963: 84).[2] In many situations the absence of that level of respectful inattention could be said to constitute disrespect. An obvious example would be when a frontline office worker facing the public at a service desk does not acknowledge a customer who has justifiably approached that desk. By contrast, we might laugh or squirm slightly with embarrassment when Gerard Hoffnung (2002) offers comic advice that visitors to England should, 'on entering a railway compartment, make sure to shake hands with all the passengers'. Not only does this draw attention to the sub-theme of cultural differences in public behaviours: we recognise the absurdity of the image because the requirements of civility also imply respect for privacy. The principle of general respect for strangers is a middle way, between ignoring people and engaging with them, while being able to take either course of action at a moment's notice. The balance may be fine: confidence tricksters, salespeople, and adept beggars focus on exploiting people whose readiness to engage may be stronger than their civil inattention.

An alternative moral position to the deferential is to suggest that respect is, like civility, a default attribute of any human relationship unless one or other party proves themselves to be unworthy of it. We do not have to admire someone in order to have respect for them. This is hardly a new meaning of 'respect', but its widespread application may be new.

Of course, this raises questions of defining what it might be that makes anyone *unworthy* of respect, and how such norms develop and gain acceptance. What are the implications of not being worthy of respect? Does it mean that there are certain things that individuals or the state are allowed to do to those deemed unworthy? For example, on what grounds should we treat prisoners with respect when they might be said to have failed to demonstrate it themselves? Are there degrees of respect, and if so what are the cultural codes that we use to share our understanding of them? And what can we learn from the notion of negative respect – of respect among anti-social people, a kind of honour among thieves? These issues of moral philosophy will shadow many of the issues raised in this book: they are largely beyond our scope but they merit a few contextual remarks here.

It would be comforting to think that all human cultures have regarded respect as a default value, but the history of warfare on our planet should caution us from such a naïve view. Nonetheless, I see no difficulty with the proposition that it has become an aspirational foundation for our civilisation. We have international agencies and initiatives promoting human rights, civil liberties, the rights of the child, of women, of gay and lesbian people, of workers, of aboriginal Indians, and so on – marked in most cases by powerful and reasoned texts – and these imply a *fundamental principle of mutual respect* among human beings in a global context. It may be necessary to keep reasserting and defending this principle, but it would seem to be a valued measure of being civilised. And as Richard Boyd notes:

---

[2] Goffman contrasts civil inattention with 'not seeing' – treating people as if they were not there at all. He also suggests that civil inattention is a 'courtesy' but "no recognition" is typically allowed' (83–4).

Regardless of the stipulations of the law, a sense that we are all part of one moral collectivity or public can only exist when we are in the habit of treating one another in ways that observe the formal conditions of civility.

(Boyd, 2006: 865)

I would therefore articulate a principle of civil relations that by default everyone is held in respect, with the undoubted capacity to lose it and the consequent requirement to regain it. Through our institutions and customs we have the responsibility to help people regain that status; unlike the fundamental principle, this responsibility is recognised in theory and developed in the government's *Respect Action Plan* (Respect Task Force, 2006). In the next section we trace the short pre-history of this unusual government credo.

Respect as a theme of policy

The reliability of civil and pro-social behaviours, among people who do not necessarily know one another, is felt to be in crisis in the UK. The predicament appears to arise from fractured forms of social relations, less dependable norms of behaviour, and less visible networks of power. The government's response has been to launch a belligerent attack on anti-social behaviour, supported by insistent rhetoric on the side of its victims in disadvantaged neighbourhoods.

There are different views on the genesis of the respect agenda, but if we are to understand how the notion of 'respect' has become politically salient, and believed to be so widely applicable across the UK, we need to reflect a little on this history. It can be seen as a development of the government's approach to crime and disorder generally (Burney, 2005) and the recognition that there might be widespread low-level anti-social behaviour and incivility that has escaped attention but which afflicts many people almost routinely. This line of policy development might be seen as somewhat untidy, if only because it seems such a belated recognition of a familiar social problem, with the rhetoric strident, and the definitions unclear.

Alternatively we can identify a path among the various policy themes on which the light of respect has been played in recent years, such as education, the liveability of public space, community involvement, social cohesion, faith and ethnicity, parenting, housing, support for young people, and local government reform. This joined-up view is reflected in the ministerial involvement in the *Respect Action Plan* from the Home Office, the Office of the Deputy Prime Minister (now the Department for Communities and Local Government) and the departments for Education and Skills, Culture, Media and Sport, Health, Work and Pensions, and Environment, Food and Rural Affairs.[3]

There is no reason to reject either account of this history, since they are clearly complementary and reflect the importance attached to this theme by the present government. In what follows I emphasise the key non-criminological policy sources, partly because the first approach has been thoroughly recorded by Elizabeth Burney (2005) and also because of the need to begin to loosen the tightly embedded association of respect and civil behaviour with research and policy on crime. In any historical summary of policy since 1997 in this area however, it is as well to keep in mind the increasing emphasis placed on *early intervention* (SEU, 2004; Treasury, 2005).

The original neighbourhood renewal strategy was published by the Social Exclusion Unit in 1998 to complement the New Deal for Communities and Sure Start programmes. Essentially, these three

---

[3] *Respect drive targets troublesome families*, Government press release, 10 January 2006.

high profile programmes were about addressing complex multiple problems in areas where poverty was concentrated. Through the 18 Policy Action Teams established in the neighbourhood renewal strategy, the Social Exclusion Unit sought to understand those difficulties and to provide practical action plans in order to transform the life chances of people who experience exclusion. The action plans, championed by individual government departments, would do this by tackling issues like worklessness, bad housing, inadequate transport, drugs, crime and educational under-achievement. As the work developed, jobs were created, housing was improved, many schools recovered and in some cases crime figures fell.

Significantly, anti-social behaviour was highlighted in the 1998 strategy and responsibility for addressing it was given to one of the 18 dedicated Policy Action Teams (PAT 8). It was recognised that anti-social behaviour is perceived to be a serious problem by a much higher proportion of people living in deprived neighbourhoods than elsewhere (PAT 8, 2000: 1.26).

The team's recommendations came under five main categories:

- assigning clear responsibility
- promoting prevention
- enforcement
- resettlement
- combating racial harassment.

(PAT8, 2000: 6.7)

The perception that there is a widespread and even increasing problem of anti-social behaviour has persisted long after the work of the PATs has faded. This is partly because anti-social behaviour is a problem by no means confined to the most problematic estates. It is commonly experienced in town centres, in and around schools, on public transport and highways, and in suburbs throughout the country. Incivilities may be perpetrated as much by 'respectable' people as by the stereotypical groups with whom it is most commonly associated (Phillips and Smith, 2003, 2006). Anti-social behaviour is routinely visible on our television screens and reported in our newspapers, especially local ones. It is a pre-occupation of fiction in various media.

While PAT 8 was reporting nationally, Crime and Disorder Reduction Partnerships[4] were being set up and getting to work in local areas, looking particularly at enforcement options. The rhetoric was about the practical policing of deviance. Not many of us can have been expecting a philosophical approach at this point, but that is what we got.

In 2003 former Home Secretary David Blunkett (2003a, 2003b) published two papers promoting the values of civil renewal in terms of interdependence, mutuality, solidarity and respect. While claiming a central part of the political terrain for the Home Office, these themes seemed suddenly to yank policy back to certain principles of Labour politics that had become slightly unfamiliar. Blunkett identified basic social order, decent behaviour, and the socialisation of the young into 'community norms', as crucial missing ingredients in many disadvantaged areas. The wide sweep of his policy attention took in community involvement, social entrepreneurship, citizenship, community ownership of assets, renewal of the public realm, police reform, and reform of the criminal justice system. (See also a similar but less wide-ranging contemporary paper by Hazel Blears (Blears, 2003).)

---

[4] http://www.crimereduction.gov.uk/partnerships2.htm

The anti-social behaviour white paper

Socialist notions like mutuality did not survive into the publication of the influential white paper, *Respect and responsibility: taking a stand against anti-social behaviour* (Home Office, 2003) which preceded the Anti-Social Behaviour Act 2003. Here the government made its commitment to link anti-social behaviour closely with visions of social relations based on respect and 'decency'.

> *There are a small number of families that can be described as 'dysfunctional'. Two or three families and their wider network of contacts can create havoc on a housing estate or inner city neighbourhood. It is always in areas of greatest disadvantage that this corrosive effect is seen and felt most clearly. Sometimes it occurs where there has been considerable family breakdown; multiple partners can pass through the house; children do not have a positive role model; there is little in the way of predictable orderly routine; and the lifestyle is such that it makes the lives of neighbours a complete misery. Some professionals have refrained from demanding changes in standards and behaviour from such families, in an effort to remain 'non-judgmental'. This stance alienates those living alongside chaotic families and who legitimately complain that professionals can go home to areas not beset by this kind of misery. It also fails children in dysfunctional families by not asserting their need for care and discipline by their parents.*
>
> (para 2.9)

The description is graphic, the glance back at the social exclusion agenda is clear. But it is just that, a backward glance: there is little here about explaining or addressing causes of anti-social behaviour, although it is emphasised that lack of respect always underlies it. The legacy of PAT8 may be most apparent in the way that anti-social behaviour policy is directed heavily at residents in low-income neighbourhoods. Belligerently siding with 'the ordinary decent law-abiding citizen' in such neighbour-hoods, the Home Secretary adopted an aggressive moral stance:

> *We will work alongside those who are not prepared to tolerate people harassing and intimidating their neighbours or mistreating our public spaces. We will work with the police, local authorities and schools to ensure that one family is not allowed to ruin a whole street, or one child is not able to disrupt a whole school. We must be much tougher about forcing people not to behave anti-socially.*
>
> (Foreword)

One of the two central chapters covers families, children and young people. The other central chapter deals with specific forms of anti-social behaviour such as noise, fly-tipping, abandoned vehicles, weapons, drunken behaviour, litter and graffiti, kerb crawling and prostitution, and so on. Most of us probably thought that there were already powers and legislation in place for dealing with these problems, and as Elizabeth Burney comments:

> *. . . this seems a rather roundabout way of approaching what should be routine municipal duties of keeping public space clean and tidy.*
>
> (Burney, 2005: 36)

Among the many things for which the white paper is praised or blamed, two stand out. First, in practical terms, it sought to clear obstacles to the use of powers by authorities, for example by making it easier for the police to overcome the lack of witnesses because of intimidation. Secondly, it demonstrated the way in which a government can construct, as Flint and Nixon put it, particular 'values, beliefs and sentiments identified as underpinning responsible self-government and shaping individuals' conduct' (Flint and Nixon, 2006: 940).

Objection to this role of moral coercion did not take long to gather voice, in spite of the popularity of some of the measures. Thus by June 2005, when the government extended the Anti-Social Behaviour Act to regulate the cutting of garden hedges, some commentators had lost sympathy. Tim Luckhurst (2005) wrote in *The Times*:

> The sanctimonious authoritarianism long detectable in our Government's values seems to have transmuted into a faith that human relations must be regulated by diktat.

Respect with a capital 'R'

In that year the Respect Task Force was established under Louise Casey, and the government's action plan was published in January 2006. A key political platform for the *Respect Action Plan* was the credo that the government should enforce 'a modern culture of respect which the majority of people want' (Respect Task Force, 2006: 3). It thus claims a crucial foundation in democracy, along with the popular, stabilising reference to 'tradition', while insisting unashamedly on its 'modern' credentials.

Among the measures put forward in the plan were these:

- 'Local scrutiny committees', which will have to examine problems flagged up by local people in 'community calls to action'.

- More parenting courses, with more agencies able to impose parenting orders on those parents who refuse to take up help when their children are 'out of control'.

- A 'national parenting academy', to train social workers, clinical psychologists, community safety officers and youth justice workers about advising parents.

- Powers to close any property which is the focus for 'persistent and serious nuisance'.

In April 2006 the Respect Task Force established an initiative with all Premier League football clubs and all London clubs, with the aim of targeting 'areas of need within the community, providing all young people with structured, purposeful activities while providing a hook for engaging those most at risk of anti-social behaviour'.[5] The Task Force has gone on to set up a consultation on a key area of concern, social housing, with a view to establishing a 'respect standard' (ODPM, 2006).

The anecdotal evidence in support of policy action of this kind has been abundant. It is easy to dismiss accounts of people feeling threatened by groups of young people gathering on street corners (where else are kids supposed to go, when they're not welcome at home and no appropriate, affordable provision is made for them?). But we should keep in mind that in many cases it is done quite deliberately, and the intimidation is intentional as an ostentatious display of gang power, often with large dogs and weapons on display. Similarly, specific examples of vindictive behaviour among neighbours, sometimes escalating to violence, are not hard to come by.

Since 2002, *Neighbours from Hell in Britain*[6] has catalogued a selection of the kinds of incident (and more persistent disrespectful behaviour) that draw popular recognition. The NFH website points to a number of symptoms that are familiar to the victims of neighbour bullying:

- Reluctance to go home.

- Losing all interest in the house.

- Not looking forward to weekends or evenings.

- Constantly thinking about moving.

---

[5] *Government's new signing to help deliver respect*. Home Office press release, 8 April 2006.
[6] http://www.nfh.org.uk/

- Attention switches immediately when you hear your NFH.
- Second-guessing events before they happen.
- Fear of confrontation.[7]

It has gradually become apparent that many people have experienced these symptoms over prolonged periods and their appeals against such injustice have not received adequate response. A civilised society does not ignore bullying or its effects. In the circumstances, it hardly seems appropriate for a university professor of philosophy to write about 'skewed ideas of injury' and 'the bogus value of respect':

> Victim impact statements proclaim invisible harms; these are taken as reason to increase the visible suffering imposed on the offender.

> (Neumann, 2006)

Whether or not the political gain makes us suspicious of the motives, it is significant that government at the highest level is publicising stories about people like this couple:

> Joe and Alison Bednall from Wakefield, who overcame fear and intimidation from a neighbouring family – including verbal abuse, dumping rubbish, and spitting – to help the local authority gather evidence to apply for ASBOs against the family.[8]

We should welcome a political culture in which complaints about persistently noisy, aggressive and inconsiderate neighbours gain such a high profile. But it is striking that the action plan makes no attempt to articulate or link to the fundamental principle of respect as a default human value. The explanation would seem to be that it has adopted a somewhat different, rather less inclusive, moral stance that resembles an attempt to reinvent the protestant work ethic, with a heavy emphasis on enforcement. Commenting at a seminar on respect and informal social control in January 2006, an official from the Prime Minister's Delivery Unit implied that the government's stance was largely symbolic, seeking to establish a punitive atmosphere, 'sending signals that can have a beneficial knock-on effect'.[9]

In the following sections I want to focus on three glaring problems with the government's approach: the notion of civic absence, the emphasis on shaming, and the lack of reference to broadly sanctioned behaviours that are manifestly short on respect, such as consumerism and professional disrespect.

Civic absence

Notwithstanding the key message put across by Ellickson in his (1991) study of rural Californian communities, which plays down the significance of legally established entitlements, it's important to assert that people need the reassurance of official mechanisms and access to the criminal justice system in cases where negotiation around a disagreement, for whatever reason, breaks down. This might be an official presence not connected with local representatives, as noted in the research carried out in Edinburgh and Glasgow by Atkinson and Flint (2004). Social landlords have particular responsibilities in this respect (Flint and Nixon, 2006). In Chapter 3 Liz Richardson explores some of

---

[7] Adapted from http://www.nfh.org.uk/spotlight/symptoms_victim/index.php
[8] *Residents recognised for standing up for respect.* Respect Task Force press release, 4 April 2006.
[9] The remark was reported on the Neighbourhoods weblog, 19 January 2006, at http://neighbourhoods.typepad.com/neighbourhoods/2006/01/informal_social.html

the subtleties of the relationship between authorities and residents in coping with anti-social behaviour.

Webster has published a theory of the neighbourhood in terms of contractual relationships and transaction costs, noting that:

> Contractual neighbourhoods are becoming popular because in many ways they deliver services to those within more cost-effectively and responsively than does conventional municipal government.

> (Webster, 2003: 2598)

By contrast, some low-income areas are characterised by a lack of attention by services, no visible presence on the estate, awkward conditions for communicating with authorities, and poor response times so that residents lose faith in them. In one such area I found residents, having paid their £6,000 annual service charge, needing to spend their own time and effort drawing to the attention of their landlord the accumulating needs for repair and maintenance on their estate, and finding those complaints repeatedly ignored. As a consequence, 'Residents feel disempowered and they are subject to systematic and legitimised disrespect, but it goes unregistered' (Harris, 2006: 11).

It's appropriate here to glance briefly at 'broken window' theory, which was first advanced in a widely cited article by Wilson and Kelling (1982). They hypothesised a process of degradation in areas where disorder went unchecked, leading in time to increased levels of crime. The argument was that if authorities repair the broken windows and maintain a basic level of order, criminals will be deterred. This theory became the foundation for zero-tolerance policing which in some US cities appeared to have a measure of success in reducing serious crime, and in the UK it would have appealed to policy makers who were emphasising the need for early intervention. However, the theory has been challenged by two key pieces of work in particular, reported by Sampson et al. (1997) and more recently by Harcourt and Ludwig (2006). The former study suggested that physical signs of disorder do not predict neighbourhood crime levels nearly as reliably as low levels of collective efficacy. The broken window hypothesis is discussed in more detail by Philip Connolly in Chapter 5.

From our point of view, reflecting on the role of authorities in contributing to an environment that is conducive to civil interaction, it's worth making a non-theoretical point here. Whether or not physical signs of disorder predict crime, what they *do* predict is just that, physical disorder. The question arises, why should people have to live with that? Where broken windows are not repaired, and other maintenance is not carried out, residents are being subjected to disrespect on the part of the official services established and funded to maintain order.

The damaging failure by any administration to address its local responsibilities will tend to be multiplied where people make proportionately greater demand on those services and where they experience exclusion, for example through poverty, ill-health, or poor communication skills in their second language. In the case study referred to above (Harris, 2006), this failure was deeply disrespectful because the efforts of residents to engage with the authorities – responding to the exhortations of government rhetoric about community involvement – were to no avail. In such contexts, what Herbert (2005) calls the 'responsibilisation'[10] of local people through neighbourhood governance is likely to be seen at best as distasteful when official agencies are failing to fulfil their basic obligations. Civil renewal requires civic renewal.

---

[10] The term is most strongly associated with Garland's (2001) work on the culture of control.

Shame all round

A key feature of the enforcement stance in the government's approach is its emphasis on systematic shaming. The intention is that through the use of legal powers and the power of popular news media (especially local newspapers) to draw attention to contraventions of acceptable behaviour, perpetrators of anti-social or disrespectful behaviour will be corrected or removed by the system and potential perpetrators will be dissuaded from following suit. But in building policy on a platform of public shaming, the government lays itself open to the accusation that it is engineering conflict for political ends, rather like having a war to boost popularity, in this case a kind of civil war. It calls relentlessly for more prisoners to be taken. Its language, the language of zero-tolerance, is belligerent.

It's clear that shaming in a relatively private context can work. A former probation worker told me:

> *Feeling ashamed, as a private feeling, can be a strong disincentive to delinquency. I've sat in on a meeting between an offender and victim (with offender's family also there) and the shame and embarrassment of the offender was palpable and potentially transformational – the most difficult thing I've ever done, he said.*

Unfortunately it can also be counterproductive, particularly in an unequal society and particularly in a public context. Fear and shame, as Richard Sennett (2003) points out, are poor motivators and often have the opposite effect to that intended. Theorists of the Catholic confession might defend the private version; but many probation workers, victim support workers and social workers have picked up the pieces from the occasions when it doesn't work. Reintegrative shaming is widely acknowledged as very powerful where there is community cohesion to buffer its psychological effects. Brewer and colleagues researched the part played by informal social control in the management of crime within exceptionally tight-knit communities in Belfast. They noted:

> *Shame is less effective as a sanction in a highly mobile and anonymous society where people lack social bonds with their neighbour.*

(Brewer et al., 1998: 574)

It's worth pausing a moment to reflect on why shaming should be problematic. Public shaming glorifies deviancy, for many offenders and also for many of its willing spectators encouraged by media and authorities. It also reinforces negative self-concepts among people who have been failed by those around them. Shaming doesn't work because it's not based on respect. The notion of shaming someone publicly is essentially disrespectful. It's legitimised dissing. Hence we have a profound irony: we have policy using a device which is not respectful, in order to promote respect.

Consumption and disrespect

The *Respect Action Plan* embodies a very partial approach to civil relations. As we have noted, the call to enforce civil responsibilities to fellow citizens emphasises anti-social behaviour and tends to play out mostly in low-income neighbourhoods. You don't need to be an unreconstructed Marxist to detect an imbalance. The government's agenda completely fails even to acknowledge that our society is riddled with the sanctioned disrespectful behaviour of 'respectable' citizens. The commonplace contemporary classic of such behaviour is the SUV arrogantly left by an able-bodied executive on a disabled parking slot. But we are not short of examples. For instance, are low-paid employees of a large company supposed to retain respect for a fat-cat director awarded (by their colleagues on the board) an enormous salary increase or handout? Is it at all likely that when the fat-cat dies, the employees and their families will be out there doffing their caps as the funeral car passes?

I recently stood and observed a woman taking a couple of children to school. They sought an opportunity to cross a moderately busy minor road near my neighbourhood, waiting for a gap in the traffic. The SUVs slugged by. With the children clutching her hands, the woman first negotiated round a car parked uncompromisingly across the pavement, then peered between other vehicles for a safe opportunity. It was an unremarkable moment, but it illustrates an accumulated systematic insensitivity to everyday needs – the needs of a carer for the safety of children within the neighbourhood, the case for a walkable route to the local school, the right to a bit of pavement to be reserved for pedestrians. A short time later I found a post-it stuck to the windscreen of a car at the same point: it read 'Are you always this considerate to elderly people and pedestrians?'

Behind this vignette there is no public or political recognition of how consumerism, the system of consumption, implicitly condones the exaggerated use of cars and the unsustainable consumption of resources. But the message is that if you do not consume, you are less important and you are failing as a citizen. In the words of Bannister and his colleagues: 'The culture of respect is manifest largely as a mode of conduct – namely, consumption' (Bannister et al., 2006: 924).

The system of consumption upholds our economy. But it seems reasonable that a regard for environmental sustainability, so seldom practised by the private sector, should be regarded as a key component of rounded respect among human beings, if only because one measure of being civilised would seem to be the ability to give consideration to the needs of future generations.

Consumerism encourages the barely civil anonymity of occasions of trade (no interaction at the checkout, compared to neighbourly chats at the corner shop) and the cocooned rampant disrespect of road-rage. It stimulates and supports non-local connections between people, at the expense of connections between residents at local level. People who consume more tend to live their lives less locally. The essential face-to-face informal context for respect is thereby eroded.

Sarah Lochlann Jain provides an ethnographic account of an American mother using her four-wheel drive SUV for errands, and notes:

> This was an urban environment designed for smooth consumption and in contradiction of accidental meetings, social interaction, or modes of transportation other than private automobile. It was an environment made easy but non-negotiable through its series of non-human actors: roads, parking, shoes, strollers.
>
> (Jain, 2002: 400)

Tracy, the woman whose progress across this constructed landscape is described, apparently appreciates the fact that she is 'not going to bond' with the staff in shops and services:

> Also enclosed within this geography of efficiency is the near structural impossibility of other types of interaction: one will by definition not run into or meet a neighbour at a drive-thru bank. The roadside architecture structures kinds of possibilities for civic interaction in ways that increase efficiency ('down moments', quick errands) and decrease accidental meetings.
>
> (Jain, 2002: 394)

One feature of our lifestyles which such examples highlight is what I call the 'swollen home'. The swollen home is one that is *deeper* to inhabit because of the seductive power of television and other home entertainment devices, by which people lead their common lives separately; and *extended*, partly through play equipment or outhouse facilities such as workshops, partly through portable private entertainment technologies, and most potently in the sense that the car is so often an extension that almost seamlessly incorporates the comforts and privacy of the home. Driving or riding in a car, in this mentality, can be so disturbing for people who are unready for potential contact with the Other, they feel the need to opt for the lofty SUV position and of course the darkened windows to minimise the vulgar glare of the public realm. Are these not disdainful, these dark windows, which declare 'I don't wish to have to acknowledge you'? Do they not represent a pinnacle of the detached disrespect of individual consumption? Our officially sanctioned respectable way of life – consume more, only engage with others at your own discretion – seems to work in precisely the opposite direction to the trumpeted intentions of the respect agenda.

Professional disrespect: a personal vignette

Having been fortunately healthy for most of my life I have been largely protected from the practised disempowerment and disrespect at which the medical profession is apparently quite expert. I recently had to visit a consultant's representative in a hospital and the experience was a short sharp shock in human relations. Since I am still fairly mobile, being sent about the hospital to have this and that measured in different rooms was not a problem to me and I made sure I maintained a smile and courteous relations with the staff who dealt with me. Then I was shown into the consultant's room. He asked me a question, and as I began to answer I realised he wasn't paying attention to what I was saying. Then after a few seconds he began to speak, talking quite loudly over me and ignoring my efforts to finish what I was saying. This happened at least twice, perhaps more – I was quite dazed by it and the conversation completely lost shape for me.

Two things were striking. First, that he didn't even make a show of taking an interest in me. Secondly, that although I am a relatively educated, articulate, white male adult speaking my own language in my home town, I was quickly reduced to a kind of bewildered compliance. When he dismissed me I felt meek and dazed.

In sharing with others what I thought was an extraordinary occasion, I have since found that this is, anecdotally, close to the norm for many people. While sympathising, people have been a little bemused at my surprise. How does this happen? I'm not particularly assertive but I have upset senior civil servants by being stroppy in their meetings: yet here I was completely off my guard and disarmed straight away. Perhaps the imbalance in the power relations between the citizen and the medical profession is so entrenched (Sousa and Eusebio, 2005), and arrogance on the part of the latter so widespread, that no-one realises this is systematised disrespect. What is it like for people whose English may be poor, who may have problematic or even frightening symptoms of illness, who are intimidated by administrative or medical environments, or lack assertiveness? In the circumstances, it's not surprising if people get frustrated and perhaps angry. Many visits to doctors and consultants are repeat visits and one often hears of people having to steel themselves, to prepare themselves mentally for a mini-ordeal.

For people whose lives are highly localised within their neighbourhood, this kind of disrespect is likely to have a significant effect on their morale and their sense of how society regards them. It's officially protected disrespect and its impact is insidious. People with power and responsibility within society are routinely abusing it in minor ways by not showing respect to those in their charge. Bullying teachers and surly officials are part of the same syndrome. It's important to make this point in order to contextualise the relentless finger-wagging of those in positions of power against those who experience disadvantage and exclusion.

Figure 1.2   Robotics Class Rules

'Be nice and get along with everyone'

I visited an after-school community project some years ago where young people around the age of 10 were working on a robotics project. At the time I met them they were messing with papier mâché, shaping the bodies of the robots whose electronics they would subsequently programme. With their teacher's help, they'd established the ground rules for working together: 'Robotics Class Rules (not to break)'.

These are guidelines for mutual respect in a practical context. You can sense the process from the product: young people think about how they'd feel if someone was negative about their work, and come up with a measure to resist such behaviour. It's a tiny but potentially profound experience of democratic empowerment and responsibility, which incorporates a sense of ownership over the rule-making process and hence over the sense of respect. It's reasonable to suppose that once these rules had been developed, by the young people themselves, nobody really needed to refer to them, but they were pinned up on the wall to give them an authoritative status. Doubtless the rules have since been taken by some of the young people into the complex arenas of later life.

But listening more generally to young people talk about life in their neighbourhoods, we get the sense that many lack anything approaching an equivalent process. There is plenty of material pointing to the risks that young people face either within the home, or from other young people outside the home. (See, for example, Skelton, 2000; Waiton, 2001; Barnes and Baylis, 2004; Seaman et al., 2005; Deakin, forthcoming 2006.) The latter phenomenon is most powerfully illustrated by their references to youth gangs, where respect blurs into tight allegiance, group members enjoying mutual respect but outsiders routinely, sometimes ritually, disrespected. (Young people's experiences in gangs are described in some detail by Aydin Mehmet Ali in Chapter 7. See also Alexander (2000)).

Young people in all societies struggle with the need to gain respect simultaneously from adults on the one hand, and from their peers on the other. These two struggles are sometimes conflicting, because growing up is like that – sometimes respect will be withheld by other kids where it is bestowed by adults, and vice versa. And all this takes place at an age when *self-respect* is very much still under construction – not a good context for emotional bulldozing. We ought at least to acknowledge this and explore ways of working round it.

But government policies can be seen to be at best unhelpful. Longstanding calls for investment in youth work and youth centres have been ignored, while the anti-youth media hype has been allowed to flourish – indeed encouraged – by our politicians. The *Respect Action Plan* makes no acknowledgement of the predominant source of children's fear on the streets – which is other children. What it does is to accentuate the sense of adult disapprobation without offering a basis of mutual respect on which to build. Research carried out in 2002 by Nicola Madge (2006) suggests that children acknowledge that they are not always as polite and respectful to adults as they might be. But she adds that they reflect on the need for adults to reciprocate (p. 46). As the Children's Commissioner Al Aynsley-Green (2006) puts it:

> Children and young people are used to being spoken about . . . what they experience far less is having their views and ideas listened to and respected. The respect agenda must also include a responsibility for adults – parents, doctors, nurses, teachers, neighbours, relatives and friends – to treat children and young people with respect. They are often vilified as a group and tell me that they are not listened to as individuals.

The problem is illustrated by a comment on a recent television programme about 'Britain's yobs'.[11] One local activist working to engage young people away from anti-social behaviour remarked that 'they don't seem to fear anything any more'. The phrase probably has the ring of truth for many people. The same sense is expressed a little more quaintly by journalist Tomos Livingstone reporting a friend's explanation: 'The rise in anti-social behaviour . . . is down to the fact that not enough people tut at youngsters anymore, and they're consequently not embarrassed about smashing car windows and so forth.'[12] The use of the word 'fear' in the first quote may be instructive, suggesting an 'old testament' model of unquestioning acquiescence to a greater authority.

The question arises, to what extent do we want children to 'fear' authority? It's a fine line perhaps, but I suggest we should give more thought to the language we use in these situations. Many young people are stifled with fear of other kids in their neighbourhood and what they need in their relation with the adult authoritative world is exactly the opposite – a sense of respectful support. Rather than being preoccupied with instilling a sense of fear, whereby we risk taking away people's readiness to change, we should be concerned with promoting pro-social behaviour and inclusion.

This is not to suggest that when young people behave in anti-social ways, there should not be the possibility of an authoritative response, as there should for anyone else, either from among local residents or from some official presence. But before the latter is needed, rather than publishing and publicising a demonstrably partial analysis of respect based on an old-testament-style authority, should we not be exploring how we establish the neighbourhood equivalent of 'robotics rules?'

---

[11] *Britain's yobs*. Channel 4 television broadcast, 24 April 2006, http://www.channel4.com/news/microsites/D/dispatches2006/yobs/index.html

[12] Tomos Livingstone, *Time Government heard the 'tut-tuts'*, 20 May 2006, IC Wales, accessed at http://icwales.icnetwork.co.uk/0100news/newspolitics/ 25 May 2006.

Chapter 2

Networks, Intervention and Retaliation: Informal Social Control in Four English Neighbourhoods

Jacqueline Barnes

Introduction

The government's *Action Plan* for the respect agenda highlights the role that parents might take, but the focus for parents is on their 'critical role in helping their children develop good values and behaviour' (Respect Task Force 2006: 3) with discussion on developing parenting services nationally, applying parenting orders and tackling 'problem families'. This places the emphasis on the relevance of parents for the children they are directly responsible for, those living with them. This is clearly a worthwhile focus, though possibly over-punitive in its emphasis. However, it does not take into account the interaction between families and their local communities. The chapter in the plan on 'strengthening communities' (p24–9) focuses more on local policing, housing management, and the provision of a national non-emergency number for reporting incidents that might not be served by the emergency services. What has been left out is the important interface between parents and the community represented by the impact that the efforts of adults (both parents and others) can have in setting standards and managing the behaviour of children and youth out and about in neighbourhoods. While their role may also extend to controlling the behaviour of adults in neighbourhoods, this chapter will focus in particular on the role of residents in managing the behaviour of youngsters. Presenting research from four localities in England, it will discuss parents' views on whether this should be their role, whether they think that neighbours would act to control other people's children, and if not, what prevents them.

First, some background into why it is thought important that adults in a neighbourhood should be responsible, at least in part, for the behaviour of local youngsters other than those in their immediate household. Some may argue that if the children's parents cannot instil the right values and actions, then it is the place of formal services – schools perhaps or the police – to get children to behave in an acceptable manner, time to bring in someone with 'real' power. Others would disagree, pointing to pressure from other community members as equally, possibly even more important. If youngsters in a neighbourhood do not act in a manner that indicates respect for those around them, then this should be conveyed to them. If one is seen dropping litter, spraying a message on a traffic sign, or behaving in a threatening way to other children, then those adults who witness the incident have a responsibility to let the youngster in question know that their behaviour is not acceptable, that it goes against what is deemed appropriate by those in the community. If they instead always walk 'on the other side' then how is a child to learn that the behaviour is wrong? This pressure from other citizens in the context of shared values has been called 'informal social control', a central dimension in the theoretical conceptualisation of community social organisation or disorganisation (Bursik and Webb, 1982; Sampson and Groves, 1989).

The essence of social disorganisation theory, developed by sociologists at the University of Chicago in the early 1900s, is that variation in crime and delinquency over time and among areas is explained by the absence or breakdown of institutions (e.g. family, school, church and local government) and communal relationships between neighbours that traditionally encouraged cooperative behaviour (Jensen, 2003). Chicago was at that time a booming industrial city, increasingly populated by recent immigrants of diverse ethnic backgrounds. Rapid growth and change were viewed as 'disorganizing' or 'disintegrative' forces contributing to a breakdown in the teaching and learning of those prior 'social rules' which had inhibited crime and delinquency in the European societies from which many immigrants came (Thomas and Znaniecki, 1918). The theory, which is also discussed by Philip Connolly in Chapter 5, commonly refers to the absence of organisation among people in relatively small units (neighbourhoods), but has also been used to explain variations in crime among larger areas such as counties, states and nations.

Social disorganisation in an area is said to influence the health and well-being of residents through its impact on social capital, meaning the values that people hold, the resources that they can access through relationships with local friends and a shared sense of identity, trust and reciprocity (Edwards et al., 2003). Coleman suggests (1993) that the norms, values and expectations of a community, particularly an informal community, rely on social capital arising from dense social networks that have continuity over time. Residents of communities lacking social capital will not be as likely to reinforce social norms through intervening to control unwanted behaviour; they will be reluctant to get involved because they do not have a strong sense that neighbours would agree with their actions or do the same for them, if their child was misbehaving. This lack of involvement in reinforcing 'appropriate' behaviour is then predicted to result in further social disintegration and negative outcomes for families and children. Informal control is the key to maintaining a community rather than relying on formal structures. This can be accomplished by intervening when adults act in an anti-social manner – possibly fighting in public, or having abusive arguments. It can also be achieved through adult involvement in leisure-time youth activities so that they can be available to step in if behaviour becomes unacceptable and, through public intervention such as control of unruly street-corner congregation, challenging youths who seem to be up to no good (Coulton et al., 1996).

This is quite circular in that social disorganisation – a relatively high level of crime, poor upkeep of the fabric of houses and the streets, a great deal of litter and mess, people having disputes in public, and so on – prevent the establishment of social networks necessary for the generation of social capital, which allow the confidence to implement informal control. In the face of disorder people tend to withdraw into their homes or 'shells' due to feelings of fear, mistrust and suspicion. Yet without the networks, social disorganisation may develop and increase. The downward spiral continues as increased social disorder is interpreted by residents as an absence of shared norms prompting many to withdraw from local life due to fear and mistrust (Aneshensel and Sucoff, 1996). This fosters feelings of alienation, powerlessness, anxiety and depression, which in turn lead to further social withdrawal.

Networks are also weakened or prevented from forming by other features of a neighbourhood such as many people moving in and out of the area, a wide mix of local residents who may speak a number of different languages and have differing customs and religious beliefs. Sampson (1992) has argued that community disorganisation is of primary importance to parents because of the role it plays in facilitating or inhibiting the creation of social capital, and that lack of social capital is one of the primary features of socially disorganised communities. He emphasises that the connectedness of social networks among families and children at local level provides children with the norms and sanctions that could not be brought about by a single adult.

Thus a key component of a 'healthy' community, one with respect, is informal social control of children and youth by local adults – the collective supervision to prevent behaviour that the community has deemed to be against their values. Most commonly this strategy has been discussed in relation to controlling local anti-social behaviour (Furstenberg, 1993), especially monitoring and surveillance of youth, peer groups, and gangs. Based on the belief that human nature is essentially good, the informal systems aim at promoting communitarianism by appealing to people's morality and conscience. People are encouraged to moderate their personal emotions and behaviour, evade their self-interests and, ultimately, to develop a sense of obligation to the community in which they live (Jiao, 2004). This may be seen to have oppressive and negative overtones if applied to managing personal behaviour as intimate as having only one child, as has been the case in China (Dewey, 2004). However, there is more agreement that it can be a positive way to manage the anti-social behaviour of youth, peer groups and gangs through monitoring and surveillance.

Social disorganisation theorists propose that local communities are complex systems of reciprocal friendship and kinship networks, and informal ties rooted in family life. Informal social control depends on shared norms about appropriate parenting and child behaviour, and norms that value protecting neighbours from criminal victimisation. But shared norms are not useful unless there is one extra ingredient – a willingness to act on these norms (Nash and Bowen, 1999). Following the lives of a group of youngsters identified when they were first delinquent, Sampson and Laub (1990) note that the theory of informal social control predicts that crime and deviance will result when an individual's bond to society is weak or broken. Lack of social networks and attachments are associated with a risk for the development of criminal behaviour (Sampson and Laub, 1990). Similarly at the community level, as local social networks begin to weaken, cohesion between neighbours is further reduced so that a downward spiral is expected in terms of the behaviour that is left unchecked. Local people's sense of collective efficacy declines as residents come to believe that they no longer share common values and norms and are unable to enforce sanctions or effect change. This breakdown in cohesion and collective efficacy can have serious negative consequences for children and youth as an important mechanism of control evaporates. Highly disordered neighbour-hoods with low levels of reciprocal friendship or perceived norms may discourage residents from attempting to implement control of youth due to feared retaliation and lack of support, leading to a rise in delinquent behaviour.

The Families and Neighbourhoods Study

Why and where?

Much of the research related to informal social control has taken place elsewhere, mainly in the United States. The Families and Neighbourhoods Study was designed to explore the utility of this and other theoretical formulations relating to parents and communities in English towns and cities. The over-arching aims of the research were to try to uncover what it is about a community or neighbourhood that assists parents in their function as child carers and what may be counter-productive to parenting and to child development. One element of that was to investigate local social networks, local shared values about parenting and about intervening to control local youth, and the likelihood of such intervention taking place. Ideally this study would have taken place in 20 or 30 localities, spread throughout the United Kingdom, but in order to look in detail at the experiences and feelings of parents, their children and the communities it was decided to focus on a small number of areas, making them as different as possible from each other, to provide a range of backgrounds for family experiences. The main focus of the study was on deprived areas, where more problems related to parenting and child behaviour are likely to be found.

The Indices of Multiple Deprivation (Noble et al., 2000) were used to identify the 20 per cent most deprived electoral wards in England and then to select neighbourhoods including some of these wards. The study includes one deprived area in a large city, a neighbourhood that is also typified by rich ethnic diversity (City[1]); one deprived area in a mid-sized town (Town) and a small deprived rural area on the coast (Small Town). Finally, a fourth, affluent neighbourhood, a suburb of a large city was selected (Suburb) so that some deprived/affluent comparisons could be made, and to allow for the possibility that findings could be applicable across neighbourhoods other than those with marked deprivation.

City is part of a local authority that covers approximately eight square miles, adjacent to the centre of a large city. The area is a lively mix of shopping streets, markets, housing and parks with a rich mix of ethnic groups. Principally there is a large population of Bangladeshi origin and a smaller, though still substantial proportion with African/Caribbean backgrounds. The housing is a mixture of older (Victorian) low-rise flats and houses, and some modern high-rise blocks.

Town is an area located near to the centre of a mid-sized town, situated on a river estuary. The town is the largest urban area in predominantly rural surroundings, notable mainly for agriculture and recreational open spaces and waterways. The area has some small rows of shops, and several parks but is predominantly residential, the housing mainly council owned and almost exclusively low-rise, much dating from the immediate post Second World War period, with many terraced and semi detached houses and some small multi-occupancy buildings. Many of the residents report that they were born and grew up locally.

Small Town is unique in many ways both in its physical make up and the community itself. It is bordered by a wide-open beach and open fields and marshlands, with much of the area lying under sea level, but the local residents have little in the way of amenities. While small it has three distinct 'zones' identifiable by their physical and social differences – the village, generally made up of small bungalows/ chalets set in neat little roads; the seafront, wooden and asbestos built beach huts constructed between the wars as holiday homes but mainly converted to become permanent homes; and the Estate, mainly built in the 1970s and 1980s with detached bungalows and three or four bedroom houses. Many of the residents moved to the area and few are locally born.

Suburb is located five miles to the north west of a city centre, an affluent, leafy residential area with a number of churches but few shops. There is one large open area bordering the suburb but no parks with amenities. The housing stock is dominated by detached residences, either older stone properties or newer brick built houses, with some culs-de-sac and gated areas. Only a small proportion of the residents are social renters.

Who, and what was asked?

In each locality approximately one third of the respondents were the parent of an infant, one third had a child of four to five years, just starting in a reception class, and one third had a child of 11 to 12 years who had just started in a secondary school. Only responses to some of the neighbourhood questions will be presented here.

---

[1] All localities are kept anonymous, partly to protect the identities of respondents but also to facilitate thinking that is general rather than specific about these particular neighbourhoods.

Two neighbourhoods (City and Town) were of sufficient size to recruit parents of 100 infants, 100 children in reception class and 100 beginning secondary school. In the two smaller areas the target was to recruit 30 parents of each age group. The recruitment strategy differed depending on the age of child. Mothers with infants were recruited with the support of health visitors. Following approval by the relevant Local Research Ethics Committees, a researcher talked to families in waiting rooms of child health clinics and GP-based mother and baby clinics, to find out if they would like to participate. Mothers of children about to enter infant or secondary school were recruited with the assistance of local schools in the target wards, sending out letters that they could respond to if interested.

All respondents (the child's primary caregiver, and in the majority of cases the mother) were visited at home and given a structured face-to-face interview lasting approximately one hour, which included questions about the neighbourhood, their family, their own background, their parenting and their current health and well being.

Shared values, parenting norms

First the parents were asked whether they thought that locally there was agreement about parenting. One question was phrased positively – 'my neighbours and I think alike about parenting', and the other negatively, 'I disagree with my neighbours about how to discipline', and they were asked whether they agreed or disagreed, or were not sure. In Suburb the parents were confident that they and neighbours agreed about parenting, endorsed by 80 per cent, and did not disagree about discipline, refuted by 91 per cent. In the three disadvantaged areas there was less consensus, but it was still the case that more than half in each area expected agreement about parenting, and did not expect disagreement about discipline (see Figure 2.1). Parents were also asked whether children locally were adequately supervised or whether they were allowed to move about in the neighbourhood too freely, referred to overall as local monitoring – though clearly this does not encompass all aspects of parental monitoring such as asking one's child who his or her friends are. There were stark differences between Suburb and the other three areas in response to the statement 'Too many children are allowed to run wild', endorsed by 64 per cent in City, 58 per cent in Town and 56 per cent in Small Town but only 5 per cent in Suburb. Clearly children did not run wild in Suburb, perhaps because they had plenty of space in their homes and gardens or because their parents kept them busy with a range of (potentially expensive) extra-curricular activities. Similarly, while 99 per cent of Suburb parents endorsed the statement 'Parents in this neighbourhood take good care of their children', this was so for less than half in all the other localities (City 48 per cent, Town 43 per cent, Small Town 44 per cent).

They were then asked whether neighbours should be involved in the control of children in the area, or conversely whether they should mind their own business. They were also asked if they thought that nowadays another adult **would** verbally correct a child's behaviour if the parent was not around. For Suburb parents these questions may be more hypothetical than for the others, since they clearly do not expect many children to be roaming unattended in their neighbourhood. In City and Town just under half thought that local people should *not* mind their own business (43 per cent and 47 per cent respectively), though this was the case for more than three quarters in the Suburb (76 per cent) but only one third in Small Town (31 per cent, see Figure 2.2), suggesting that the nature of the neighbourhood may influence thoughts about community vigilance. If the area is too small (and the Small Town area comprises several small neighbourhoods) then perhaps it is hoped that people

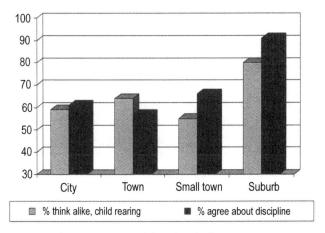

Figure 2.1   Percent consensus about parenting and discipline, by location

will keep their thoughts and actions to themselves, whereas in the affluent suburb there was an expectation that everyone would look out for each other. Nevertheless, minding or not minding one's business is not the same as controlling children. Asked if adults had the right to correct a child if the parent was not present there was surprisingly no difference based on disadvantage, with agreement from about half in City, Town and Suburb (55 per cent, 51 per cent, 45 per cent) but again those in Small Town were not likely to say that adults had this right, in their view (18 per cent, see Figure 2.2). It is interesting then that, when asked if adults would intervene locally, this was at a similar level in Suburb and Small Town (43 per cent, 37 per cent), but lower in City and Town (33 per cent, 23 per cent). The actuality of people intervening may be influenced by the size of the neighbourhood, and the likelihood that people might know each other. Both Suburb and Small Town were relatively small areas compared to City and Town, and had easily identifiable boundaries, whereas the other neighbourhoods merged into larger residential settlements.

To investigate local informal social control in more detail, respondents were asked how likely it was (with choices from very likely to not at all likely, using a five point scale) that neighbours would intervene in 14 different scenarios involving a five year old child, either to ensure their safety and prevent them from harm (five questions), to limit misbehaviour (four questions) or to prevent

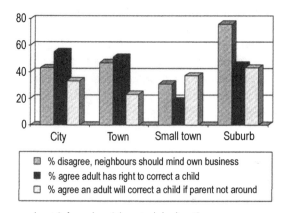

Figure 2.2   Local consensus about informal social control, by location

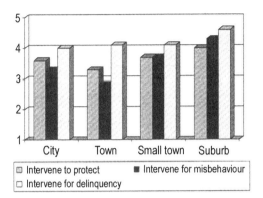

Figure 2.3   Mean score (range 1 false to 5 true) for informal social control, by location

delinquent acts (five questions). It is important to note that the age of the child was specified as five years, if they had asked about a teenager then the replies might have been different.

In all four areas young children displaying delinquent behaviour (e.g. has a knife; stealing from local household) were expected to elicit more reaction from local adults than situations where they were seemingly at risk of neglect or injury (e.g. wandering alone) or were misbehaving (e.g. hitting another child; see Figure 2.3). The behaviour most likely to lead to intervention was the scenario of a young child with a knife, and the one least likely to lead to expectations of intervention was a young child picking flowers from a garden. When delinquent acts were described, the average response was near the top of the five point scale (on average approximately four with five representing very likely and one representing not likely) in the three disadvantaged areas, and even closer to very likely in Suburb. In contrast the average response for incidents where a child was vulnerable (at home alone, had fallen off a bicycle) or misbehaving (throwing rocks at a dog, hitting a child of the same age) was close to the midpoint indicating that parents were not sure that they knew if local parents would intervene or not.

So far informal control has been presented only in terms of the four different neighbourhoods, and the extent of disadvantage present, but the study was designed to investigate what factors – either within the neighbourhoods or in relation to the respondents themselves and their personal experiences in the neighbourhoods – might explain more or less informal control. Parents were asked about the level of crime in their locality (nine crimes such as mugging, drug dealing, burglary or car crime), about the extent of general disorder (14 factors such as litter, alcoholics, gangs, burned out buildings), about their own personal exposure to crime, either as the victim or knowing someone personally in the neighbourhood (12 items such as being mugged, hearing gun shots, fight with weapons), and about whether they were afraid for themselves or their children to go out, in the daytime or after dark (score from 0–4). Scores on each of these scales were correlated with the informal control scale scores. All these aspects of social disorganisation were negatively associated with the likelihood of informal control, and in particular they suppressed the likelihood that intervention would occur for delinquent behaviour (see Table 2.1).

It should be noted, nevertheless, that one additional aspect of local disorder was the most strongly associated with lack of informal control, a scale reflecting how much retaliation was predicted from local children, teenagers or parents. Three questions were posed about verbal retaliation asking for a true to false (five point) response to the statement 'Children (teenagers, parents) might yell or swear at someone who verbally corrects their behaviour (their child)'. Three additional questions asked in a

Table 2.1   Associations between informal social control (ISC) and neighbourhood risk and protective factors

	ISC for Delinquency	ISC for Misbehaviour	ISC for vulnerable to abuse/neglect
Risk factors			
Disorder	−0.23	−0.16	−0.16
Crime	−0.21	−0.16	−0.15
Exposure to crime	−0.20	−0.14	−0.14
Personal fear	−0.12	−0.14	−0.11
Expect retaliation (total)	−0.30	−0.42	−0.37
Expect retaliation (parents)	−0.30	−0.44	−0.36
Expect retaliation (children)	−0.29	−0.42	−0.31
Expect retaliation (teenagers)	−0.27	−0.36	−0.32
Protective factors			
Shared norms, parenting/discipline	0.16	0.19	0.21
Shared norms, monitoring	0.29	0.37	0.40
Local social networks	0.17	0.10	0.16
Local social participation	0.13	0.14	0.18

similar vein about physical retaliation from children, teenagers or parents. These six items plus one additional question about parents getting angry if a neighbour verbally corrects their child were added together to make a scale ranging from seven (no retaliation) to 35 (a great deal from all age groups). This total score was strongly and negatively associated with all three kinds of informal control (see Table 2.1). The amount of retaliation expected from each age group was compared, and in all locations most retaliation was expected from teenagers (see Figure 2.4). In Town and Suburb the least retaliation was expected from children (lower than that from parents) while in City least retaliation was expected from parents and in Small Town equal amounts of retaliation were expected from children and parents. Nevertheless, while retaliation from parent might be lower than that from teens, the amount of retaliation expected from local parents was the most strongly associated with lower informal control, although correlations between ISC and retaliation from all three age groups were significant (see Table 2.1).

The theory of informal social control places strong emphasis on its relationship with shared values and norms, strong local social ties and local social capital, represented by shared values and shared

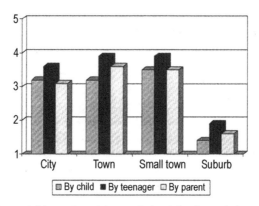

Figure 2.4   Mean score (range 1 false to 5 true) for retaliation following verbal control of a child, by location

opportunities for neighbours to help neighbours. Questions pertaining to shared norms have already been described and these were associated with ISC (see Table 2.1). In particular when there was a feeling that local parents were effectively monitoring their children, in a way that reflected the respondents' own views about how closely children should be controlled – or allowed to roam about in the neighbourhood, then there was a greater expectation of informal control, supporting the theory. Shared norms about parenting and discipline were also positively associated with informal control, but to a lesser extent. Information on local social (non-family) networks and local participation that might lead to the development of social capital (e.g. sharing information and favours with neighbours, watching each other's property, socialising together) was also obtained and these were both associated with expectations for more informal control (see Table 2.1). As with local norms about parenting, these associations were not as strong as those reflecting the more problematic aspects of the neighbourhoods.

But all these aspects of a neighbourhood are likely to be related to each other. If there is a great deal of crime locally, or much disorder such as violent arguments between neighbours, one is likely to feel more fear, and may be less inclined to socialise with neighbours or ask them to watch property. If there is more disorder locally one might also predict more retaliation following the verbal discipline of a local child. Thus it was important to find out what was the main factor associated with more or less informal control, taking all the other relevant factors into account. This can be accomplished by using multiple regression. Factors that are associated with the extent of predicted informal control, based on correlations, are all entered together into an analysis, which then takes into account the relationships between each potential predictor. When this was done, entering not only those factors described here but also the personality and current mental health of the parent giving the responses, and their own personal use of discipline, an expectation of more informal control of children by neighbours was predicted by only two factors – a lower expectation of retaliation (Beta $-.28$, $p < 0.001$) and more non-family local social networks (Beta $.16$, $p < 0.001$).

Open-ended interviews

Less structured second interviews were conducted with a random selection of the parents, and some of their remarks illuminated the quantitative findings, as they described their conflict between thinking that it was a good thing to intervene, to protect a child in distress or prevent those causing trouble from continuing, but that this came at a cost. For example, one mother in Town described how she herself had intervened:

> I walked to the bus stop once, just after she [her infant] was born, and there was a little boy in the park no more than eight, and there were two boys about twelve years old pulling him from side to side until he ended up on the floor. I thought, I'm not having this. The other mothers in the park all ignored him. So I picked this boy up and I told the two other boys to go, and I walked this little boy home.

However, two others from the same locality explained why they were reluctant, and avoided intervention:

> I get scared what they might do and I daren't tell them off in case it makes them worse, they might go and target you then.

> The lady opposite . . . reported the teenagers racing up and down the road on a moped like mad without a helmet and she got a brick through her window.

Similar remarks were made in Small Town:

There was an incident recently with two boys fighting, one was beating the other one up, he was on the floor, and a lady came out because he was on the floor crying, she went over and got told to f'off, 'none of your f'ing business' was what she got.

In City there was general anxiety about being around youngsters when they were out and about:

A lot of the kids aren't very nice in this area any more. I won't walk past them on my own at night time, put it that way.

There was also anticipation of problems if one stepped in to prevent trouble:

There was a group of them (teenagers) in the building and they were there smoking, doing drugs or whatever down there and I said 'you don't live in here, what are you doing in here? Go out.' They shouted 'Get the f*** off' and there was a lot of them and just one of me, so I thought 'Oh I'd better just keep at that'.

But it was certainly not a universal. Residents of the same area were ready to act, expecting that parents would be grateful, as they themselves would be, if their child was protected:

Last night, I had to tell a little boy off who was outside putting water-bombs in the middle of the road. I said, 'No, you mustn't do that!' and his Nan was inside doing the washing up. I reckon she heard me (laughs). But you've got to be careful, you don't want to step on anyone's toes, but you don't want a child to be hurt. Everyone knows each other, so [neighbour], for instance, if she saw one of mine doing something silly on his bike, she would shout at him, but I wouldn't mind because it would be for his own safety.

Parents in Suburb were the most confident, emphasising the fact that they expected neighbours to have similar values:

It's just so safe for children. You've got to be careful because you can never say anything's too safe, but it's just the fact that everybody knows each other, so people look out for each other . . . (the children) accept that we are all friendly around here.

I just think the people, generally speaking, are decent people. We are all like minded and I think we all look out for one another's children as well.

So parents living in neighbourhoods that are typified by more economic disadvantage, more crime and disorder, and problems of fast migration in and out of the area, leading to lack of strong social ties, do face challenges. They may need more than guidance from the government about how to give respect and instil it in their children, though it would be reassuring if the response that was given by this mother from Town was more typical:

Yes, it's very friendly here. It's friendly and basically people try to help each other. If you have a problem you just ask and they always help . . . Neighbours will keep an eye on my son for me.

Cultural issues

Clearly one's views about local parents will be influenced by a range of factors, but one factor that may be of particular importance when considering the Respect agenda is that of ethnic or cultural background. Unlike cities in the USA, many UK cities have neighbourhoods with a rich mix of different cultural groups. In the Action Plan discussion of 'What is the issue?' it is noted that:

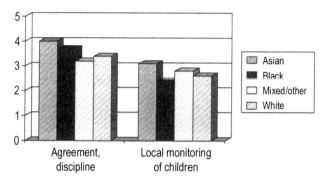

Figure 2.5 Mean scores for consensus about parenting (1 false, 5 true) in City for respondents from different ethnic groups

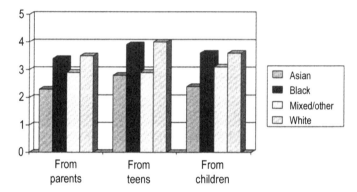

Figure 2.6 Mean score for expectation of retaliation (1 false, 5 true) in City by respondents from different ethnic groups

Ethnic and cultural diversity is a source of strength and dynamism in our society both nationally and locally. But without a shared framework of respect and rules, people can be susceptible to the argument that differences in culture and lifestyle are undermining community cohesion.

(Respect Task Force 2006: 5)

In one of the neighbourhoods studied it was possible to examine potential implications of ethnic diversity for informal social control. City included a substantial proportion (51 per cent) of respondents who were of Asian background – the majority of these Bangladeshi, and also a proportion who were of Caribbean, African or UK black background (7 per cent) and more than one third (38 per cent) who were white British, with the remainder either describing themselves as having mixed backgrounds or other groups (4 per cent). Overall the respondents of Asian background were the most positive about local parents in terms of the extent of agreement about discipline, or supervision of their children (see Figure 2.5) with the white residents the least positive about their neighbours. This was also seen in their responses to questions about the likelihood of retaliation from children, teenagers or local parents, if a child was controlled by a neighbour (see Figure 2.6), with white and black respondents expecting similar (higher) levels of retaliation. Finally, the Asian respondents predicted more informal control to stop delinquency, misbehaviour or to help a child at risk of abuse or neglect than the white or mixed background respondents (see Figure 2.7).

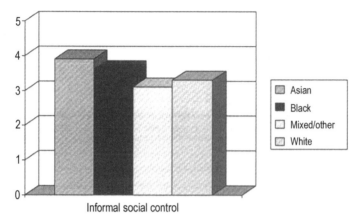

Figure 2.7 Mean score for expectation of informal social control (1 false, 5 true) in City by respondents from different ethnic groups

What might be the implications for a mixed community such as this? The Bangladeshi parents were in the majority so may have been more confident about local families because they thought that they know what other parents' views might be. They may also have met more people through local contact in shops or during community activities designed to support their own culture. However, there is a less positive explanation, indicated by some of the comments made during qualitative interviews, that it was not the Asian parents who were particularly positive but the other groups who were more negative, and that this was in part due to the ethnic difference, and to being in the minority. A number of the white and Caribbean, African or UK black parents made remarks that indicated a negative view of Asian youth, talking about gangs, and they were particularly likely to make this kind of comment if they had been resident in the neighbourhood for some time.

> I read in the newspaper that a man got murdered just over the train station, you know. They go around in gangs and you see groups of boys . . . I think Asians keep their girls in the house but they allow their boys to do anything . . . When I first lived here it wasn't this kind of community, there wasn't an Asian community . . . I'm not against Asians or anything like that, but I think . . . well it's an Asian community what can you do, there are more of them than you . . . My little boy doesn't really have any other West Indians to mix with . . . They wouldn't do anything say if there was a Rastafarian, they wouldn't close the school for my culture, but because there is an Asian community in this area so that is how it is.

These differences in the ways that the local community, and its young people, are perceived will have relevance if any crime reduction or respect building initiative is introduced. It may be useful to find out about differences in local perceptions by way of local surveys or focus groups and then build on positive perspectives, while understanding why some residents feel less positive about their neighbours, either because they feel that 'their neighbourhood' has changed or because they simply feel in the minority, a voice not taken seriously.

And the children, what do they say?

So far all the information described in this chapter has been derived from parents or other caregivers. The children in these areas also had some ideas about what they wanted from a neighbourhood which are important to keep in mind. Some of the secondary aged children (11 or 12 years old) in

City, Town and Suburb were questioned in small groups. They were asked what they wanted from their neighbourhood and several explained that they wanted to be able to spend time away from their homes, with their friends. They hoped that their neighbourhoods would provide space so that they could 'hang out' away from family, an important aspect of autonomy for this age group. Their comments reflect those of the boy of 15 who won a High Court fight to challenge the legality of a curfew zone in his neighbourhood of Richmond, in South West London, arguing that he was a 'model student' who should not be treated like a criminal (BBC News, 2005). These teenagers discussed what they would like in terms of shelters to spend time, even in bad weather, sport facilities and parks or open spaces where they could feel safe. However they expressed a range of fears and worries about being out in their communities, even in the affluent Suburb:

> Yeah you get gangs of boys they don't do nothing but they talk dirty, they call you dirty names. (City)

> I know some of the boys, they think they are all hard and that, because some people are scared of them and that because they don't like going past them just in case they are going to do something. (Town)

> In the day it's safe (large open area), but in the evening there's quite a lot of teenagers. And people go on motorbikes there. (Suburb)

Much is being said in the media about children carrying weapons when they go out, and this is generally precipitated not by wanting to carry out aggressive acts, but to protect themselves. They also expressed fear about being in areas that were poorly lit. These youngsters were the same ones that, seen in a group from a distance in their 'hoodies', could become an object of fear for adults. Not many people think in the same way as the Archbishop of York, who himself wore such a garment while giving a sermon, urging people not to judge teenagers by their fashion choices (BBC News, 2006a).

Discussion and thoughts for the future

It sounds positive to think that adults who are out and about will intervene to stop misbehaviour or delinquency, or protect a child who is at risk of abuse. But we should remember that this type of strategy can get out of hand, becoming vigilantism that gives adults an excuse for themselves engaging in behaviour that is unacceptable, arguing that they are controlling others. It can lead to the entrenchment of already negative views about youth formed on the basis of their clothing – the infamous hoodies – in a generalised perception that *any* young person is up to no good and should therefore not be allowed to wander freely in the community. There can be repercussions if responses are inappropriate, an example of which can be found in the case of a grandmother in Bournemouth who was arrested after challenging youths who kicked a football against her car. The difficulty was that she herself made use of physical methods, giving an 11-year-old boy 'a clip round the ear' (Sanderson, 2006). Other incidents have tragic consequences, as with the teenage boy who stepped in to prevent a fight between friends outside his school (BBC News, 2006b).

In March 2005 the government appointed Al Aynsley-Green as the first Children's Commissioner to promote the interests of children and young people in England. His reflections are useful in exploring the debate about how to 'control' children and youth in a positive manner. He asks 'How welcome are children and young people in our streets, shops and playing fields?' going on to indicate that perceptions may be distorted by the media, saying 'We have been told that 70 per cent of press articles about young people are negative and perpetuate thuggish behaviour' (Aynsley-Green, 2006).

Comments made by some of the young people interviewed for the Families and Neighbourhoods Study suggest that they would like to be welcomed in their neighbourhoods, but that they do not feel protected or included. As other contributors to this volume suggest, the continued social, spatial and moral isolation of young people is at best unhelpful. Many practitioners have sought to promote intergenerational projects of various kinds,[2] and such work would seem wholly appropriate for support under the aegis of the Respect agenda. It is unrealistic to regard the government's emphasis on youth volunteering, while welcome in itself, as much more than a partial contribution to the necessary re-integration of young people into society.

What is highly relevant in relation to the respect that adults in neighbourhoods might show to each other is the finding that the one aspect of a neighbourhood likely to limit informal control is fear – not just fear of teenagers but fear of young children and equally fear of their parents. Increasingly – as one incident follows another – we hear of events that illustrate the reality of what may happen when a peacemaker, or someone pursuing a burglar or car thief gets too close to their target. Recent stabbing deaths include a young man who felt that a man on a train was behaving in a threatening manner to his female companion (Pavia and Smith, 2006; Winterman, 2006), a young woman who seems to have pursued someone attempting to steal her car (Cowan and Lewis, 2006), and a teenage boy who tried to prevent a fight between two other youngsters (Martin and Alleyne, 2006). Undoubtedly many acts of intervention take place all over the country all the time, but those with tragic consequences receive media attention, they act as a warning – better not say anything, you may be the next stabbing victim, better to walk on, stay on the other side of the street, keep reading the paper, avoid eye contact – despite exhortations for more intervention (Furedi, 2006).

That we might fear those in the act of perpetrating crimes is understandable, but it is of more concern that many parents fear other parents. Controlling a child is likely to lead to a potentially violent confrontation with both the child and then, when they run home to describe the incident, with that child's parent. It is difficult to think of ways that trust in other parents can be improved by government intervention. The parents in Suburb were the only ones interviewed who trusted others, who expected that values would be similar, and that these values would include joint concern about children's behaviour. For most, the child is now more often someone to be defended at all costs, whatever might have taken place. Perhaps if less focus was placed on parenting orders, parenting classes, and telling parents that they are the ones who need to change their children (or else) then parents would be less defensive. While schools focus on educational targets; while the training of teachers concentrates on new (or old) ways to teach reading, spelling or mathematics, possibly less energy is left for thinking about how to inspire children and how to manage their behaviour. Informal control and formal systems each work more effectively when both are in place.

It was also found that informal control was more likely when parents knew more of their neighbours and supported them in small ways, sharing information, looking after keys and so on, or socialised with them. Schools can play an important role in facilitating initial contact between parents in a neighbourhood through social events such as international food evenings, concerts where youngsters can display their musical talents, or outdoor activities such as fun runs or five-a-side football. Though many of the respondents in Town had been born locally, attended local schools and had many family members in the vicinity, this is generally the exception rather than the rule in most neighbourhoods. Local families will come to learn more about each other, including the ways that they use discipline or their strategies for keeping track of a teenager's ever changing social network,

---

[2] See information provided by the Centre for Intergenerational Practice, http://www.centreforip.org.uk/

taking part in a quiz night at their child's school or going on a coach outing, than they will if their only contact is hooting at the car in front as each drops off their child at the school gate. Encouraging attendance at schools in walking distance, with many children who live near classmates, should increase the likelihood of families becoming more familiar with each other. The concept of the school being the hub of a community has been discussed in recent DfES documents. For example *Building Schools for the Future*[3] suggests that this initiative, which aims to rebuild or renew every secondary school in England over a 10–15 year period, will benefit parents and other community members:

> *Creating educational and leisure facilities for the whole community, not just pupils, is a fundamental part of the BSF programme. So you and your neighbours will also be able to use them for sports and evening classes.*

Cross-referencing between this kind of initiative and those developed by other government departments, particularly the Home Office, could highlight the potential impact of developing social networks in a neighbourhood. Many of the respondents reported that they had been controlled by neighbours when they were children if they were seen misbehaving. While it is possible that this 'golden age' of neighbourliness may not have ever been that great, and we may be irritated by the oft-quoted saying 'It takes a village to raise a child' (e.g. Clinton, 1996), there is a nugget of truth. It need not take a village, but it may help to know that there are many people out there in your own neighbourhood who would step forward if they felt that a child or youngster was in need of some re-direction.

[3] http://www.bsf.gov.uk/

Chapter 3

Incentives and Motivations for Neighbourliness

Liz Richardson

Background

In the late 1990s Michael Young and Gerard Lemos proposed that social landlords introduce a 'Mutual Aid Compact' for their tenants (Young and Lemos, 1997). This would be a voluntary agreement that tenants signed up to, promising to respect the place where they lived, their neighbours, and to provide practical help to neighbours where possible. As a concept it received a very mixed reception on both ideological and practical grounds. However, the debate it provoked illustrated the high level of interest in whether it is possible to 'make' people be better neighbours. Could a public agency stimulate or even enforce the lending and borrowing of cups of sugar? Would this lead to landlord-approved tea drinking? And would that mean that the housing management service could then also put its feet up in terms of tenancy enforcement and anti-social behaviour?

Questions over state and agency intervention to promote social networks are not new, and have not gone away (6, 2003). But the Mutual Aid Compact proposal seemed symbolic of a paradigmatic shift at the time. This shift in thinking was in favour of formalising informal relationships, and in favour of state intervention – 'if they won't, then we'll make them!' It arose partly out of the frustrations of many advocates for community building about the slowness and difficulties of creating and maintaining communities. This idea of formalising local social relationships grew alongside a shift in thinking in the social housing field and elsewhere about rights and responsibilities. The argument was that if social housing tenants have responsibilities that match their rights, one of those responsibilities is to their neighbours on behalf of their landlord.

One practitioner who was hacking out a path in this perilous moral territory was Tom Manion of Irwell Valley Housing Association. Widely vilified in the profession in the early days, he argued for a radically new approach to changing people's behaviour that was based on an individual reward and punishment model, called Gold Service, as a route to strengthening neighbourhoods and communities, rather than a traditional community building model. Now, in the early 2000s, there are at least ten social landlords offering reward based schemes covering around 100,000 social rented homes in different parts of the country including Wales and Scotland. Gold Service is only one approach, and complementary (or competing) agency approaches to changing people's behaviour to be more responsible citizens have also blossomed.

This chapter describes research which looked at four different experiments to increase people's willingness to behave co-operatively towards each other, to support social norms, and work with the authorities to tackle instances of problem behaviour. The idea was to look at projects designed to strengthen informal social controls, and increase people's willingness to do something themselves to tackle un-neighbourly behaviour of all kinds. This could include changing their own behaviour, 'going and having a word' with adults or young people directly, or reporting more serious infractions to the authorities.

The four types of intervention we looked at in our research were:

- Good neighbour declarations, otherwise called community or estate agreements, led by public agencies.
- Good neighbour projects led by community organisations.
- Schemes that reward positive behaviours, with sanctions for negative behaviours.
- Local authority wide strategic work.

The chapter will offer a brief description of the study, then explore five interesting practice findings and recommendations from the research that have relevance for those actively trying to tackle anti-social behaviour and increase neighbourliness in low income areas.

The study

The study focused on the operation of three schemes in particular neighbourhoods, and at a fourth set of initiatives operating across a whole local authority area. The first neighbourhood was in Salford, Manchester, where the study looked at *Irwell Valley Housing Association's Gold Service*. *Gold Service* is an initiative by the local housing association to provide individual cash bonuses and faster maintenance services to tenants who pay their rents promptly and have no breaches of their tenancy agreement. The second scheme is *Sanctuary Housing Association's Good Neighbour Declaration*. The study looked at one estate in Hackney, north London, where this was in place. The *Good Neighbour Declaration* takes a mainly symbolic form, with the association asking residents to sign up to a personal contract on how they will behave. The third scheme is *The Blackthorn Good Neighbours Project*, a community based voluntary project on a council estate in Northampton. *The Good Neighbours Project* is rather a collective incentive scheme designed to provide facilities and services that help local individuals and households to get to know each other more and thus to develop greater neighbourhood solidarity and cohesion. In addition we looked at one neighbourhood where there were no neighbourhood-specific schemes taking place, in *University ward in Middlesbrough*. The local authority had been active across its area in setting up many different forms of anti-social behaviour initiatives.

We gathered detailed background material on each of the estates, interviewed staff working in the neighbourhoods, and carried out focus group interviews with a range of residents including young people. These provided the context and the material for a household survey undertaken in the four areas sampling a representative 10 per cent of households. In addition we mapped similar work taking place nationally, shown in Figure 3.1.

Practice findings and recommendations

A fuller explanation of our research, methods, and theoretical model can be found in Bastow et al. (forthcoming 2006). Here we explore some of the research findings that are most relevant for practitioners in social housing attempting to improve the neighbourhoods they manage by encouraging tenants to behave in a more neighbourly way.

1. Good neighbour agreements led and implemented by agencies

- **Monsall Future Partnership, Manchester:** Joint estate agreement of a common set of standards and targets for service delivery to tenants and residents of all the partner landlords. In return tenants sign up to a Community Declaration.
- **Manningham Housing Association, Bradford:** Mutual aid compact with residents agreeing to help each other out when needed.
- **Manchester Housing:** Community Agreements defining reasonable and unreasonable behaviour.
- **North Tyneside Council:** Estate agreement covering anti-social behaviour, repairs, estate management and vandalism.
- **Whitefriars Housing Group, Coventry:** Develop community or estate agreements in which residents agree and set down rules expected in a neighbourhood, block or street.
- **Metropolitan HT Community Covenant, Brent:** Since 2002, all new tenants are asked to sign a community covenant, which covers expectations of behaviour.
- **London and Quadrant HT:** Develop estate agreements for small areas or streets as requested/appropriate.
- **Richmond Housing Partnership: Meres Estate Agreement, Barnes:** Obligations were jointly drawn up by the RA and RHP. Residents received a 16 page booklet to sign and return, people that signed up given a window sticker to display. Over 75 per cent of households have signed up.
- **Southern Housing Group:** Good neighbour declaration in small estates where appropriate/requested.

2. Good neighbour agreements led and implemented by community organisations

- **Cottington Close EMB, Lambeth:** Good neighbour declaration in tenant management organisation (TMO) of 247 homes, set up in 1995.
- **Sutton in Ashfield Neighbourhood Watch, Nottinghamshire:** Innovative/proactive neighbourhood watch scheme led by residents.
- **WATMOS TMO, Walsall:** Not a good neighbour agreement but have a participation agreement covering involvement in the TMO.

3. Schemes that reward positive behaviours, with sanctions for negative behaviours

- **City of Edinburgh 'Just Rewards':** Offers bonus bonds, special deals on products, a 'One-Off Rent Arrears Double Deal', and community double deals. Eligibility to join based on rent being paid on time and no breaches of tenancy. Covers roughly 22,000 homes.
- **Kirklees Neighbourhood Housing:** Tenant reward scheme in the Arms Length Management Organisation (ALMO). Launched Jan 2005, eligibility to join based on rent being paid on time and no breaches of tenancy. Benefits include: prize draws, discount card etc. Covers 28,000 homes.
- **Derby Homes 'Homes Pride+':** Scheme in the ALMO covering roughly 15,000 homes. Faster repairs and additional services for long standing tenants. Launched Jan 2005. Benefits include £100 'golden goodbye' voucher for good tenants to redeem at the end of their contracts.
- **Metropolitan Housing Trust 'Rewards for Residents':** Housing association in their Midlands region has 'Rewards for Residents' initiative. Motto is 'who cares wins'. Launched 2005, gives rewards to tenants in over 2,500 homes who pay their rent on time and comply with terms.
- **Charter Housing:** Housing association in Wales covering 3,600 homes offering tenants reward scheme.
- **Glasgow Housing Association 'Gold Service':** Ardenglen, Glen Oaks, and Wellhouse Housing Associations are three local associations within GHA. Introduced Gold Service in 2002. Tenants who comply with tenancy terms get enhanced repairs, bonus bonds and other benefits.

Figure 3.1   Examples of similar work around the country

- **Castle Vale Community Housing Association 'VIP Gold':** Offers discounts at local shops, discounted home insurance etc for clear rent account and sticking to tenancy conditions. Also open to all residents, i.e. home owners and people renting in the area. Residents who do not have a rent account with the HA must not have caused ASB. Covers 2,500 homes in West Midlands.

- **Longhurst Housing Group 'Just Rewards':** launched 2005 offers cash and benefits for sticking to tenancy terms. Manage 6,500 rented homes in the East Midlands.

- **'Testway Housing Incentive Scheme (THIS)':** High Street vouchers, enhanced home improvements and a Community Fund in return for clear rent account and no breaching tenancy. Covers 5,000 properties in Hampshire.

- **Crawley Homes 'Rewards for You':** Scheme in the ALMO covering 8,500 properties in the South East. Members get vouchers, list of approved contractors, community grants, discounted insurance for adhering to terms.

Figure 3.1 *Continued*

1. **Action by the authorities and landlords enables people to do more not less, and agencies should act first before asking residents to play their part.**

In our research we wanted to test out what factors had most effect on people's willingness to do something to help tackle anti-social behaviour – changing their own behaviour, going and having a word, or reporting incidents to the authorities. A big question was how much a sense of 'community spirit' in a neighbourhood made a difference.

The residents did not have a single definition of neighbourliness, but these were neighbourly places. They had high levels of social trust. These neighbourhoods passed the 'key test', with 39 per cent of respondents saying that they looked after keys for a neighbour at least once a year. In all four areas the vast majority of respondents regularly said hello to their neighbours, and three fifths also regularly did a favour for a neighbour – although between one in six and one in four respondents say they never did favours. Levels and types of neighbourliness varied between the areas e.g. in Hackney doing favours for neighbours was much rarer, compared to Salford where far more respondents said that they visited with neighbours in their home. Across all four areas a quarter (25.5 per cent) took part in local social events more than once or twice a year.

We analysed the links between 'community spirit' and people's willingness to 'get involved' or do something. We looked at three indicators of neighbourliness and 'community spirit':

- Levels of participation e.g. doing favours, going to social events or local meetings.

- Positive perceptions of the neighbourhood e.g. knowledge and trust of other people.

- Personal stake in the neighbourhood including length of time people had lived there, and intention to stay living there.

People's commitment to their neighbourhood and levels of community engagement were not the most powerful factors in explaining whether they would take action against anti-social behaviour. Our results showed that these community ties were outweighed by other factors in explaining whether people would take action against anti-social behaviour. In particular, people's perception of the authorities and fear of retaliation were more important factors, as shown by the thick broken dotted line between 'worry and low confidence' and 'willingness to intervene', and by all the different lines between perception of the authorities and the other factors in Figure 3.2. The thicker

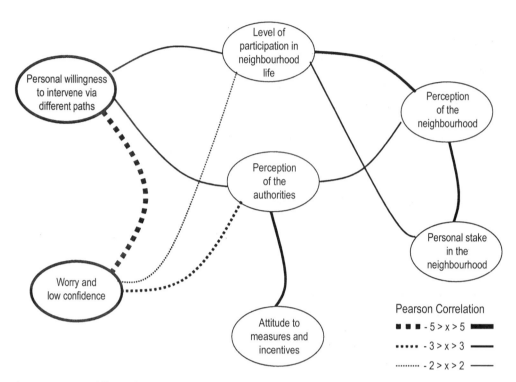

Figure 3.2   How different factors influence people's willingness to take action themselves

the line is the stronger the correlation or link, a broken line means a negative relationship; an unbroken line means a positive relationship.

But community ties were still relevant factors in whether people were willing to act. The most important one was people's level of participation in neighbourhood life, including helping out neighbours as well as going to meetings. People's personal stake and perception of the neighbourhood only had an effect on their willingness to be active citizens through their participation in the life of the community, or their perceptions of authorities.

The finding that community ties are outweighed by perceptions of the authorities indicates the scale of the challenge of tackling un-neighbourly behaviour. People's obvious commitment to the neighbourhood and friendly contact with neighbours is not enough by itself to change their behaviour to protect that neighbourhood.

Strong community ties do not necessarily produce collective resources such as social control (Wilson, 1987). It has been recognised that 'collective efficacy' (Sampson, 2004) although a powerful force, needs the underlying conditions of law and order and management of neighbourhoods to be in place before it can operate effectively.

Our research showed that people were more prepared to act if they felt that agencies were pulling their weight. As Harris suggests in Chapter 1, what he refers to as 'civic absence', i.e. lack of attention by services, no visible presence on the estate, awkward conditions for communicating with authorities, and poor response times, appears to diminish the neighbourly response to incivilities. We look at conditions for communication between residents and authorities below.

So, a positive perception of the authorities was strongly linked to more willingness to act. We assessed perceptions of the authorities based on the extent to which residents trusted officials to

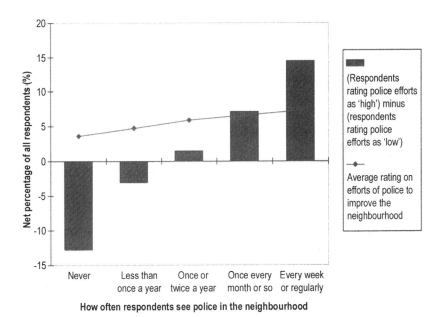

Figure 3.3 The influence of how often respondents see police in their neighbourhood on ratings of police efforts to improve their neighbourhood

back them up, and how hard people felt agencies were trying to improve things in the neighbourhood. Perceptions of whether authorities were pulling their weight were improved where there was a more visible street presence in neighbourhoods. Therefore having more frontline staff visible, 'keeping an eye' on neighbourhoods, will contribute to residents' willingness to do something themselves. Figure 3.3 shows this using police visibility, but the results showed the same pattern for other street presence, including street wardens, caretakers, other housing management staff, and other uniformed and local authority staff.

Some practitioners working in low income and disadvantaged neighbourhoods are concerned about doing more. They are worried that increased action by agencies leads to residents making less effort not more. In our study areas, part of the rationale for some of the schemes being introduced was to put more responsibility for tackling minor neighbour nuisances onto tenants and away from the landlord: 'we clarify responsibility about what the landlord can and can't do'. Over-dependence on outside bodies is a genuine concern and worry for authorities and for many residents too. However, our research showed that if agencies do more to enforce rules, to maintain physical environments and a visible presence in a neighbourhood, then people are more rather than less willing to do something. Indeed, in some of the neighbourhoods the idea that residents should kick-start the process of co-operative behaviour threatened to create a stalemate situation between residents and agencies.

If residents see agencies making an effort, they will do more themselves. Agency action added to the residents' capacity for mutual self-help; it does not replace it or diminish people's own sense of responsibility. Therefore social landlords must make sure their own enforcement and preventative work is properly in place before asking or expecting residents to play their part.

2. **People are willing to do their bit to tackle anti-social behaviour, but they are fearful even when doing so. There is untapped potential for stronger alliances between residents and agencies to tackle anti-social behaviour.**

Based on the stakeholder interviews, agencies wanted help from residents to form a coalition against miscreants, but felt that residents as a whole were unsupportive for a number of reasons, in particular:

- In some neighbourhoods there was a history of a closed culture, and a code of non-co-operation with the authorities, although things had changed in recent years.

- Residents were apathetic.

The following quotes from workers we interviewed illustrate these points:

> *It was definitely an area that was a hard nut to crack, very much closed doors. There wasn't a community feel particularly.*

> *People know the names of criminal families, nephew no. 25, but it's a real no-no to talk to housing officers or anyone in authority.*

These comments are based on direct experience of these neighbourhoods over a number of years, and present a reality in those places that was described to us by residents and staff in detail, and with some horrific accompanying examples of closed communities protecting criminal cultures. However, the fact that this has been the case seemed to overshadow a different reality experienced by residents. Some of them felt beleaguered by anti-social behaviour, wanted to tackle the problem, wanted agency backing to tackle the problem, but felt let down by agencies, and were fearful of retribution if they did try to help the authorities by reporting. Despite acknowledgement of this in the research by professionals, the implications for agency responses had not been fully thought through in some of the schemes.

Residents said they had found it difficult to help the authorities because of problems all the way along the reporting chain that de-motivated them in reporting incidents:

- Lack of secure ways to report incidents.

- If they managed to make a report the authorities did not respond effectively, or at all.

- Where authorities did take action, there were knock on effects like displacement.

- Where action had been successful, resources had been withdrawn, so the gains were not sustained.

These criticisms coincided with the survey findings that 'Making it easier and safer to report ASB' is ranked top of a list of seven options for improving neighbourliness and reducing anti-social behaviour (see Figure 3.4). Better enforcement, i.e. punishing anti-social behaviour with fines and penalties, was rated third.

Indeed, one of the major contributions of the community based Blackthorn Good Neighbours Project to community safety was not to bring the community together, although it did do this. Instead, it was to allow a way for the police to connect with the community, build relationships and develop the alliances that enabled serious criminal problems to be tackled, shown by a dramatic drop in crime rates in the area after intervention by the police and local authorities. In this case the potential was tapped and produced results.

Despite the difficulties residents faced in safely reporting problems, many were still willing to do this. Strikingly, just under two thirds of respondents who said they *would* report young people[1] would

---

[1] We also asked the same question about adults' behaviour.

| | Number of times each option scores top out of 7 and bottom out of 7 | | |
	Scores top	Scores bottom	Net score (top *minus* bottom)
Make it easier to report anti-social behaviour	444	101	343
Upgrading local homes	418	132	286
Punishing anti-social behaviour	371	155	216
Encouraging community events	225	203	22
Establish written rules of behaviour	164	293	− 129
Reward the community	108	298	− 190
Rewarding individuals for good behaviour	101	380	− 279

Figure 3.4   How respondents ranked a list of seven options for improving neighbourliness and reducing anti-social behaviour

worry about the consequences of doing so, would not feel confident about intervening, and did not trust authorities to back them up. The people who did report things expressed a high degree of mistrust for official back-up, and a fear of potential retribution from the perpetrators.

Fears about retaliation came across strongly in the focus groups:

If I saw vandalism happening? Not say a word in case I got a mouthful.

I've said it before. I said don't do that, and they kicked the shit out of my fence.

I said to them, is that your car? They said yeah, but I didn't pursue it because he had this screwdriver.

10 years ago if you'd have said to me I'd have walked away from something I wouldn't have believed you. It's very hard when you have to turn your back.

Residents were concerned enough to act, even when they said they are not confident in doing so, and were therefore potentially easily dissuaded. We suggest that there is untapped potential for stronger alliances between residents and agencies to create better conditions for pro-social behaviours in disadvantaged neighbourhoods. There would appear to be a set of missed opportunities for residents and agencies to work together. The agencies in the study areas were aware of the need to maximise these opportunities.

3. **What landlords think they are doing is not what is really happening for residents. Therefore landlords should ask more questions about how residents see the issue and possible solutions in order to develop more effective interventions.**
The mechanisms that agencies think they are using to create change are not seen in the same way by residents. The perception that agencies had of the impact of an initiative often contrasted with the residents' perceptions. These mutual misunderstandings could lead to the wrong initiative being put in place, the creation of ineffective projects, frustration for residents, or the right initiative being promoted in a way that doesn't appeal. Therefore landlords and other agencies should ask residents more about how they understand interventions and why they would be motivated to change behaviour in order to develop more effective interventions.

One of the schemes in particular illustrated this. The way the landlord understood the scheme was that:

- It encouraged people to examine the way their behaviour impacts on others.
- It enabled residents to challenge each other at an early stage without having to go to the landlord for help. It was therefore suited to tackling neighbour 'annoyances' that may otherwise blow up into more serious disputes.
- It clarified people's roles and responsibilities, and put more responsibility back onto residents for sorting out their own disputes.

A housing worker summarised their point of view like this:

I think people are more aware of the need to think about others. (The scheme) *has been educative. People don't know how they live their life affects others. Sometimes people need to be made aware.* (The scheme) *brings an awareness to people, it helps people to stop and think and resolve issues at a low level without* (the landlord) *having to get involved. Does it give people the courage to intervene? There are those who will go and knock, others just think that everything is the responsibility of the landlord. In the first instance we always say – just talk to your neighbour, you have to get along if you live next door. You're the best person to resolve this, if the landlord gets involved it raises the stake.*

However, we found that:

- Residents were willing to admit to minor wrongdoing themselves in contrast to the agency's perceptions that 'people are ignorant of how their life affects someone else'. For example, 14 per cent admitted to occasionally making 'noise indoors that might bother your next door neighbour', and another five per cent admitted to doing this quite or very often. Overall in the survey across all four areas between 10–29 per cent agreed that they at least occasionally left rubbish, dropped litter, made noise that would bother neighbours, played loud music, let children play outside noisily, parked in someone else's space, or have a messy house or garden. Nationally surveys also show that around one in five (17 per cent) will admit to things like dropping litter (MORI, 2006);
- Residents in the household survey were more likely to think the scheme worked by 'making me feel that there is more backing from the authorities' (42 per cent) than that the scheme worked by 'making it more obvious if I don't follow the rules' (27 per cent);
- In the focus group the emphasis was on reporting to the authorities or an outside body, but residents were clearly feeling frustrated by a lack of response, not understanding that the scheme was deliberately designed to reduce the level of landlord response. One resident commented:

  Have you ever tried Victim Support because they helped me, every time I call (the landlord) *like you say they does nothing, I go to Victim Support instead and they contact* (the landlord) *so maybe you should try them, or better still your MP and it would be dealt with in two weeks . . .*

- In the household survey nearly 60 per cent of respondents had not heard of the scheme, and of those that had heard of it, most had only heard 'a little' or they were not sure what it was. Therefore it is difficult to argue that the scheme was the main driver in people becoming more considerate to their neighbours.

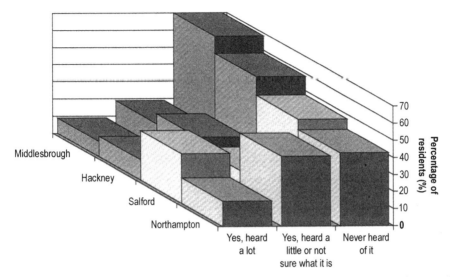

Figure 3.5   How far respondents were aware of local schemes (and Middlesbrough Council's general work to improve social behaviour)

4. **For people to become more neighbourly, they do not always need to be aware of schemes. But better awareness helps promote co-operative behaviour by citizens. Therefore agencies need to communicate more effectively with residents about citizenship measures they are taking.**

Awareness levels of schemes to promote neighbourliness were low, even where membership of schemes was high. Levels of awareness of schemes or initiatives are shown in Figure 3.5.

Figure 3.5 shows that the three neighbourhood focused schemes were better known than the local authority-wide strategic work in Middlesbrough. However, this is more than understandable, given the wide range of different projects within Middlesbrough's Community Safety Strategy, some of which are publicly branded but many of which are not.

The interesting example is that of Irwell Valley's Gold Service in Salford. There are two lessons here:

- Gold Service has been proven to be effective in reducing rent arrears and the number of empty homes (available to let), and has increased the proportion of rent collected (Lupton, Hale, and Sprigings, 2003). Membership of Gold Service is over 90 per cent of Irwell Valley tenants. In our survey, just over half Irwell Valley tenants in our sample said that they had heard of the scheme. It is very likely that some were members but did not identify themselves as such. To be effective, Gold Service does not require tenants to be able to name the scheme, or even know if they are a member, as long as the tenant keeps to the membership rules in terms of their behaviour, because it uses the direct levers of reward to alter behaviour.

- However, Gold Service's direct levers only extend to behaviours under the 'control' of the landlord, such as paying rent, or damaging property. Other forms of behaviour require residents to take action voluntarily, and therefore need to know that schemes exist for them to work. Our first finding was that if residents see agencies making an effort, they will do more themselves. Therefore low levels of awareness will potentially hold back the positive effects of schemes that do not have strong mechanisms along the lines of Gold Service-style reward schemes.

Individual cash incentives are a strong lever but, as we discuss below, are not popular or well thought of by British people, may cost around £70 per household per year of which three quarters is paid back to the household,[2] and may feed into a 'peer effect', or the community safety equivalent of 'keeping up with the Joneses'. For example, people doing up their front gardens in Salford:

> *It started in (X street), one person did it, then gradually they all started. It was a bomb site before, now they're doing it and people already doing more.* (They think) *well if they can do it it's not that hard. It doesn't cost a fortune to paint the fence and put in some little pots.* (In X street) *it started when we had the hanging baskets last year, there was a knock on effect. What kicked it off was how people follow on from each other.*

On one hand, Gold Service gets results despite members not being clear what it is. This shows that people did not necessarily need to be aware of what was being done to them for it to be working. However, to repeat, our first finding was that if residents saw agencies making an effort, they were more willing to do more themselves. Additional peer effects need people to know what their neighbours are doing, or not doing. Also, some initiatives need people to be aware that it exists for the scheme to work. For all of these reasons our fourth recommendation is that agencies need to communicate more effectively with residents about citizenship measures they are taking. They need also to take into account the difficulty, as shown by our awareness results, of branding initiatives in a memorable way.

5. **Rewards for neighbourliness are effective in specific ways, but were not intuitively popular or a priority with residents. Therefore they should be used as part of a package, discussed fully with residents, and actively promoted.**

Incentives and rewards for neighbourly behaviour have been shown to be effective in specific ways, but were not intuitively popular or a priority with the majority of residents. The main point is that they were not the striking measure in residents' minds. Both community rewards and individual incentives came bottom of the pack when we asked people to rank measures to tackle anti-social behaviour, shown in Figure 3.4. It is not surprising that residents put other measures such as better reporting or upgrades to housing first, nor is it out of line with the relatively modest role that incentives could play in altering behaviour.

So our respondents had not spent much time thinking about rewards. When we specifically asked people in the focus group what they thought of individual rewards, the response was mixed. In the focus groups, there was some moral resistance to the idea of rewarding individuals for simply doing what they ought to be doing. For example, one participant suggested that '*not getting evicted!*' was reward enough in itself. Residents in the focus groups said:

> *If* (you) *introduce rewards it's like saying we don't expect you to behave so here's a reward if you do. We should be expected to behave and if we don't – then it gets tackled.*

> *It's not good to reward because being a good neighbour should be normal, should be part and parcel of the responsibility of having a house. You should be punished if you don't.*

---

[2] See Audit Commission website for more information about costing reward incentive schemes at www. audit-commission.gov.uk/housingefficiency/ incentive.

In the area where rewards had already been implemented the discussion focused on implementation problems, with some well-behaved people apparently unfairly excluded from the scheme. In all the focus groups there was concern around the contested issue of setting down criteria for rewards: 'You may be a good tenant then go home and beat up your wife every night.' (This tension between private and public unacceptable behaviour is also referred to by Kevin Harris in Chapter 4.)

In the household survey there are broadly three clusters of responses:

- A 'punitive' set containing the majority, with people who strongly support punishments and rules, put their faith in cracking down on people behaving badly, and generally dislike the idea of rewards or incentives;

- A 'community' or 'collective renewal' set, with people who supported things like physical renewal or more community events; and,

- An 'incentives' set with fewest respondents who tend to dislike the punitive policies and community policies.

Incentives are not a stand alone measure, and should be used as part of a wider strategy to build viable neighbourhoods and tackle negative social behaviour (Lupton, Hale, and Sprigings, 2003; see also Audit Commission, 2005). Guidance by the Audit Commission reinforces the point that 'reward incentive schemes have the potential to be inequitable to customers if not developed and implemented effectively'. The Commission also points to potential barriers within housing organisations to effective implementation of incentives schemes, and suggests ways of engaging with the concerns of staff in housing organisations (Audit Commission, 2005). As well as discussions internally with staff, agencies that want to develop incentives schemes will need to engage with residents, discuss the ideas, promote the concept, and back their actions up with enforcement measures.

Concluding remarks

There is much in the government's Respect agenda that has resonance with the findings from our work. This suggests that policy is moving in line with reality on the ground, despite concerns over the moralistic overtones of this policy expressed elsewhere in this collection.

We found that, much as they would have liked to tackle problems directly, the problems of severe anti-social behaviour were just too much for communities. These were neighbourly places, but what agencies did, or did not do, had a stronger influence over people's willingness to do something themselves to tackle incivility than neighbourhood ties. This does not need to take away from the government's support for community building and community organising. But it backs up the emphasis in the Respect agenda on a front line visible presence in neighbourhoods, as well as proactive management of neighbourhoods. This front line presence, in the form of neighbourhood wardens, caretakers and 'super caretakers', neighbourhood policing, housing officers and so on, emerged in our research as critical to residents' decisions about what they did to help the authorities, or to challenge neighbours themselves. Our work indicates that the push for more ground level staff to be eyes and ears in neighbourhoods is not simply a retro fashion for newly styled park keepers, but a genuine boon for struggling places, which also offers entry level jobs to local people.

Our household survey found that rules and punishments were the most popular set of measures. Problems with the reporting and enforcement chain dissuaded people from helping the authorities, including the lack of action and the time action took. However, residents in our focus groups were critical of tough enforcement measures where this led to a displacement of the issue rather than a genuine resolution. Therefore the government's proposals to speed up and make more drastic enforcement measures should receive a cautious welcome with conditions attached.

We saw that incentives, while not instantly sellable, could have a positive effect. It is welcome that the Respect agenda makes reference to incentives in social housing, and incentives for young people. What is needed now is some more thought about whether and how incentives could be applied in other spheres.

So better enforcement, done well; and incentives, widely applied, both get a thumbs up. What has arguably less focus in the government's new Respect policies are ways for these ideas to be discussed and negotiated. The community solutions favoured by some respondents described above may not be an immediate solution to the problems of neighbourhood disorganisation; but this approach, more than the others, allows spaces for negotiation and the accommodation of alternative views. Indeed, in the focus groups we found that people wanted more focus groups. While weekly focus groups may not be a realistic option, the concept of better information flows to residents, stronger accountability of authorities to service users and residents, and increased transparency of decision making are practical propositions. The Respect agenda has been criticised for its populist leanings. This research suggests that it could have resonated more clearly with the views of local people, if a more balanced and sensitive approach had been adopted.

Chapter 4

'Do You Live on 'ere?' Neighbouring and Respect

Kevin Harris

Attention, Slimebag!

The Belgian scholar Jan Steyaert took this image on a street in Antwerp. It shows a standard bottle-recycling facility, with the ubiquitous blue plastic bag on the ground alongside. At the front of the recycling container someone has placed a board with a message painted on it, which reads in Dutch 'vetzak verboden te storten'. The English translation is: 'Don't leave litter you slimebag.'

What's going on here? Antwerp is a historical city in one of the more advanced, wealthy and equal societies in the world, yet here someone seems to be struggling to find the ground to negotiate their differences.

We can suppose that one person has paid scant regard to the tidiness of their shared environment; and the other clearly sets greater store by it. We can surmise that the latter has observed untidy

Figure 4.1 Personal message about litter: Antwerp, Belgium

behaviour (or just its evidence) over a period of time, by a single individual, to the point where in exasperation they were moved to express their displeasure in this form.

There are a number of points we can make about this little vignette:

- First, it comes across as an instance of *controlled aggression* at neighbourhood level. The language is harsh and if we heard such phrases used in the street we might be alarmed at the prospect of a confrontation.

- Secondly, it's *individual*. The term 'you slimebag' is singular and implies that a particular individual is being addressed.

- Thirdly, the message is *anonymous but personal*, which brings a slightly sinister sense to it as an example of human communication.

- Fourthly, it's an unambiguously *public* message. We can suppose that the writer of the board may have felt they had no private way of expressing this message; or else that if some form of direct approach were possible, they may have been fearful of the reaction it might have provoked. Perhaps the writer seeks affirmation somehow from other residents: but how do they add their views?

- Fifthly, it assumes that there are *norms of behaviour* to which the litter perpetrator is not adhering. The board is a challenging declaration of values. It says you should live this way, not that way.

- Sixthly, it's *not dialogue*. There's no entreaty, no 'please'. Just a command, in a manner presumably intended to shame. The mode of communication limits the possibility of negotiation, and the language pretty much rules it out completely.

- Finally we can say that it suggests *ownership and responsibility*, on the part of the board-writer; an implied sense of responsibility on the part of others (local or non-local) who do *not* leave litter; and a corresponding *lack* of responsibility or ownership on the part of the perpetrator. The board tells us that the perpetrator is felt to have been disrespectful in this neighbourhood and the language suggests that they are not felt to merit much respect themselves as a consequence.

Is it fair to say that this little story is trivial? How trivial is it, when we can suppose that the board-writer has possibly been expressing a boiling irritation, probably built up over a period of time, and has gone to some lengths to transmit their message? Perhaps such differences in perception and behaviour in themselves are trivial in the grand scheme of things. Incidents like kids kicking footballs against the walls of other people's houses or inebriated adults shouting outside late at night – these are familiar features of human life lived in close proximity. We have phrases in English that express the natural history of contiguous negotiation – give-and-take, living cheek-by-jowl, rubbing along, taking the rough with the smooth, ruffling feathers, rattling cages, and so on.

What matters is how we accomplish the negotiation of such disagreements and frictions, what processes we have to hand to help us reconcile our conflicts. In that context, the *vetzak* vignette is perhaps symptomatic, because it exposes so clearly a weakness in our social fabric.

As a communication event, the board and its message would seem to be effective in publicly asserting certain values, in the face of their visible rejection. But it would seem to be a very inferior way of seeking to instil a sense of respect, responsibility and ownership in someone who drops litter.

What alternatives might the board-writer have turned to?

- In most towns and cities there are bye-laws with penalty fines against littering, and a council department responsible for keeping the streets clean in spite of such behaviour. In some centres there are surveillance cameras that would cover this sort of location.

- In a small, tight-knit neighbourhood with dense, overlapping social ties, someone would quite likely have known who the perpetrator was, and had a quiet word with them or their family perhaps.

- We can imagine the board-writer having conversations with fellow residents, tutting together at the bus stop or outside the baker's. Others join in and agree, and they discuss a more concerted campaign, perhaps trying to recruit others to a very visible clean-up event.

- In a connected, networked neighbourhood, a comment posted online might have broadened awareness of the problem and produced a collective response.

But in this case, none of these options appears to have been available or identified. The task of policing low-level disorder, and keeping the street clean, has been beyond the authorities and their regulations. As in so many places, the decline of dense social ties in the neighbourhood has reduced the possibilities of informal social control and no social network has been mobilised. No appropriate communication system exists here for residents to share information and views about local issues. The board-writer feels a need to re-enforce social norms, and possibly fears a descent into anarchy, but lacks a channel through which to express this. Hence the sense of desperation in the message.

This then is how we might characterise the issue of respect in the neighbourhood – infrequency of interaction, a high percentage of unknown others, weak social networks and informal control, transgression of norms, attempts to reassert norms, and no appropriate communication channel to help residents establish, assert or modify such norms. In this chapter I examine various aspects of shared life in neighbourhoods, with a view to providing an understanding of the context for local social relations.

'Do you live on 'ere?' Social relations in the neighbourhood

Many years ago as a student I was delivering questionnaires on a London housing estate when a resident called across the street, 'Do you live on 'ere mate?' It was his way of making sure I understood that it was not my territory, I was a visitor, possibly not a guest, and had been noticed. As is illustrated by cul-de-sac residents in the case study reported in Chapter 6, very often the territory close to the home is perceived not so much as public space but as 'community space', and can be interpreted as such (see Brown and Werner, 1985 : 543–6).

A neighbourhood is a residential area where residents tend to have a sense of belonging but usually all citizens have a right of access.[1] It's here that people learn the public practices of everyday life, the accommodation of the Other, the necessary giving and taking and rubbing-along in relative proximity as identities are shaped and hardened. Neighbourhoods have histories and churning secrets, whose nature is seldom legible in the physical design or the visible condition. The neighbourhood is a nursery where civil relations grow, or fail to grow. It is the primary arena where life takes place.

---

[1] A neighbourhood to which access by outsiders is severely restricted is an enclave. Usually these are still neighbourhoods, indeed sometimes the creation of 'community' is an overt reason for limiting access. See Keller (2003).

When we consider civil and uncivil relations more specifically in the neighbourhood context, we need to reflect on some particular features. First, there is the greater likelihood that others who we encounter will be known to us, or to someone we know. Secondly, we may have a heightened sense of territorial ownership and belonging. Thirdly, there is greater likelihood of some damaging repetition of uncivil behaviours, with consequent distress. And finally we should also ask, if respect for others is not learned and rehearsed in the household and in the neighbourhood, where and how will it be learned? The practice of respect is a public issue not satisfied by the privatisation of social life.

In this book we advance the argument that civil relations, represented by the default value of 'respect', are fundamentally underpinned by informal relations at the most local level, the neighbourhood. Neglect of the practice of neighbouring and of informal social control will weaken and threaten civil relations across society. And it works the other way: if, as we have discussed in Chapter 1, there is a decline in civil relations across society generally, it is likely to have an impact at neighbourhood level, and this is the local context to which many people who experience exclusion are largely confined. While those who can afford to, will establish social relations on the basis of a geographically dispersed network, those who cannot are typically limited to relationships among those around them. It follows that people who experience exclusion are likely to be disproportionately affected by any general decline in the quality of civil relations. Faced with un-neighbourly anti-social behaviour, if you can't afford to gate yourself in or buy access to a broader social network like a golf club, chances are you're stuffed.

The concept of neighbourhood is not susceptible to neat definition, but that hardly renders it invalid. I regard the neighbourhood as the socially charged spatial environment that a resident recognises closest to the home, which may be a few houses or several hundred.[2] The Chicago school of sociologists tended to regard the neighbourhood as a subset of 'the community', which suggests that everyone lives in a neighbourhood and every neighbourhood is part of a community. I'm not convinced that everyone lives in a neighbourhood: some folk for example live in a tangled confusion of poorly integrated buildings, traffic-generated design afterthoughts and spaces that are occupied by a stuttering flow of renters, lodgers and non-residents for short spells. By extension, it is hard in such environments to sustain much neighbourly behaviour. Nor is it clear that every neighbourhood is part of a community. The C-word should be used with discretion, especially when a geographical area is what is really meant. People usually have communities, or at least social networks, to which they feel they belong, but often a spatially defined one is the last or the least in a short list.

Our argument carries some urgency but it is not new. In part it was put forward by Jane Jacobs several decades ago in the context of urban planning. She famously drew attention to 'the casual public sidewalk life of cities', and noted:

> The sum of such casual, public contact at a local level – most of it fortuitous, most of it associated with errands, all of it metred by the person concerned and not thrust upon him by anyone – is a feeling for the public identity of people, a web of public respect and trust, and a resource in time of personal or neighbourhood need. The absence of this trust is a disaster to a city street. Its cultivation cannot be institutionalized.

(Jacobs, 1961: 67)

The absence of respect and trust to which Jacobs refers is an unknown that shadows deep beneath any civilisation, it is the dreaded antithesis. In our own time its outlines have been sketched by Elijah Anderson as a tension between 'the decent' and 'the street':

---

[2] Paul Hilder (2005) has done a little definitional research and finds that in some senses the term applies to 'perhaps 4,000–15,000 people'.

Neighbors are encouraged to choose between an abstract code of justice that is disparaged by the most dangerous people on the streets and a practical code that is geared toward survival in the public spaces of their community.

(Anderson, 2000: 134)

This latter code, the code of the street, is according to Anderson 'a kind of adaptation to a lost sense of security of the local inner-city neighborhood' (p323). This reminds us that a key function of the neighbourhood is to nurture human development in a secure context. Through his ethnographic study Anderson identifies complete indifference to neighbours, and being inconsiderate of their concerns, as 'a defining trait of street-oriented people' (p47). Before we consider behaviours more closely, we need to assess changing attitudes towards neighbourhood.

There goes the neighbourhood?

For many of us, the notion of neighbourhood conjures up a 'retro' model, which we might describe as comprising close-knit encounters of the traditional kind. Here we have the familiar notion of the tight-knit, coherent neighbourhood of mutually supportive people with a strong sense of place-based identity. Such environments are routinely served up as part of the staple in TV drama series and social documentaries. But of course they weren't usually much fun if you were gay or from an ethnic minority. Highly cohesive local communities can be intolerant and culturally stifling. And as Doreen Massey has pointed out,

The old coherences had really been constructed by the smothering of internal diversity – the male dominance of the coalfields, looked back on by some as an exemplary solidarity, was a clear case in point.

(Massey, 1994: 119)

Philip Abrams explains why the celebrated close-knit community was effectively the product of dubious external forces. Writing in the late 1970s about the traditional neighbourhood type of social network, he notes that:

Internally, the networks of the traditional neighbourhood were indeed marked by collective attachment, reciprocity and trust. Externally, they were no less plainly marked by constraint, isolation and insecurity . . . The so-called natural helping networks of the traditional neighbourhood – not actually natural at all, of course – developed as a response to certain highly specified social conditions which one would not wish to see reproduced today.

(Bulmer, 1986: 92)

Thus we can be neither surprised, nor necessarily disappointed, if contemporary neighbouring is quite distinct from the 'compulsory solidarity' (Crow et al., 2002) associated with the context of overlapping ties, strong kinship networks and shared disadvantage. An analysis of 22 years of US data by Guest and Wierzbicki confirmed the suspected trend away from predominantly local ties:

Neighborhood and non-neighborhood ties are becoming disassociated over time, so that individuals are becoming specialists in localized versus non-localized social interaction.

(Guest and Wierzbicki, 1999: 109)

As Philip Connolly outlines in Chapter 5, increased transport and mobility options have undoubtedly played a huge part in reducing the relative significance of neighbourhood ties. Such options have facilitated more dispersed employment, and hence have undermined the ways in which workplace ties and neighbourhood ties get re-enforced. Towards one extreme, we find localities characterised by high levels of mobility and transience (although often with a core settled population) in which routine exchanges of greetings and information have become fewer and the sense of trust and security has atrophied. Towards the other extreme we find what has been called the 'secession of the successful' in gated communities and armed enclaves.

So comparatively we depend less on relationships in the neighbourhood than used to be the case. It is instructive to take this analysis a little further, as Talja Blokland does in reviewing changes in a particular Rotterdam neighbourhood over a generation. In an important summary of the key issues, she says:

> *The most significant changes are* **the diminished need to be neighbourly** *and the increased opportunities to relate to fellow neighbourhood residents* **at one's own discretion**. *Neighbourliness is less uniform, and the mutual familiarity of neighbourhood residents has gradually become less public. Generally, therefore, mutual attachments are fading among neighbourhood residents, in keeping with common-sense perceptions. Contrary to common sense, however, the cause of this decline is not that people are unwilling to help each other or are less social or helpful than in the past or compared to the ideal country village. Rather, it is attributable to the social structure, which increasingly accommodates* **structured choices according to personal discretion**.

> (Blokland, 2003: 122–3, emphasis added)

We should note that the ability to exercise discretion in one's choice of social ties is not equally distributed across society: this is an issue of power to which we will return in a later section.

The disregard for neighbourhood

We can explore this understanding of the 'diminished need to be neighbourly' for a moment by considering some of the effects of increased personal discretion in the maintenance of personal social networks.

Many people whose mobility is less constrained, appear to have little *use* for neighbourhood. The relative strength of personal social networks – dispersed kin and friendship ties, work and leisure ties, often supported by the technologies of remote communication – has come to equate more closely with 'community' than have purely local ties. Where there is little perceived value in investing in neighbourhood ties, the logical development is the gated community, from which residents have to make highly purposive outings by making trips to typically enclosed, self-contained shops or attractions. As Larry Ford describes it:

> *The trip likely consists of getting into a car in the garage at home and getting out in the garage of the final destination*

> (Ford, 2000: 205)

thus minimising almost to zero the possibilities of serendipitous encounters with diverse others. We drive more and walk less:

> *For every five steps we took ten years ago, the average person is now taking four steps and that is bound to have an effect on our lifestyles*

> (Franklin, 2002)

The implications of this *disregard for neighbourhood* do not arise just in planning and health, but also in other policy areas such as transport, school catchment, citizenship, the housing market, regional economic development, and of course, crime and anti-social behaviour. We will make little progress in appreciating this issue if we fail to take account of the ways in which 'similarity of interest is more important in forming relations than similarity of setting' (Hampton, 2002). In short, for those who have choice, the emphasis of time and effort tends to be on personal social networks, not local connections. Our understanding of local social relations and neighbouring has to take this into account and not imply that 'traditional neighbourhood' is either recoverable or necessarily desirable.

This is not to relegate neighbourhood relations to insignificance, of course. People still have to live and interact in proximity and it could be argued that, in a context of increasing mobility with networks supported by communication technologies, the need for local community, though different, is more acute than ever before (Harris, 2003). At the neighbourhood level we are talking about physically accessible face-to-face ties, which have certain advantages over ties that may be stronger but are remote – advantages that may escape our notice until they become dangerously sparse. Further, there are arguments that democracy and civil renewal depend heavily on the local experience of the public realm, on the everyday experience of civility and civil interactions: if these are diminished, democratic society is diminished.

The policy question that arises is how we stimulate and sustain viable neighbourhoods that complement people's personal social networks, their 'personal communities' (Pahl and Spencer, 2003) – contributing to positive social capital, meaningful citizenship, and the experience of safe and creative neighbourhoods. How do we strengthen and re-integrate neighbourhood relations into a context where personal social networks now tend to dominate people's motivations? How do we promote and sustain viable neighbourhoods in which local social relationships can flourish as an accepted extension of individual behaviours?

Neighbourhood without community

Separation in lieu of the negotiation of life in common, rounded up by the criminalization of residual difference – these are the principal dimensions of the current evolution of urban life.

(Bauman, 2000: 94)

I have stayed in gated houses a few times and been struck by the way in which the barriers – fences and electronic gates – function not just as obstacles for intruders and discouragement for passers-by, but as disincentives to going out. Popping out for a run in a Brazilian city required being 'let out' by the maid, and let back in again. Taking a walk in a South African suburb similarly required a relatively elaborate ritual and, notwithstanding the pleasant green environment, wasn't very agreeable either. Houses are well-defended with daunting fences and serious cameras peer back at you, notices proclaim armed-response services, and ferocious dogs are encouraged to broadcast their awareness of your presence.

And if that isn't enough to reduce face-to-face connection among residents to an occasional nod from passing cars, one home-owner has added a disturbing touch of their own: a skeleton hangs from a tree deliberately in full view of the road. This is the most emphatic statement of division I have ever witnessed on the local scale. If you are not like us, this is what could happen to you. We choose polarisation. Antagonism is acceptable.

'Community' for residents of such areas is presumably quite different to 'community' for the black people who service their needs. The notion of safety and security on the street – only black people walk here – is discarded and not seen as the responsibility of residents. The responsibilities of residents are personalised to the point of little more than self-protection, so that 'community' is found not in the locality but in spatially dispersed networks (Wellman and Frank, 2001) – sports and social clubs, business associations, dispersed kin and friendship networks. The telephone and the car become indispensable and help to cocoon the home from the space around it, while making it accessible to controlled contact from beyond. Thus people move *into and out of* the neighbourhood, but seldom *within it*. Withdrawal from the neighbourhood and its public space amounts to a profound message about trust, as Elizabeth Frazer points out:

> *For if people's values and modes of conduct are just their own then we lack a stable basis for predicting how others are going to behave and thereby we lack security.*

> (Frazer, 2002: 47)

It's likely in such contexts that the discretionary practice of neighbouring is reduced to the sterile minimum required for the purposes of defence, perhaps augmented with occasional encounters which, given the barriers, are necessarily structured. And the organic behaviour we call neighbourliness (a more subjective notion of course) has little fertile soil in which to grow.

The importance of neighbourliness

If neighbouring is what happens, positive or negative, when people live in proximity – unless they refuse to have anything to do with one another – then neighbourliness is a more qualitative notion. It suggests some intention and implied benefits.

Neighbourliness requires neighbouring: mutual recognition among residents through repeated informal encounters over time. These encounters will typically be varied and unscheduled, although to some extent they may be defined by routines. One simple outcome from such a level of interaction is likely to be a shared sense of stability and security. Neighbourliness assumes certain conditions, such as:

- A *public realm* in which people move about (and in a manner that does not make recognition impractical or meaningless, as is often the case when cars are involved).

- A *non-threatening culture and environment* in which the impulse to express recognition or to interact is not felt to be unwelcome.

- *Recurrence* of interaction, in an environment which people have cause to revisit (not necessarily routinely).

- A readiness among local people to occupy that space, to promote *community presence* – Philip Connolly discusses this in Chapter 5 as 'being there'.

- A fundamental dependence on *informality*[3] (together with an assumption that recourse to formal entitlements is an ultimate option if needed).
- A degree of *consistency* in such interactions over time.

Relationships between neighbours depend on occasions, of various kinds. These might include, for example, conversations in public places from impromptu and serendipitous encounters; conversations in semi-public or semi-private space – over the garden fence, at the doorstep, while washing the car outside the house, etc; and instances of material, instrumental, or emotional support (issues of reciprocity become significant at this level).

When we seek to understand the nature of civil relationships in neighbourhoods, we quickly discover that mutual respect between residents, and informal social control generally, are finely balanced on the pivot of privacy. Judgements that keep one's neighbouring behaviour acceptably and predictably settled between privacy and interference pervade most interactions, either consciously or instinctively. This is illustrated by a respondent's comment in research carried out by Crow and his colleagues:

> *We did actually have someone, you know, who used to beat his partner up quite violently, and you try and turn a blind eye, don't you? You just listen to it because in this house you can't help that, at 2 or 3 o'clock in the morning. Then he started doing it early in the evening when the children were awake, so we had no choice but to call the police. It's none of our business, but when the children are in, then that's something else, isn't it? . . . We assumed it was drink.*

(Crow et al., 2002: 137)

Rather than being diminished by proximity, the violent man's right to privacy seems to be accentuated, and notions of responsibility to the victim are easily trumped by parental responsibilities; the dilemma of interference only becomes problematic when the managed experience of children comes into the equation. The researchers conclude:

> *The construction of a good neighbour as someone who is prepared to condone domestic violence highlights the tension that exists between the ideal of privacy and independence and the reality of having to respond in some way to the often intimate knowledge of neighbours' lives that proximity necessarily brings.*

(Crow et al., 2002: 137)

The relationship between privacy and neighbourliness is subtle and significant. People expect to be able to withdraw from social contact, and they appear to value neighbourly behaviour that is non-invasive. Keller, in her study of a specific housing development in the eastern United States, found 'a clear-cut relationship between high ratings on privacy and strong liking for the community' (Keller, 2003: 155). Similarly Dana Cuff observes:

> *The notion of neighborliness often connotes the benign, minor kindnesses bestowed among co-residents that punctuate a steady state of general disregard.*

(Cuff, 2005: para 2)

Both Abrams (Bulmer, 1986) referring to UK practice, and Blokland (2003) referring to Dutch practice, are clear that frequent visiting in people's homes is not felt to be good neighbourly behaviour. This

---

[3] See Misztal (2000) and Gilchrist (2004b). Note also how important the word 'casual' is in the classic works of both Jacobs (1961) and Oldenburg (1989).

contrasts with the implications of much of the US research, which places greater emphasis on visiting as an indicator of neighbourliness and suggests rather more blurring between neighbourhood relations and friendship. There is potential for confusion here, so it is as well to be clear: friendliness, a key component of positive neighbouring, is by no means the same thing as friendship. There may be good psychological reasons why we rarely mix the two. As our knowledge of other people increases, the greater the likelihood that we will discover a significant difference of opinion, perhaps a political or ethical difference: serious differences of opinion among people living in proximity are best avoided. In the UK tradition, friendship and neighbourliness are quite distinct. (See Abrams on the sociology of informal neighbouring, in Bulmer, 1986, Chapter 5.) A similar distinction has been made between *sociability* (which requires only a minimal level of acquaintanceship) and *socio-emotional support* (referring to more intimate relationships such as friendship and kinship ties) (Unger and Wandersman, 1985: 142).

Peter Mann, in his 1954 paper on research in Cheshire, describes some behaviour in terms of 'overneighborliness'.[4] This is the extreme form of what Mann termed 'manifest' neighbourliness, characterised by overt forms of behaviour such as neighbours going out together on trips. The concept emerges elsewhere: for instance in a short study of neighbourliness in Manchester, Harris and Gale (2004) found critical use of the phrase 'living in each other's pockets'. An example comes from an interview with a resident:

> My house became the local drop-in. It got too much. All day there was four or five people in the house – I couldn't get my housework done and there was no privacy. I was trying to bring up two sons at the time. They'd come in mine and drink all me tea, sugar and coffee, it went on all day, sometimes they were there until late at night.

(Quoted by Harris and Gale, 2004: 34)

Mann noted that a high degree of manifest neighbouring can mistakenly be taken as indicative of social solidarity among all residents, and he contrasted it with 'latent' neighbourliness, 'characterized by favourable attitudes to neighbors which result in positive action when a need arises' (Mann, 1954: 164).

Non-invasive neighbouring can of course be difficult to distinguish from avoidance, which may in turn imply isolation. More negatively, neighbouring can be confrontational: in this form, the individual or family provocatively disturbs norms of privacy through anti-social behaviour such as playing loud music, training up a threatening dog, or being abusive or violent.

We can thus identify a spectrum of neighbouring, at either end of which there is a point at which it becomes anti-social. Negative anti-social neighbouring however is quite different to 'over-neighbouring', which is characterised by a lack of sensitivity to generally accepted norms of privacy. A suggested model of the spectrum is provided at Figure 4.3.

The benefits of neighbourliness

Whether or not neighbourly behaviour can be described as genuinely altruistic (Bulmer, 1986), to some extent people will always need motivations to learn to live in proximity. A key reason has to do with property values, and this is sometimes felt to be an explanation when differences are found in social relations between home owners and renters. The extent to which awareness of the effects of disorder on house values is a secondary rather than a primary motivation for neighbour responses is

---

[4] Although Mann's research was conducted in England, it was published in a US journal and spellings are American.

Provocatively negative	Passively negative	Passively positive	Passively supportive	Interactive and supportive	Intrusive, 'nosy'
(anti-social, disturbs norms of privacy, may be confrontational, felt as threat to stability)	(no acknowledgement, possibly deliberate avoidance, non-social, may imply isolation, atrophy of social relations)	(non-committal acknowledgement, accentuates privacy, 'I keep myself-to-myself')	(recognition, hesitant inquiry, minimum conversation, possible readiness to help in time of need, not clarified)	(convivial expression of interest, apparent readiness to help and support in time of need, balanced with sensitivity to personal privacy)	(proactive interference – perceived or real – excessive inquisitiveness, lack of sensitivity disturbs norms of privacy)

Figure 4.3 The spectrum of neighbouring. © *Respect in the Neighbourhood.* K. Harris (Ed.) Russell House Publishing, 2006

a subject for research and debate. Temkin and Rohe, in their study of social capital in Pittsburgh neighbourhoods, have a comment on this:

> *Community development practitioners developing social capital may not specifically have property values in mind when building community. However, neighborhoods with higher levels of social capital should have lower crime rates and provide a healthier social environment for their residents. To the extent these are perceived as amenities, this social environment should be capitalized into the value of housing within the neighborhood.*
>
> (Temkin and Rohe, 1998: 65)

It's worth noting that neighbourliness, as a form of social capital, is a common good which has externalities: its benefits can be felt by those who do not invest in it. Policy should not see neighbourhood relations as a closed system. The benefits accrue in the social, cultural and economic spheres, and of course in the promotion of the civic within the public realm. In this sense, neighbourly behaviour potentially benefits all residents including those who maintain minimal relations with others around them. The main benefits that neighbourliness can offer include the following.

- *Safety and sense of security*. This can be reflected in a general sense of ease or discomfort, as well as in crime and disorder. Informal connections between neighbours provide a basis for sharing information, raising alerts, and mobilising a response if needed. The popularity of home zones is in part down to the rediscovery of the street as a secure environment for play. In some neighbourhoods street play is rare or impossible, sometimes because of design and traffic issues but also sometimes from a sense that street life is unsafe or at best uninviting.

- *Instrumental aid, support, and the flow of information*. A basic level of neighbourhood interaction – a nod or a grunt in passing – facilitates the possibility of further interaction by establishing the grounds for reciprocity. Where neighbourliness is evident we would expect to find people sharing materials such as tools, helping one another occasionally with simple tasks, and in the course of various interactions, passing information and providing the context for sharing experience. Reciprocity is the foundation for mutual respect (Sennett, 2003: 219). However, reciprocity in the exchange of favours reflects trust in complex ways: for example, in the urban neighbourhoods they studied, Williams and Windebank (2000) found that people preferred not to take material help from friends or neighbours, and if they did, they preferred to pay for it.[5]

- *The neighbourhood is still, for many people, the primary environment for sociability and civil engagement*. This applies to many young people, older people, and those who are unemployed or who live alone. By extension we might say that for many people, relations in the neighbourhood are a key factor affecting quality of life (Airey, 2003). It could also be argued that there is a social divide between those who proactively inhabit (i.e. contribute to and invest in) neighbourhoods, and those (such as some who are cash-rich time-poor) who don't; and that the secession of the latter diminishes the primary sociability of those who remain.

- *Establishing and defending norms of behaviour*. A stable and consistent ecology is crucial for individual growth. A viable neighbourhood constitutes the ecology for the practice of acceptable norms of behaviour. Such norms will change over time and may be tested up to or beyond their limits (for example by young people or by criminals) but it remains fair to say that the neighbourhood has a role to play in socialisation which no other context can offer.

---

[5] For more on issues associated with reciprocity see for example Plickert et al. (2006), and Ghate and Hazel (2002).

- *Priming local residents for their own defence and development*. It is difficult to see how effective community action – for example against some perceived planning or environmental threat – can be mobilised quickly without a context of informal and repeated interaction among residents.

Neighbourhood stability: disorder

Research into the effect of neighbourhood disorder in Illinois identified a clear relationship with neighbourliness:

> People who report that they live in neighborhoods with a great deal of noise, dirt, drugs, crime, graffiti, vandalism, and danger are significantly less likely than others to visit and talk with neighbors or to help neighbors out.

> (Geis and Ross, 1998: 242)

Perceptions of disorder include the appearance of private and semi-private spaces, in terms of litter and debris for instance. It has been found that members of households with high ratings for 'yard attractiveness and good sidewalk maintenance' were more likely to be personally acquainted with their neighbours (Greenbaum and Greenbaum, 1981). Wikstrom and Dolmen (2001) found strong association of low social cohesion and low informal control with high levels of disorder; while Ross and Mirowsky (2001) found that perceived disorder accounted for the poorer health of residents in disadvantaged neighbourhoods.

Such findings are part of an extensive debate about neighbouring and disorder, in which there is sometimes a question about the degree to which cause and effect are confused. We should be wary of assuming a simple linear relationship between orderly neighbourhoods and people of a neighbourly disposition, in either direction. Do sociable people who proactively inhabit their neighbourhoods also have an active distaste for disorder? (It wouldn't necessarily follow that less sociable people somehow relish disorder.) Is an orderly neighbourhood likely to attract sociable people, disproportionately? Both may be partly or largely true. Does an unstable environment attract a higher proportion of less sociable people, who are therefore less likely to engage with one another with a view to bringing about change? I have spoken to residents of run-down tower blocks who hold this view. It does seem fair to say that neighbouring implies at the very least a modest recognition of the concerns of others, and so does helping to minimise disorder.

In extensive research in Baltimore, Ralph Taylor found that stability and class (particularly the former) have strong impacts on attachment and involvement, and thus indirectly had an impact on responses to disorder. He suggests that:

> In more stable neighbourhoods residents know one another better; consequently they rely more on others to deal with minor problems, and express fewer security-related worries because the environment is more predictable.

> (Taylor, 1996: 53)

Sampson and colleagues, also using large-scale research data, similarly found clear benefits accruing from neighbourhood stability:

> Regardless of concentrated poverty, racial/ethnic composition, and person-level covariates, stable neighbourhoods exhibit considerably higher levels of reciprocated exchange and intergenerational closure than do unstable neighbourhoods.

> (Sampson et al., 1999: 656)

Other researchers have contributed further insights. Janowitz found that 'community leadership' was 'strikingly associated with residential stability', with an average of 22 years at the same address (Janowitz, 1967: 120–2). Neighbourhood satisfaction, loyalty, and attachment to neighbourhood have all been found to be indicators of stability over time (Temkin and Rohe, 1998). Chung and Steinberg (2006) confirmed that residential instability is associated with less neighbourhood social cohesion, but neighbourhood cohesion is not directly related to offending. Barnes and Cheng (2006) draw attention to the effect of the perception of neighbourhood disorder on parenting. Friedrichs and Blasius (2003) clarify that residential stability is not the same as presence: exploring the question of whether more time spent by residents in the neighbourhood – measured by the share of time out of 24 hours – would increase the propensity to accept deviant behaviour, they found that it does not necessarily do so. Living in a stable neighbourhood does not necessarily mean that residents are there most of the time, as a day-time walk round many suburbs would remind us.

Neighbourhood responses to incivilities or deviant behaviour are not always going to be similar. Examining responses to disorder in areas of Edmonton, Alberta, Hackler and his colleagues (1974) found that residents of less stable areas which had high neighbourliness scores were inclined to call for an external, official response to disorder; whereas in the more stable areas, residents preferred informal intervention over formal intervention. There may be some correspondence with research reported by Atkinson and Flint (2004), who looked at informal social control in affluent and deprived areas in Scotland. In the deprived areas the call for more beat police was 'linked to a need to control crime through an official presence that was not directly linked to the local community who feared reprisals and labels of being a *grass*' (2004: 341).

It does seem that neighbourhood stability is of particular significance. Taylor (1996: 68) even suggests that policy makers should prioritise it over regeneration, and we will return to this in our final chapter.

Neighbourhood stability: transience

> Folks round here don't come from round here.
>
> (Eddie Izzard)

Length of residence is probably the most important feature of any definition of neighbourhood stability. The 2002 social capital analysis of General Household Survey data showed that:

> . . . the positive correlation between length of residence and high levels of neighbourliness remained after all other factors were taken into account.
>
> (Coulthard et al., 2002: 30)

High levels of mobility are therefore likely to be of concern to policy makers. According to a Cabinet Office paper on geographic mobility, every year some 10 per cent of households move (Donovan et al., 2002). A more recent government report acknowledges that 'In areas of high mobility, it can be difficult to create cohesive communities' (DCLG, 2006: 20). While it is fair to say that relative stagnation of population may be unhealthy, it's also important to remember that some areas will be disproportionately experiencing churn on a highly disruptive scale. Some years ago I visited an estate where I was told that, at the local primary school, there was an 80 per cent turnover of pupils year-on-year. It's difficult to see how we can expect teachers to teach, or community development to be possible, in such a context.

It's commonsense to observe that a sense of permanence is an important component of belonging and readiness to invest in local social relationships: people who do not expect to stay long are going to be less inclined to invest in their surroundings. Furthermore, Wilcox and her colleagues found that 'population instability was positively and significantly related to violence', adding that concentrated disadvantage had a significant effect on physical incivility (Wilcox et al., 2004: 198). And Ellickson, in a study that strikingly mixes the ethnographic and the legal, notes that '. . . the lack of a prospective long-term future relationship makes disputants less likely to resolve their differences without the help of third parties, and hence more likely to resort to legal and political action' (Ellickson, 1991: 39n). Thus informal social control will be weakened by geographic mobility. The impact of high levels of neighbourhood change can be particularly acute for older people, as they become generally less mobile and more dependent on support (Phillipson et al., 1999).

Informal social control

We come then to the central concept in the ways in which neighbours deal with the transgression of norms: informal social control, often described in terms of 'eyes on the street'. Atkinson and Flint put forward this definition:

> *Informal social control consists of two primary mechanisms: the existence of collective norms and values within a 'community' and the ability of that community to regulate its members and to realise collective goals such as controlling group processes and visible signs of social disorder.*
>
> (Atkinson and Flint, 2004: 335)

As we have noted, informality is a key component in neighbouring. Informal recognition of other residents, casual greetings, and non-committal encounters in neutral places, are part of the shifting material that helps to build meaningful connections between people. These seemingly trivial behaviours accumulate over time to form the basis of trusting relationships which can be drawn on in time of need. They serve to establish and re-enforce norms, and help people to identify and deal with threats. The relationships can accumulate to provide a communication network which people are likely to deem reliable where important information is concerned (Harris and Gale, 2004: 20).

But even with minimal recourse to formal mechanisms, a neighbourhood is still a social system. In order to function – i.e. to minimise damaging conflict among its members – certain conditions (norms of behaviour) pertain and need to be reinforced. Where they are transgressed, the first option for reasserting control is usually an informal one. Ellickson's research in rural US neighbourhoods led to his hypothesis that 'members of tight social groups will informally encourage each other to engage in cooperative behaviour' (Ellickson, 1991: 167).

Much of this book is about adjusting to changed perceptions in the ways in which we exert informal social control in our neighbourhoods. Various examples illustrate this:

> *Years ago everybody minded everybody else's business, if you saw a child misbehaving you disciplined it.*
>
> (Brewer et al., 1998: 577)

> *If they would only take a little telling off people and werenae so cheeky to folk. They throw stones at folk's windows and everything.*
>
> (Airey, 2003: 132)

(He) knows he can come to my house and say, . . . I've had a problem with (your daughter) . . . and will you sort it out, and (he) knows that I will. But many people will not accept any complaint about their children and will simply challenge you to phone the police or the council.

(Harris and Gale, 2004: 27)

A lot of kids are allowed to run wild around here, they smash up the phone boxes and break bottles. They are allowed to do what they want.

(Barnes and Baylis, 2004: 97)

It's the youngsters from 13 upwards that spit and fight and to me that's not acceptable, they like to start the trouble, to be rude to you for you to start back.

(Barnes and Baylis, 2004: 100)

Understandably, most of the literature considers informal social control as a valid and valued mechanism for controlling crime and anti-social behaviour. There are three other perspectives which we need to mention. The first is to acknowledge that at certain levels, the norms expressed by the processes we are talking about can be manifested as what Evans calls a 'neighbourhood dogma' – views having an established shared local currency which amount to something more than loosely shared norms. Evans notes that this dogma may be transmitted or publicly displayed, sometimes in ritualistic ways that amount to a powerful unofficial code (Evans, 1997: 45–6. See also Brewer et al., 1998).

The second is that certain events, including a neighbour becoming a victim of crime, may stimulate other manifestations of 'community': Chapter 6 offers a case study in which this appears to have happened. In some cases a certain negative event, or a series of them, constitute the catalyst for residents exerting positive social control: the transformation of the Pembroke Street estate in Devonport, previously riven with routine vandalism and now recognised by the Home Office as one of its 'Guide Neighbourhoods', is a case in point (Watson, 1994).

The third alternative angle is to recognise that the concept of 'community' in neighbourhoods necessarily includes informal information and communication (Harris, 2006), and that this is intimately related to the processes of informal control. The communication channels that carry information about breaches of acceptable norms also carry subtleties about those norms, and much other intelligence besides. Brewer and colleagues describe 'the grapevine' as 'the mechanism by which the local moral economy is socially disseminated' (Brewer et al., 1998: 580).

Much of the research into informal social control confirms its contribution to community cohesion. Developing the notion of *collective efficacy*, Robert Sampson has researched and written extensively about the conditions under which people succeed or fail in maintaining local quality of life.[6] Collective efficacy is the combination of social cohesion and readiness to intervene in the common interest:

Socially cohesive neighbourhoods will prove the most fertile contexts for the realization of informal social control. In sum, it is the linkage of mutual trust and the willingness to intervene for the common good that defines the neighbourhood context of collective efficacy.

(Sampson et al., 1997: 919)

Basing their arguments on British data, Sampson and Groves (1989: 797) claim that 'communities with sparse ties among friends and neighbors generate a weakened system of social control, which, in turn, facilitates predatory crime'. Conversely, as Unger and Wandersman (1985: 143) put it, 'neighborhoods that have a high degree of social interaction may be more likely to control crime

---

[6] Useful brief summaries of the notion of collective efficacy can be found in Halpern (2005) p124–6, and Sampson and Morenoff (2006) p190–1.

informally'. (A high level of interaction is not the same as a network of strong ties: recent work by Shafer and colleagues (2006) suggests that strong networks do not contribute to collective efficacy, nor do they have an impact on the perception of disorder.) Some low-income or deprived neighbourhoods are relatively cohesive, but on the whole too many odds are stacked against their residents. Where kinship and friendship networks are strong, we would expect to find a degree of informal control (Atkinson and Flint, 2004); but, as Sampson and colleagues found in their extensive Chicago study:

> Shared expectations for the informal social control of children were considerably lower in neighbourhoods of concentrated disadvantage.
>
> (Sampson et al., 1999: 656)

Readiness to intervene

In research reported in this volume, Jacqueline Barnes explores some of the detail of people's readiness to intervene in cases of anti-social behaviour or incivility. As an implied measure of social change this question has popular appeal. In the television programme *Britain's Yobs* previously referred to,[7] the reporter suggested that 'increasingly we don't intervene', although this assertion was unsupported. At about the same time, a security company gained some media publicity by claiming that 64 per cent of UK respondents lacked the confidence to challenge a group of 14-year-old boys vandalising a bus stop, and that 30 per cent said they definitely would not. The finding was apparently based on a Europe-wide survey (ADT, 2006). Similarly, in advance of the publication of the *Respect Action Plan*, MORI announced that '55 per cent of people have asked someone they did not know to stop behaving rudely' (MORI, 2006). Undoubtedly, readiness to intervene is an important measure of how civil we are as a society, and we need research with rather more subtlety than these popular surveys allow. We should be able to distinguish, for instance, differences in behaviour according to whether or not the perpetrators are known and whether the location is the witness's own neighbourhood. Some insights from the social identity approach reported by the ESRC Violence Research Programme will be of value here: the research clarifies how 'bystanders are only influenced by fellow bystanders if they see them as members of a common group' (Levine et al., 2002: 3). The ease with which various components of our identities (home-owner, parent, car-driver, Muslim, dog-owner, football-supporter . . .) can be interpreted from half-clues by others looking for commonality may therefore be an important factor in intervention, particularly if they do not recognise us as neighbours. We also need to explore how the fear of retaliation relates to the theme of risk aversion (Hillman, 1993; Waiton, 2001; Adams, 2005).

Of course, there may be many reasons why we do not intervene. Are the perpetrators armed or do they appear under the influence of drugs or alcohol? Would the authorities, residents or other passers-by support an intervention? Did I really see what happened? Three general explanations for not intervening can be found in the qualitative research by Barnes and Baylis: fear of reprisals; the view that 'it's not up to me'; and the attitude 'well, I used to do it' (See Barnes and Baylis, 2004: 101). Similarly, motivations to take action can also be varied and complex, and not necessarily purely altruistic. I spoke to a man who had stopped a row from developing into a fight on an underground train, modestly claiming, 'primarily for my own selfish interest, not wanting to get to work late because if they had started fighting the train journey would have been delayed'. The instance was

---

[7] *Britain's Yobs*. Channel 4 television broadcast, 24 April 2006, http://www.channel4.com/news/microsites/D/dispatches2006/yobs/index.html

of additional interest because he was well aware that, as a black man with a strong African accent, dealing with two white men in the centre of London, his intervention had an effective element of shock for those he addressed.

While this instance may have had the advantage of anonymity and surprise, being prepared to intervene in the neighbourhood, by contrast, is likely to be enhanced by established familiarity with the perpetrators. One participant in the Manchester review expressed it like this:

> *What counts is who they will listen to. Different people in the neighbourhood have different degrees of neighbour clout.*

> (Harris and Gale, 2004: 27)

'Neighbour clout' was this resident's way of describing the kind of respect that he feels is appropriate for dealing with challenging behaviour. It reflects a perception of status among other residents, and how they're viewed by others for different reasons. Lack of neighbour clout could be an important unofficial indicator of potential disorder at local level.

Formal and informal

It would be misleading to present informal social control as entirely independent of formal control mechanisms. As I argue in Chapter 9, any proposed revival of respect and civil relations at local level will depend on both. But there are two insights from the literature which I want to use to shed light on the relationship between them. The first is the emphasis that Ellickson, a legal theorist, puts on the primacy of informal approaches:

> *Neighbors in fact are strongly inclined to cooperate, but they achieve cooperative outcomes not by bargaining from legally established entitlements . . . but rather by developing and enforcing adaptive norms of neighborliness that trump formal legal entitlements.*

> (Ellickson, 1991: 4)

In other words, for Ellickson, formal back-up in cases of disagreement may be far less important than legal systems would imply or government would like us to believe.

Secondly, the research by Atkinson and Flint (2004) highlights a seldom examined issue about spatial scale. While they found that residents in deprived areas were more inclined to seek recourse to formal social control, it depended on the location. As one respondent pointed out, an incident requiring intervention beyond the immediate neighbourhood could be decidedly problematic because of fears of retaliation:

> *Right on your doorstep you'll stop them because it's yours. Once you get away from your own doorstep, in that middle ground, that's where I bite my tongue . . . Everybody is going to know who you are . . .*

The researchers suggest that 'informal social control at the level of the wider neighbourhood, which government policy seeks to enhance, is the very social and spatial scale at which residents are least willing to intervene in the governance of others' (Atkinson and Flint, 2004: 342. See also Evans, 1997).

We should reflect back to the earlier point that cohesive neighbourhoods can be oppressive towards those who by virtue of some difference are condemned to outsider status. Where informal social control and the readiness to summon formal control are strong, deviance from norms is less likely to be tolerated. Quoting a national study which looked at anti-social behaviour orders and acceptable behaviour contracts in mixed housing areas, Elizabeth Burney notes:

Police officers dealing with troubled neighbourhoods often face community demands for far more extreme action than they would contemplate. Enforcement is an easier concept for people to grasp than negotiated solutions. One practitioner quoted by Nixon et al. (2003: 102) said: 'At residents' meetings that's all I ever hear about is 'why isn't the borough doing more ASBOs?' and so I talk about ABCs and then they say 'we don't want that soft crap, we want ASBOs'.

(Burney, 2005: 122)

It could be argued that such attitudes challenge the findings of Ellickson (1991) discussed above.

One problem with much current government policy on local issues is its unvarying implicit assumption that 'community' equals consensus. We can't keep preaching this trite gospel. Residents in a locality seldom come together to discuss or decide on anything specifically to do with their neighbourhood in any significant proportion of their number, other than occasionally in housing ballots. There is undoubted merit in notions of neighbourhood governance that imply decision-making by residents required to reach consensus, or implied consensus, on issues such as the provision of amenities and policing. The principle is sound, the rhetoric often fanciful. As Crow and Allan pointed out twelve years ago, in practice, consensus cannot be taken for granted (Crow and Allan, 1994: 162). A more reflective use of the concept 'community' will lead us to an understanding that cohesion is not the absence of conflict, but rather, as Alison Gilchrist puts it, 'a collective ability to manage the shifting array of tensions and disagreements among diverse communities' (Gilchrist, 2004a: 6).

While it's apparent that informal social control is a mechanism for defending one's own and communal territory (Barnes et al., 2006: 31) it's important to keep in mind three other points. First, as we have noted, informal social control depends upon and helps to maintain local communication channels. Secondly, introducing formal surveillance systems in place of informal systems is an admission of failure and not a lasting solution to the problems of incivility or anti-social behaviour in local areas. Thirdly, if there is anything to be said for trying to minimise the prevalence of NIMBY ('not in my backyard') attitudes and generating more of a WIMBY ('welcome in my backyard') culture, it is precisely the kind of social development to which policy could and should be contributing.

Occasions, encounters and errands

I have referred to the significance of informality and perhaps it is the more informal manifestations of neighbourhoods that we most need to understand. The opportunity for people *to encounter* one another on their own terms is perhaps the single crucial feature of neighbouring that has received least attention.

One starting point is to pay more attention to 'occasions' and opportunities for encounter, such as queuing at the post office or walking the dog – the kinds of scenario where people bump into one another with a degree of regularity and predictability, but without formality. In this respect it's worth reflecting on the extent to which the phenomenon of the neighbourhood errand – to post a letter, to buy a loaf – has become endangered, again diminishing the extent to which neighbours encounter one another serendipitously or semi-routinely. If the stamps, the letter-box, the baker, the bottle-bank and other traditionally local resources are all available non-locally at the supermarket, and you 'have to' go there anyway, those errands are more seldom run. Neighbourly encounters are likely to be less frequent and, critically, are likely to be concentrated on a smaller and narrower proportion of the local population, such as older and younger people. These are the particular effects of auto-dependent urban sprawl, which 'reduces social capital primarily because it reduces opportunities for spontaneous social interaction' (Freeman, 2001: 70).

Victoria Nash distinguishes between situations in which people are just exposed to the presence of others, and situations in which they are required to interact and co-operate with others. She notes that both are required for a healthy public realm and for building diverse local social networks:

> *Without the everyday mundane encounters of passing people in the street, queuing together in shops, talking to the man who runs the post-office, it is impossible to imagine how any level of generalised trust can arise.*

> (Nash and Christie, 2003: 34)

Local third places (neutral meeting places) (Oldenburg, 1989) play an important role in the promotion of sociability, the diffusion of information, the establishment of norms and commonality, and the development of a sense of trust and security. The classic examples of third places are coffee shops, pubs, corner shops and hair salons. Various other kinds of place such as markets, launderettes, public libraries, gyms and parks can fulfil this role, as of course do some kinds of event such as pub quizzes and football kickabouts.

In order to promote civility, our neighbourhoods need spaces that encourage and provide for lingering in conversation, while also allowing the individual to pass on with a polite nod or short greeting or even to avoid unwanted encounter. That means places have to be easy to move through, have a clear uncluttered image, and be easy to understand (DETR, 2000). Our spaces need to be inviting but escapable. They should be legible without being over-determined.

Place, belonging and boundaries

Social geographers like to remind us that places are constructed through social relationships. This raises the question of the extent to which a residential area loses its identity if social interactions decline below a certain point. And how would we know? Elsewhere (Harris, 2006) I have described an estate where residents appear to sense imminent decline caused by 'civic absence', a looming drugs culture, and weak community presence reflected in reduced informal interactions. In Chapter 5, Philip Connolly stresses the importance of walkable environments, noting how various aspects of perceived safety, such as street lighting or ease of crossing roads, can have a powerful effect on people's willingness to walk in the neighbourhood and hence can impact on opportunities for casual encounter. Research by Leyden, (2003) confirms that, as we would expect, residents in walkable neighbourhoods, with more places to walk to, are more likely to know their neighbours. In this section I want to refer briefly to some other issues about the physical design and appearance of neighbourhoods.

While it might be easy to exaggerate the extent to which design can contribute to the experience of neighbourhood, there is a great deal of recorded work to build on. Barton and his colleagues articulate the potential contribution of good urban design:

> *. . . responsiveness to the existing context, compatible mix of uses, appropriate buildings to accommodate activities at the right rent, appropriate location and levels of accessibility, all brought together in a place which is attractive and feels safe – can create conditions where a sense of neighbourliness and belonging is more likely to develop.*

> (Barton et al., 2003: 184)

There are subtleties in the ways in which our environment affects encounters. Research by Christensen and her colleagues in East Jutland, on the relation between design of spaces and opportunities for people to meet, suggested that:

> the design of the neighbourhood has some influence on the **frequency** of neighbours' encounters and meetings. Furthermore, the design of the neighbourhood decides whether these meetings and encounters take place as a result of a gradual and voluntary approach – or whether they take place suddenly and abruptly, as soon as one opens one's front door.
>
> (Christensen et al., 2002: 4, emphasis added)

Another example is provided from recent research into the views of residents on the design of new housing. On one estate, the children's play area had been sited in a location without good informal surveillance: a very basic error. A resident commented:

> It's attracting nuisance with a lot of kids from other estates who are vandalising it. The swings were never put up. Had they put it in where the houses would be looking on to it, the adults could keep an eye on the play area and the kids.
>
> (CABE, 2005: 21)

The Swiss educationalist Marco Huttenmoser argues for far more emphasis on neighbourhood space in child care:

> In the past we have overestimated the 'power of upbringing' and demanded too much of parents. Bringing up children not only needs competent parents but also needs the right space. And space – as I believe – has to become the new paradigm of child raising. For younger children space means space outdoors, a suitable neighbourhood.
>
> (Huttenmoser, 2005)

While space for children usually requires some form of direct surveillance, with young people over the age of about ten, as I suggest in Chapter 1, there are more complex needs. Conflict and disharmony can characterise the ways in which young people use their local spaces as they learn the skills and lessons of negotiation, avoidance and integration with their peers. Research by Tucker and Matthews illustrates how this is not just an urban or suburban phenomenon: with a shortage of appropriate space, rural villages are often zones of social tension (Tucker and Matthews, 2001: 167). Spaces need to be designed not only *for* young people and *with their involvement* (Worpole, 2003): it's also appropriate to consider the potential of new spaces for intergenerational interaction. A Finnish play equipment company has provided an example, by recognising that:

> Yards and parks should be designed as meeting places for three generations, where parents and grandparents don't simply sit on benches or fiddle with their mobile phones, but move around with the children . . . Playgrounds are ideal places for people of all ages to improve their motor skills. At the same time, they provide a natural environment for interaction and cooperation between different age groups.[8]

Environmental design can also have an impact on the relative *permeability* of the neighbourhood, contributing perhaps to a sense of exclusion or exclusiveness (as with gated communities, or culs-de-sac, which we consider in Chapter 6); or to a fractured sense of coherence or lack of identity.

As my chapter title suggests, there is a language of belonging and association, which reflects some of the subtleties of behaviour around being 'resident'. One cul-de-sac resident in the research

---

[8] *Playgrounds, shared exercise places for adults and children.* Lappset news release, 11 May 2005, http://www.lappset.com

reported in Chapter 6 mentioned that neighbours' relatives who visit regularly come to be recognised by other residents and included in pavement conversations. A sense of local identity and belonging is often recognised as a component in community development, but we might ask how significant it is in relation to neighbourliness. People might express a low level of attachment to their neighbourhood but still exhibit neighbourly behaviour. Conversely, where we find high levels of attachment to a locality it's quite possible that we might not find a great deal of neighbourly activity going on. In an affluent area with homes set well back from the street, levels of neighbouring may well be minimal, with attachment high, unless there is some crisis that puts both under pressure. Whatever the shades of difference here, it does seem to be the case that neighbourhood ties are a stronger predictor of civic involvement than is place attachment (Lewicka, 2005). Liz Richardson's research reported in Chapter 3 suggests that residents' sense of attachment is not a key predictor of their readiness to take action against anti-social behaviour. Similarly, Wedlock (2006) found that sense of attachment was not as strong a predictor of low levels of crime as was a sense of community.

The notion of boundaries is always implied in the discussion of 'community'. Community is a 'boundary-expressing symbol' which can cover a range of meanings 'precisely because it allows its adherents to attach their own meanings to it' (Cohen, 1985). We can identify three kinds of boundary which will have an impact on people's sense of belonging in neighbourhoods: physical boundaries such as roads and railways; administrative or 'enacted boundaries' (Suttles, 1972: 242); and perceptual boundaries (particularly to do with a sense of safety and associated with times of day). In combination these will have a complex impact on people's social reach and hence on their neighbourhood relations. In any detailed exploration of the sense in which the experience of boundaries relates to neighbourly behaviour, it would be important to look at age and gender differences.

The rural view

Most of our discussion has implied an urban or suburban context, not least because issues of incivility are accentuated where people are concentrated together, and that is the context on which most research is focussed. While some studies such as Berry et al. (1990) and Ellickson (1991) have looked at certain aspects, the literature lacks an exploratory comparative analysis of rural and urban neighbouring practice.

Neither overt respect nor manifest disrespect are uniquely urban experiences. Phillips and Smith (2006) in their Australian survey of incivilities note the greater likelihood that uncivil city centre episodes would be 'deeper' events, with follow-up reactions and interactions; but they also found a surprising proportion of episodes reported from small towns, suburbs and rural locations.

There are some important points to take into account. In rural areas in the UK, change is probably more rapid now than in the past and, with minimal institutional support, can be that much harder to absorb:

> *Like their urban counterparts, many rural residents may simply practise everyday 'avoidance' of neighbourly responsibilities, expectations and uncomfortable sources of anxieties, but such visible manoeuvres may matter more in rural spaces, especially to those who already feel different.*

(Parr et al., 2004: 414)

It may be possible to generalise from the implications of the research into mental health in rural areas reported by Parr and colleagues. They note how local people with mental health problems may end up crossing a line where locally acceptable 'eccentricity' becomes locally unacceptable 'deviance'. 'The prevalence of detailed local knowledge about such individuals, fuelled by sustained surveillance of their behaviour' can catalyse a process of exclusion, thus overturning the potentially supportive nature of the local social network (Parr et al., 2004: 411). Furthermore, the development of befriending schemes in rural areas certainly suggests that traditional models of rural support now require some kind of formal structure in order to meet needs: it's possible that to some extent they always did.

Residents of rural neighbourhoods, as much as urban ones, have always experienced and had to adapt to divisions, but Simmons in his review of rural poverty suggests that the nature of polarisation in the rural context has changed:

> A century ago, it took the form of the lower orders touching their forelocks and hoping for the best. Now, forelock-touching belongs to the past and polarisation has become the gap which has opened up between the indigenous country-dwellers and those who, in steadily increasing numbers, have come to settle in the countryside.

(Simmons, 1997: 118–19)

The issues of rural cohesion in terms of an autonomous, defended lifestyle are illustrated in Holloway's (forthcoming 2006) research into rural racism and the discourse around a ritual public bonfire featuring a mock gypsy caravan, in Sussex in 2003. She found that the lifestyle of gypsy travellers, like that assumed of asylum seekers:

> . . . was seen as insufficiently white in cultural terms to fit in to a rural area, threatening as it did the privileges of whiteness enjoyed by the settled community.

(Holloway, forthcoming 2006)

Thus questions of belonging, allegiance and 'commitment to community' arise and have to be negotiated, often with a stronger emphasis on kinship than is common in urban areas. From research with young people in the Scottish Borders, Jamieson's (2000) categorisation of some examples as 'attached migrants' (often but by no means exclusively middle-class young men) and 'detached stayers' (often working-class young women) suggests subtleties and levels of complexity that challenge stereotypes.

Poverty, social networks, choice and power

I have referred to the role of increased choice in people's preferences for extended social networks over place-based connections. But not everyone is able to exercise a great deal of choice in the selection of relationships. So we would expect neighbourhood relations to vary as they reflect socio-economic differences. We would also expect to find differences in motivations and attitudes towards neighbouring, although this is by no means the same as noting, for example, that wealth or poverty can characterise neighbourhoods. Thus Sampson and Morenoff in a study of low-income neighbourhoods in Chicago suggest that there is 'a durable structure in poverty areas that erodes shared expectations, trust in mainstream institutions, and collective capacity' (Sampson and Morenoff, 2006: 201).

Here I want to refer to some nuances that are apparent in the literature. The first concerns the nature of social ties. Geis and Ross clearly show that living in a low-income area does not in itself discourage ties with neighbours (Geis and Ross, 1998: 242). However, it is widely assumed that it is not the lack of ties, but their extent and range, which is of significance. Campbell and Lee showed that people with high socio-economic status 'have large but shallow neighbor networks, while more economically disadvantaged respondents are involved in smaller networks comprised of more durable ties that are frequently activated'.

They add:

> *The economically advantaged claim larger networks by virtue of their integration into broader society, but do not require strong links to neighbors for day-to-day support.*

> (Campbell and Lee, 1992: 1092)

Automobility is of course a key factor, because there is a strong relationship between heavy car use in a neighbourhood and the nature of residents' social ties (Freeman, 2001).

People who live in deprived neighbourhoods are more likely to experience a sense of powerlessness and to tolerate deviant behaviour: Friedrichs and Blasius found that:

> *. . . it is not the local network but the total number of network persons that leads residents to reject deviant behaviour, and forceful deviant behaviour in particular.*

> (2003: 819)

Where people lack choice, low levels of place-based ties can be particularly constraining, as they lack both the dense overlapping networks of the past and the sparser overlapping networks needed today (Taylor, 2002). Lupton and Power argue that, in a declining neighbourhood where people are disinclined to interact with one another or to instigate action for change:

> *Community spirit is not necessarily lost – rather it becomes more contained within smaller groups. Residents often refer to a strong sense of community within tightly knit kinship groups or long-standing friendship networks.*

> (Lupton and Power, 2002: 135)

This sense of retrenchment will be familiar to most community development workers. The researchers note that informal social control is undermined 'because residents are less confident of shared norms and standards that can be collectively promoted or enforced' (135).

The sense of powerlessness associated with social exclusion is related to neighbouring, probably as both cause and effect. The concept of empowerment tends to fade from discussions of social capital, (Wood and Gwyther, 2002) but in this book, from the doffing of caps to the construction of street etiquette, we are concerned to reassert the significance of power relations in the understanding of behaviour.

Democracy depends upon communication and community (Calhoun, 1998; Friedland, 2001). Non-participation in civic life may have roots in 'the habit of non-participation' – the sense in which people grow up and pass through family life, school life and early employment without expecting to have any say in the decision-making processes that affect them (Harris, 1999: 68). If levels of recognition in neighbourhoods are low and discouraged, civil relations and civic participation may be stunted for many people from an early age. The significance of neighbourliness in this respect is confirmed in the Illinois study of Geis and Ross. They found that people who visit and talk with their neighbours and help each other out reported 'significantly lower levels of powerlessness' (1998: 242).

The impact of built form on the sense of power is explored by Dovey (1999), who discusses various ways in which architects and planners manipulate spatial behaviour. The issue, he says, is not whether but how they do so.

Neighourhood variety: cohesion and diversity

Chapters 7 and 8 explore the implications of broader cultural differences in local behaviours. In this section I want to add a few points to stress the significance and complexity of these issues.[9]

Harmonious relations in the neighbourhood tend to reflect an equilibrium between homogeneity and heterogeneity. Where a population is too homogenous, there is a risk of becoming insular and losing the ability to assimilate new ideas and to adapt to changes (Gilchrist, 2000: 151). Residents in more diverse populations, on the other hand, may find it hard to identify common interests, and different expectations of shared norms – for instance over parental discipline, or loud music – may form disincentives or barriers to interaction. These imbalances may be important: reflecting on neighbours' willingness to intervene, Hackler and colleagues suggest that norms have to be held nearly universally, otherwise they're likely to be ineffective (Hackler et al., 1974: 335).

At the same time, we should be wary of a tendency to characterise neighbourhoods as more homogeneous than they are. Janet Foster (1997), in an analysis of neighbourhood networks on a London housing estate, shows how heterogeneity and diversity can impact in different ways in such a context; and that people can have quite ambivalent views on the degree of neighbourliness that they claim or recognise. She also reports that the anticipated possibility of hostility from other residents clearly affects openness to diversity. A key implication is that while solidarity (or cohesion) and diversity (or heterogeneity) as social forces seem to pull in opposite directions, under certain conditions people establish a functional ecological equilibrium:

> The differing types and composition of networks on Riverside aptly demonstrate that different forms of neighbourliness can occur in the same setting simultaneously among different groups of people. These networks played an important role in an environment where Asian, white, black and Chinese/Vietnamese households alike lived with an underlying suspicion about their neighbours and expressed concerns about their safety.
>
> (Foster, 1997: 126)

It seems likely that the relationship between neighbourliness and diversity will become a key area for research and policy. As Richard Sennett observes, 'the sheer fact of diversity does not prompt people to interact' (Sennett, 1994: 357). And more recently a leading commentator on social capital suggested that 'more diverse places are places in which people don't talk to their neighbours much. More diversity means lower levels of co-operation within neighbourhoods'. Research suggests that informal social control through social ties may be less effective in racially heterogeneous neighbourhoods and predominantly minority neighbourhoods (Warner and Wilcox Rountree, 1997: 534). David Halpern notes:

> Ethnic and social heterogeneity has been found to act as an inhibitor of social capital, lowering trust and engagement not only between groups but within them too.
>
> (Halpern, 2005: 281)

The issue for policy will become urgent, because our neighbourhoods can be expected to become increasingly diverse. The experience of the young white girl growing up among Asian boys, referred to in Chapter 1 above, is just one graphic example of a painful confusion of cultural norms. One question that we will address in Chapter 9 is; to what extent does it imply the need to formalise the negotiation of norms?

---

[9] I acknowledge that the concept of diversity is contested, even to the point of being felt to represent disrespect. Peter Wood for instance has written that 'It can be, by turns, racist, line-jumping, people-bumping, rude, exploitative and conniving' (Wood, 2003: 303).

Chapter 5

Heelgood Factors: The Role of the Street Environment in Promoting or Undermining Informal Social Control

Philip J Connolly

Down in the street

This chapter looks at the evidence and practice for optimising the contribution of safer streets and public spaces to the overall goal of reducing crime and increasing perceptions of civility. It argues that improvements in the design, maintenance and management of these spaces contributes to this goal by increasing the availability of witnesses, potential guardians and residents acting as informal place managers in their own neighbourhoods. These improvements are also able to signal the presence of a community regulating its own local environment and thus enhance feelings of civic pride. The chapter also uses references to the streets from popular culture to illustrate that the street environment is not passive and can be transformed by its residents. Finally these references illustrate the capacity of streets to inspire people to make friends, music and even money.

The significance of the streets lies in the fact that they are the one public service that almost everyone uses each and every day. The streets are people's first point of contact with the wider environment. Thus the appearance of the streets exerts an important influence on residents' perceptions of whether their local environment is well maintained and orderly or whether it is neglected and chaotic. It is as pedestrians that residents are most sensitive to the quality of their environment; walking at three mph it can take several minutes to negotiate a convoluted underpass but travelling at 30 mph in a car you'll quickly get back onto your normal route. The streets are also the setting for people's first contact with people from beyond their family unit.

Crime (and incivility) has five usual components: an offender, a victim, the absence of a guardian, a location and a time (Cohen and Felson, 1979). Just as there are repeat offenders and repeat victimisation there are also 'hot spots' and 'hot times' for crime or incivilities. Places with more than their fair share of crime were first termed 'hot spots' by criminologists who observed that in one American city 50 per cent of calls for police stemmed from just three per cent of the police officers' beats. At www.chicagocrime.org you can drill down to any city sidewalk and read details of the latest crime incidents. It is not surprising that Chicago has pioneered this tool for assessing how desirable it is to move in or out of a neighbourhood: the city has been a laboratory for studying the ecology of crime since the 1920s. W.I. Thomas, a pioneer of the Chicago school of sociology, formulated 'four wishes' to categorise residents' motivations in relation to the environment of their neighbourhood (Thomas and Znaniecki, 1918). His four wishes were: new experience, security, responsiveness and recognition. Thomas coined the term 'social disorganisation' to describe a neighbourhood lacking the ability to solve its own problems. Social disorganisation theory has been introduced by Jacqueline Barnes in Chapter 2. It stresses that criminality is a product of three strands: high levels of turnover in tenancies; people of different languages, cultures and races isolating themselves from each other or avoiding opportunities to meet or mix together; and poverty levels that result in those on low income being preoccupied with their own survival needs.

More recently Sampson and Groves (1989) redefined these strands as: anonymity and sparse acquaintanceship networks among residents and attenuated control of public space; unsupervised teenage peer groups; and a weak organisation base and participation in social activities. The attenuated control of public space is likely to be the most visible sign of the neighbourhood's deficiencies. Each of these strands has been articulated by researchers but residents themselves often express disorganisation in terms of what they see (Crenson, 1983). Some studies have highlighted the connection between non-residential physical disorder and the fear of crime (Skogan 1990; Perkins and Taylor, 1996) but others have not (Taylor, 1999). The Scottish Centre for Social Research (Curtice et al., 2005) reported that:

> Those who believe that the environment in their neighbourhood is poor are more likely than those with fewer environmental concerns to report anxiety, depression and a generally poor state of health.

It is my own proposition that the general sense of disorder in the external environment is transmitted to the residents through:

1. safety fears arising from the fragmentation of the flow of people.

2. the mismatch in residents and their children's play needs, and the rights of through traffic.

3. their collective inability to close the gap in their own expectations and what the managers of their environment deliver in terms of its maintenance.

4. the degree of uncertainty in trying to predict the ability of the outdoor environment to support their journeys on foot.

Each of these has a design, maintenance and management component. Many problems have their origins in poor design.

A sketch of our changing streets

The design of our streets has changed over the last five decades to reflect the changing patterns of work and in particular the means by which people get to work and to other places. At one time the men would emerge from their houses at a similar time each morning and walk together to the factory, bus or train station. They would meet with others coming from the opposite direction at street corners. Corner shops selling newspapers could thrive on a plentiful supply of customers. There are residential streets close to me where the end house, much larger than the one adjacent to it, was obviously a corner shop. Stores had no need to advertise, they simply had to be open. Bakeries and greengrocers had enough custom to be able to offer fresh rolls or fruit to the early morning shift workers. These attractive aromas are now only to be found in supermarkets.

The women left at home didn't just run the home and bring up the children but they managed the neighbourhood too. The image presented in old photographs such as those found in Young and Willmott's classic study, *Family and Kinship in East London* (1957) is of women leaning over garden gates and fences, arms akimbo, exchanging news of each other's families. These women were the means by which information pulsed through social networks. It is easy to think that it is only the teenagers who are bored by the present lack of activity in modern streets but many older people with fond memories of the 1950s feel the same way too. A neighbour of mine wrote to me thus, 'It would be ideal to pop along to play group, our own play group, in our own place, I for one would love it'. She is eighty years old.

People were in relatively low car ownership and so relied more on what they could carry themselves. Consequently they made regular trips to local shops rather than the weekly or fortnightly food shop that is common today. Populated streets attract others because people like to watch other people. Greater housing densities and larger family sizes without the range of home entertainment currently available persuaded more people to use their streets for entertainment. The streets allowed for many chance encounters as well as the opportunity to meet new people, many people married the girl next door. The Beatles highlighted the vibrancy of such urban environments:

> *In Penny Lane there is a barber showing photographs*
> *Of every head he's had the pleasure to know.*
> *And all the people that come and go*
> *Stop and say hello.*

Street markets thrived and street vendors were common. Public space was more often social space in which the street was a stage for the life of the community. The increased visibility of local residents meant that they were gently persuaded both to maintain their own reputation and to respect the mores of their community. The teenagers spent more time in the presence of other adults and in turn had less opportunity to engage in anti-social behaviour. In the presence of so many potential guardians few people would attempt any violent assaults on others passing by.

The 1960s were a period of increasing car ownership. The streets witnessed the rat race as the rat run. Owners began to concrete over their front gardens to park their cars. Street edges were splayed to allow for the rapid turning of vehicles without them having to change gear. As the space for traffic increased (whether it was moving or static) people progressively withdrew from the streets. Joni Mitchell noticed the changes and expressed it in her 1970 song, 'Big Yellow Taxi'.

> *They paved paradise and put up a parking lot,*
> *With a pink hotel, a boutique,*
> *And a swinging hot spot.*
> *Don't it always seem to go*
> *That you don't know what you've got till it's gone?*
> *They paved paradise and put up a parking lot.*

The loss of 'liveable streets' was literally drawn to people's attention by Appleyard, Gerson and Lintell in 1981. They studied streets with varying levels of traffic and the extent of social interaction amongst each street's residents. The street with heavy traffic had relatively little social interaction and residents had fewer friends and acquaintances. On lightly trafficked streets residents were found to have three times as many local friends and twice as many acquaintances as those on busy streets. The researchers concluded:

> *. . . there was a marked difference in the way these streets were seen and used especially by the young and the elderly. Light (street type) was a closely knit community whose residents made full use of their street. The street had been divided into different use zones by the residents. Front steps were used for sitting and chatting, sidewalks for children playing and for adults to*

stand and pass the time of day . . . the street was seen as a whole and no part of it was out of bounds. Heavy street on the other hand had little or no sidewalk activity and was used solely as a corridor between the sanctuary of individual homes and the outside world. Residents kept very much to themselves. There was no feeling of community at all.

(Appleyard et al., 1981: 22, 24)

Children played less and less in their own streets from the seventies onwards and appeared more and more in the company of their parents and adult carers. The increase in escorted trips contributed in turn to the increasing traffic. Between 1975 and 2000 there was a 26 per cent decline in walking amongst the general population – equivalent to 110 trips per person per year. As people switched to driving, the neighbourhood's eyes and ears were increasingly in short supply. To make up this shortfall with official police patrols, police numbers would have had to rise sevenfold (Connolly, 2004).

The reduced visibility of pedestrians encouraged engineering and construction professionals to ignore them. Street lighting was designed to light the carriageway and not the footway. The standards for illumination were related to the volume of vehicular traffic and thus penalised neighbourhoods with low car ownership but with consequently higher numbers of residents needing to walk everywhere. Planners and architects conspired to create the abandoned street of the seventies and eighties. In some cases the street itself was jettisoned in favour of aerial walkways linking buildings that were at right angles to the road.[1] The green space in between was fragmented into small pieces that were difficult and expensive to care for. The term S.L.O.P. was invented to describe how it had arisen – Space Left Over (after) Planning. Walking became riskier because pedestrians were sent on long detours under subways or across footbridges to cross busy roads. Those still walking the dispersed and meandering routes were cut off from other people who might provide help and were thus vulnerable to robberies or worse. Punk rock sensed the edginess of the streets and the Jam in particular crystallised the mood in the song 'That's entertainment':

> *A police car and a screaming siren*
> *A pneumatic drill and ripped up concrete*
> *A baby wailing and stray dog howling*
> *The screech of brakes and lamp light blinking*
> *That's Entertainment.*

The street had changed from being a place of intimacy to a byword for danger. Spending time on the streets came to be seen not only as unpleasant but dangerous – policies were promoted that actively discourage spending time on the streets. These policies were particularly applied to the removal of young people, the one group in our society who in the main still use the streets. I shall now move from this sketch of the changing character of our streets to the evidence for why I believe that reducing the threat from young people (whether real or perceived) depends upon repopulating the streets, and that to support this it is necessary to remove the barriers to everyone else being out there.

Triggers of the fear of crime

The literature on the triggers of the fear of crime highlights concerns both over people 'hanging around' and the absence of other people. Concern over people 'hanging around' is usually linked to

---

[1] See Boddy (1992) for an analysis of the separation of pedestrian from motorised traffic.

after dark, in certain places and the very fact that these people are not actually doing anything (Lucas et al., 2004). In a study commissioned by the government (Crime Concern and Social Research Associates, 1999) people were asked what makes them feel unsafe when walking about their area after dark. In urban areas people hanging around tended to be the most common reason given for feeling unsafe, followed by poor lighting and places for strangers to hide. In Inner London, residents tended to avoid adjacent neighbourhoods with a poor reputation for crime, the main high road after dark, pubs and places with a reputation for prostitution, the local park after dark, alleyways and local hotels with a poor reputation. The places people specifically said they avoided in their neighbourhood were consistent with those types of localities which people earlier said caused them to feel unsafe. That is, lonely places, back or side street alleyways, subways and those locations where drunks might congregate. The more vulnerable groups in city areas (women and the elderly) perceive crime as an area problem and fear certain environments (Kinsey et al., 1986).

One US survey of women's concerns disclosed that 48 per cent named car parks, 42 per cent certain streets, 40 per cent public transport and 27 per cent parks as being hot spots for crime (Werkerle and Whitzman, 1995). These factors were between two and five times more important than the next most important factor – lifts (10 per cent). When asked what it was about these places that made them feel unsafe at night, 61 per cent named poor lighting, 39 per cent that the space was devoid of other people, 33 per cent that the place was not visible to other people, 30 per cent that there was no access to help, and 19 per cent that the place had hiding spots for other people. During daylight the most significant factor was a lack of other people (21 per cent) followed by not being visible to others and having no access to help (both 12 per cent). Poor lighting still accounted for 10 per cent of the respondents. It can be concluded that the presence of other people engaged in meaningful activity e.g. engaged in pedestrian journeys of their own, can reduce the fear of crime. Indeed there is official recognition for this. The 1994 DoE circular *Planning out crime* (section 14) stated that:

> One of the main reasons people give for shunning town centres at night, is fear about their security and safety, one of the main reasons for that fear is the fact that there are very few people about. Breaking that vicious circle is the key to bringing life about in the town centres.

Many commentators have enthused about the benefits of pedestrian movement as a deterrent to crime, most notably Jane Jacobs and William H Whyte. In her seminal book The *Death and Life of Great American Cities* (1961), Jacobs used a metaphor from the arts to describe these benefits:

> Under the seeming disorder of the old city, wherever the old city is working successfully, is a marvellous order for maintaining the safety of the streets and the freedom of the city. It is a complex order. Its essence is intricacy of sidewalk use, bringing with it a constant succession of eyes. The order is all composed of movement and change and although it is life not art we may fancifully call it an art form of the city and liken it to the dance – not to a simple minded precision dance with everyone kicking up at the same time, twirling in unison and bowing off en masse but an intricate ballet in which the individual dancers and ensembles all have distinctive parts which miraculously reinforce each other and compose an orderly whole. The ballet of the good city sidewalk never repeats itself from place to place, and in any one place is always replete with new improvisations.

(Jacobs, 1961: 60–1)

This poetic exposition is certainly persuasive but not scientific enough for many design and police professionals. Central to her message is a psychology of trust in the value of strangers which in turn demands an assessment of the available evidence.

Pedestrian movement and the incidence of crime

The relationship between the number of people and the type of crime is well known but poorly quantified. Felson (1998) made the following observation:

> If vendors of snacks and drinks seek crowds, so do pickpockets, luggage thieves and bag snatchers. Other offenders pay closer attention to the absence of people. For example, the flow of people to work generates a counter flow of burglars to residential areas taking advantage of their absence. The flow of workers home at night and on weekend produces a counter flow a few hours later of commercial and industrial burglars to take advantage of the situation.

Angel (1968) observed that opportunities for street robberies were high on streets with few people: those with sufficient numbers to produce targets without waiting around but not enough to operate as a deterrent. Further support for Angel's observation was provided by Valerie Alford (1996). Alford studied the 16 highest crime streets in the Deptford area of south east London. She found that the highest crime per pedestrian levels appeared on the local authority housing estates. Here they are higher than on the main through routes of Deptford such as New Cross Road, Evelyn Street, and Lewisham Road. The risk of being mugged would appear to be related not to the numbers of pedestrians but the rate of flow of pedestrians along it.

Cohen and Felson (1979) assert that as pedestrian street use increases, streets become safer because of the presence of guardians. The Violence Research Programme based at four UK universities attempted to discover whether bystanders do act as potential guardians and in what circumstances they intervene to prevent crime. Their study (Levine et al., 2002) concluded that bystanders play a vital role in encouraging or discouraging violent attacks. This is not just in the obvious sense of people intervening or not intervening, but also because by their action or inaction they communicate both to the victim and the perpetrator their approval or disapproval of what is taking place.

Support for Jane Jacobs's 'eyes on the street' or what Newman (1972) termed natural surveillance can be found in a number of studies. A study in Croydon compared the rate of theft per car parking space in a short stay car park as opposed to the adjacent long stay commuter car park (Liddle and Bottoms, 1991). It found that the short term car park benefited from the regular pedestrian trips to and from their owners' cars and experienced less theft. In the well documented Kirkholt study (Forrester et al., 1998) of house burglaries, 70 per cent of the burgled houses were visible to neighbours but only 35 per cent of the properties chosen were visible to passers-by.

It can be concluded that there is evidence that pedestrian movement, the arrival and departure of a stream of people mainly strangers to one another, does deter crime. The likelihood of crime in or arising from public space appears to diminish when there is an unpredictable number but steady flow of pedestrians passing by. The challenge to designers is to produce designs that will have the effect of maintaining the flow of pedestrian movement. This requires infill development that increases net residential density (Kenworthy and Newman, 1989), mixed-use development that reduces the average distance between housing and employment and even mixed-use within a single building to encourage street level activity throughout the day. Walkable neighbourhoods require local shops and amenities to support the objective of a regular flow of pedestrians. Residential streets should be designed with a vernacular architecture and hierarchy of road layout that allows people to interpret their environment (Saelens et al., 2004). Personal security is also enhanced through ensuring that a reasonably frequented pedestrian network separates green spaces in front of dwellings with residents' own front doors (Poyner, 2005). Designers should contribute to good maintenance by specifying materials that are durable and street furniture assembled from components that are easily changed in the event of them becoming faulty or damaged.

Fixing the street

Considerable attention has focused upon the role of street maintenance in crime. Philip Zimbardo (1973) recognised that high levels of crime occur in poorly managed and badly maintained street environments. To test his theory of a link he set up an experiment in which he left one car in New York's Bronx area and another in the affluent area of Palo Alto near San Francisco and filmed what happened to them. Within minutes of being left unattended the car in the Bronx was vandalised: within days it was stripped. In contrast the car in Palo Alto stood untouched for more than a week until Zimbardo damaged it himself with a sledgehammer. Observing the car over the next seven days he watched as it too was vandalised, over turned and destroyed. Zimbardo concluded that passers-by observing a damaged car assume that no one will care if it is stripped for spare parts. Seeing a half stripped car, vandals will move in and burn it. And once that occurs the sense of disorder will spread from the car to the street sending a signal that anything goes. Many researchers have noted the way that even one instance of neglect can have a mushroom effect, for example litter begets litter (Geller, 1980). In addition, areas where there are high levels of vandalism tend to be the areas where there are higher levels of offending.

Zimbardo's experiment gave rise to the criminologists James Q Wilson and George Kelling's theory of 'broken windows' (1982) which claims that one unattended broken window leads to many more. They observed that residents withdraw from a neglected and uncared-for street environment. The informal control that their presence brought is lost and the vandals who created the problems become emboldened and intensify their harassment and vandalism. A vicious cycle then kicks in, with the lack of social contact eroding community involvement and the ensuing atmosphere attracting more serious offenders from outside the area who sense that it has become more vulnerable and therefore a less risky site for criminal activity. The theory argues for attention to be paid to minor signs of decay such as litter, and prompt action to be taken to repair and maintain the street environment.

One obvious example of the broken window theory in action is the abuse of public telephone boxes in central London. If the telephone box acquires full length advertising it is easier for 'carders' to leave prostitute calling cards without being observed. Once this happens it is seldom long before, in a well-known routine, a drug addict folds the card and rams it into the coin slot, forcing a plastic pen into the coin return slot to render the phone temporarily out of order. After several hours have elapsed during which numerous people may have lost money in the machine, the addict reappears with a cigarette lighter to melt the pen and burn the paper in order to retrieve enough coins to buy drugs. The consequence is that the community has lost a facility to the local criminals; the solution is to remove the cards when they first appear and limit the commercial advertising.

As the phone box example illustrates, the theory links minor crime to more serious crime. Thus the dropping of litter stimulates the spraying of graffiti tags – the vandals' 'signatures' – which in turn creates an environment conducive to vandalism. The presence of criminal damage soon becomes less of a concern for the residents than the street robberies and so the seriousness of the forms of prevalent crime is ratcheted up. In the United States police forces have incorporated the broken windows hypothesis into their operations. They have sought to undermine the likelihood of serious crimes by tackling minor ones such as graffiti, criminal damage, prostitution and drunkenness.

There are conflicting evaluations of the effectiveness of 'broken window' type operations. A study of crime data in California conducted over a ten year period found a statistical correlation between the introduction of 'broken window' policing and a drop in property related crime. Their research also took account of social and economic factors such as unemployment and income levels (Worrall, 2002). Of course, correlation doesn't prove cause and more recently Harcourt and Ludwig (2006) have re-evaluated the same districts of New York that had implemented 'broken window theory' policing and reaped a fall in murder rates during the 1990s. They demonstrated that the decline in crime observed was exactly what experts would have expected from the rise and ebb of the crack epidemic with or without 'broken window' policing initiatives.

Now US researchers have widened their attention from the buildings and the pavements to the roads. They have begun to research the relationship between traffic and crime and found a moderate to mild relationship between the incidences of murder and traffic fatality rates for all 50 US states. These researchers (Giacopassi and Forde, 2000) speculate that the absence of traffic enforcement may send a signal to residents that the police are absent or uncaring not only about the disregarding of traffic safety rules and higher accident rates but about rates of crime in the neighbourhood generally. This raises the possibility that another sign of a neglected environment is 'rat running' traffic. Consultants for the Building Research Establishment (Pascoe, 1993) interviewed convicted house burglars and found that they viewed houses in traffic calmed streets as less suitable targets, perhaps because they were still wedded to the idea of a quick getaway, and also because traffic calming may be another visible sign of a community at work. This suggests that slower moving traffic is also a sign of order: and broken windows theory now has a daughter that some have termed 'crumpled fender theory'.

Trees, flowers and soft landscaping also play a role. Low hanging branches may provide a useful climbing frame for scaling fences, bushes a hiding place for muggers and plant pots stash places to conceal drugs. On the other hand well maintained greenery and flowerbeds can provide a counter current to the forces behind a local crime wave. A generation ago researcher James Wise (1981) suggested that the beauty of an area could provide 'a gentle deterrent to vandalism'. He cited the example of street signs that suffered less vandalism when they were surrounded by flowers. Residents living in greener surroundings report less fear of crime, fewer incivilities and less aggression and violent behaviour. A 2001 study by the University of Illinois used police crime reports to examine the relationship between vegetation and crime in inner city neighbourhoods. The results revealed that buildings with greener surroundings had fewer crimes reported. This held for property crime and violent crime (Kuo and Sullivan, 2001). It can be argued that a well maintained planting regime and cared-for healthy trees can reduce the likelihood of crime, possibly through the impact on stress levels of aggression or simply through adding to the sense of order. The way forward is not simply local authority managed pocket gardens but also resident inspired 'green thumbs' too. In the US more than two million residents are involved in neighbourhood beautification projects. Some have been so successful that residents have been able to act as guides on walking tours of their reclaimed streets. I believe that it is this sense of ownership of the streets that lies at the heart of a successful neighbourhood crime prevention programme. The willingness of people to walk their streets – especially women whom surveys repeatedly show are more sensitive to neglect – is the defining indicator of that ownership.

Politicians persist in arguing for more police officers on the streets rather than in squad cars. They understand the important dynamic that the officer on foot is able to establish with the community. In 1982 Wilson and Kelling wrote:

The door and the window exclude the approaching citizen; citizens like to talk to a police officer. Such exchanges allow them to explain to the authorities what is worrying them (whereby they gain a modest but significant sense of having done something about the problem). You approach a person on foot more easily than you do a person in a car.

The essence of the foot patrol is to reinforce the informal control mechanism of the community itself. It is a relationship that underpins community policing.

Being there

Community policing doesn't just rely on the police being visible; it also requires the community to show up too and on foot. Sadly many residents choose not to. Instead of walking even less than a mile, one in five opt for their cars instead (DfT, 2004). Many people are legitimately able to point to a street environment that excludes them. Chief amongst these are its future users – the children.

Research into the needs of children aged between three and 12 living in residential neighbourhoods has identified two major features of the street environment that are critical to children's development: the degree to which they are able to go to places on their own (Berg and Medrich, 1980; Churchman and Ginsberg, 1989); and the degree to which they are able to play outside in a safe and challenging environment (Churchman, 1980). Children play because it's fun, but evolution has taught us to play because it helps us to develop problem solving skills, supports language development and enables us to express emotions and acquire social skills (Rogers and Sawyer, 1998).

A study by Wheway and Millward (1997) shows that motorised traffic must be considered as the main obstacle to children being able to play near their home. In the same area, children living on roads where cars are slow play out, whereas they do not play out where the cars are fast (30 mph is fast). Motorised traffic circulating close to the home environment isolates young families within their neighbourhood. Apart from preventing children playing freely outside, motor circulation prevents them from moving about alone to a large extent, for example to pay visits to friends or to go to a public playground in the vicinity. The freedom of action of these children is greatly restricted. The consequences are manifold. One study (Huttenmoser and Degen-Zimmerman, 1995) found:

- Children and parents living in environments where children cannot play outside without being accompanied have clearly fewer contacts with their neighbours.

- This applies as much to contacts between children as to those between adults and children and even to those between adults.

- Concerning the last type of contacts, not only do these parents know fewer in the neighbourhood by far, but they speak less often with them, go on fewer excursions, and also do not organise as many parties together.

The obligation of always having the children near and to accompany them everywhere strengthens the bonds between mothers and children but makes it harder for children to become independent.

Even the journey to school can be an important play experience itself if children are allowed to use the street independently (Tranter and Doyle, 1995). However, the trend to escort children to school by car denies that opportunity. Between 1985–86 and 1999–2001 the proportion of children being driven to school rose from 22 per cent to 39 per cent whilst the proportion walking fell from 75 per cent to 54 per cent. Whilst children are being escorted more and more often, the range in which they are allowed to walk unaccompanied is also diminishing. It has been calculated that for a nine year old in 1990 their range of play space from home had shrunk to one ninth of what it had been in 1973 (Hillman et al., 1990). As children's play range diminishes the number of people familiar to them decreases and so progressively more and more people are simply strangers in their lives. Children are being progressively removed from the streets and traffic is the key cause. Getting them back will require giving them priority and introducing speed limits of 10 mph in residential streets. Other design features that will also contribute are non-linear streets with build outs that utilise a choice of materials including soft landscaping. Additional play spaces could be located alongside popular pedestrian routes to key community facilities.

However, exclusion from the streets doesn't stop with the children. As people age they rely more on walking to meet their travel needs. This is because their use of the car declines after retirement and failing eyesight forces many to join their fellow non-car owning pedestrians on the walk to the shops or the bus stop. However, going out for a walk can be a severe trial (Age Concern and the Pedestrians Association, 1997). Over half have a problem with cracked and damaged pavements and every year around 600,000 suffer falls that require medical treatment. Two in every five feel that there is too much traffic and have difficulty in crossing roads. Many signal controlled junctions have no pedestrian phases. Many crossings allow insufficient time to cross: the standard is based upon the 85th percentile of pedestrian walking speeds and so discounts three in every twenty peoples' needs. One in three older people (31 per cent) fears falling on uncleared snow or wet leaves. It is not surprising that on any given day two thirds of older people don't go out. Encouraging older people to use the streets will require boosting investment in pavement maintenance, more crossings and adjusting the timings on crossings (especially on main roads that connect residential areas with local shops).

Many of the problems encountered by older people are the same problems faced even more acutely by disabled people. A MORI survey for the Disabled Persons Transport Advisory Committee (DPTAC, 2002) found that 60 per cent of disabled people have no car in the household and that they travel a third less often than the general public. Improvements in walking conditions were desired by all disabled people and around half say they would go out more if improvements were made. The dissatisfaction with pavement maintenance outweighed (42 per cent) all other concerns. The most significant inducement to encourage disabled people to go out more would be a more accessible street environment with fewer trip hazards.

Finally and in terms of numbers, women are the most significant group both using and suffering from a hostile street environment. Reflecting the relative differences in their levels of car ownership, unsurprisingly women walk more than men, making 278 trips per year compared to men's 246 trips. This applies to every age group between 16 and 60 (IHT, 2000). Twice as many women as men (15.0 per cent as against 7.3 per cent) walk to work. Women also report greater difficulties and experience more problems with their street environment than men. One study reported the following:

In the urban setting, women were often 'fenced in' and threatened to varying degrees by heavy and/or fast moving traffic flows with too few pedestrian crossings, and hindered by broken, uneven and slippery pavement surfaces and excessive kerb heights (this was of course of particular concern to elderly and disabled women and those with young children). In rural areas, neighbouring villages and amenities were sometimes rendered inaccessible by major trunk roads, and where pavements were the exception rather than the rule, walking was often experienced as particularly hazardous. In both contexts, personal security was a prime consideration – and there are many examples of destinations being within walking distance but being unsafe to walk to because of the high risk of encountering threatening persons. Similarly subways and flyovers were generally disliked and avoided as unsafe and/or perceived as obstacle courses, forcing either lengthy detours or dangerous crossing of busy roads.

(Hamilton et al., 1991)

Ten years after these comments were made the *2001 British Crime Survey* (Kershaw et al., 2000) reported that 43 per cent of women avoided walking the streets in their own neighbourhoods after dark. It follows that the most important improvement would be enhanced street lighting. Kay Painter noted that improving street lighting has the most significant impact on crime when it is implemented in places that were previously badly lit, has mixed-use development, is on pedestrian transit routes, in localised trouble spots where offender and target convergence is predictable and where visibility is poor and surveillance restricted. The chief design attributes of a successful street lighting scheme are:

- Brightness of the illumination.
- The colour of lighting.
- The average level of illuminance.
- In order to avoid light pollution – the height of the luminaire.

In the well documented Dudley relighting scheme (Painter and Farrington, 1997), more pedestrians were encouraged to use the streets, particularly women pedestrians. This in turn led to a significant decrease in the prevalence and incidence of crime.

I would contend that a quality street environment is one that has been designed, maintained and managed around the principle of social inclusivity of public space for the person on foot. This in turn requires policies that will remove physical barriers to the ability of everyone to use the streets. The previous discussion of what these physical barriers are illustrates that the detail is crucial. The presence of older people, women, children, disabled people and especially those people who are a member of two or more of these groups is the most visible sign of success.

Resident involvement

Many residents have been active in recovering their streets for the use of their whole community. They have been motivated by rising levels of traffic, crime or anti-social behaviour, or simply the dereliction of green spaces in their neighbourhood. The presence of community organisations with a focus on their street environment enables residents to get to know one another better and to recognise strangers or the unusual activities of both insiders and outsiders (Shapland and Vagg, 1998). People living in 'walkable', mixed-use neighbourhoods have been found to have higher levels of social capital as compared to those living in car-oriented suburbs (Leyden, 2003). It is likely that residents, through walking their dogs and/or taking walks to local shops, churches or temples etc. add to this sum of 'collective familiarity'. In addition, the achievement of an improved environment removes one incentive people have for moving house and thus increases the likelihood that they will become long-term residents. Long-term businesses or residents can act as 'place managers' and provide an informal supervision of a neighbourhood (Eck, 1995, 1997).

One example of community organisations focused on their street environment is the home zone movement. Home zones are residential areas in which the street environment has been modified to reduce traffic speeds to below 20 mph, and to give priority to non-motorised uses of the space. The

Department for Transport's evaluation of home zones (DfT, 2005) gave some consideration to their impact on crime. Whilst the evaluation occurred during an early phase in their evolution and there are few home zones in the UK, early indications are promising. In the Morice Town home zone in Plymouth recorded crime dropped from 92 incidents in the year before completion to just nine in the year following completion. In Tameside, crime statistics for the wider West End suggest that domestic burglary has reduced by 80 per cent in the last three years and vehicle crime by 50 per cent. In several home zones an important contributory factor to the increased feeling of security was the installation of new street lighting schemes. In Southampton the reduced traffic speeds and limited access to the area were deemed to have deterred drug dealing in the area. My own view is that giving residents more control of their streets reduces the control of criminal elements and encouraging residents into their streets denies the space to those engaged in illicit trading or incivilities. The home zone movement represents a fledgling democratic movement but if it is to flourish it requires significantly more funding.

A further lesson from the home zone movement is that the street environment should not be regarded as permanent or static. Just like any other environment its users can and should be allowed to shape it. The focus of the anti-social behaviour debate has been on the way some people abuse their environment but there are creative uses of the street that can entertain and even inspire others. The film *Dogtown and the Z Boys* documented the beginning of skateboarding. It is an uplifting film of people pushing the boundaries of human skill and endeavour. The environment for their pursuit changed from surf waves to the search for comparable conditions for revamped miniaturised surf boards but now fitted with wheels. Their search moved from school playgrounds, through swimming pools drained of their contents, to the street. One of the earliest skateboarding magazines summed up the creative impulse thus: 'We saw new potential in a concrete landscape.' Skateboarding is an admirable diversionary tactic from the temptation to become involved in anti-social behaviour. However the social inclusivity of public space calls for everyone else to develop new uses of the street and play out too – or at least take a walk.

Chapter 6

Cul-de-sac Solidarity: A Case Study of Neighbours Dealing with Vandalism

Kevin Harris

It would be horrible to think you weren't welcome in the place you lived. And worse still if nobody paid much attention, if nobody took any notice.

Introduction

On the morning of 17 November 2005, all the residents in The Woods, a quiet cul-de-sac in southern England, received a hand-delivered note through their doors. It began: 'This is to bring to your attention that somebody has been vandalising our cars.'

The note detailed and dated three incidents in which tyres were apparently deliberately damaged. It concluded: 'We have since lodged all the above to the police and we are appealing to anyone who has experienced a similar problem(s) or may have seen anything suspicious to please inform us.'

This simple half-page typed letter stimulated a collective neighbourly response over the following weeks. In this chapter I use the residents' own accounts to explore, first, what it is like to be part of a neighbourly response to anti-social behaviour; secondly, the extent to which that was based on a pre-existing sense of community; and thirdly, what difference the spatial design of their street might have made to that same sense of community and to their response.[1]

The context

The Woods[2] is a short banjo-style cul-de-sac consisting of sixteen semi-detached properties built around a small spinney. All the houses are occupied and about half have children. When asked about the social mix, all respondents thought that it was either 'surprisingly' or 'inevitably' mixed: none thought it could be described either as working class or middle class. One said:

There are people in well-paid jobs, builders and plumbers, that would probably call themselves working class.

---

[1] Nine residents were interviewed using a 2-page questionnaire as a basis for discussion. The discussions lasted between about 40 and 60 minutes. The notes were emailed to the respondent for comment and revision, and to give them the chance for further reflection. Very few revisions or additions were made: most of the quotations are therefore the residents' unedited verbatim remarks.

[2] The street name and some of its details including the number of properties have been changed to protect the identities of participants in this case study. House numbers and all personal names have also been changed. Because of the sensitivity of the issue and the fact that combined remarks are easier to attribute, none of the comments other than those of the victims are attributed. All unattributed quotations are from residents of The Woods, recorded between February and June 2006.

This is the sort of location where estate agents see no point in having their signs put up, with no casual passers-by to attract. There is turnover (one household perhaps every 3–4 years or so) but it is easily absorbed. There is clearly a high degree of stability in The Woods: one resident had moved in shortly before the episode but most had been there for several years, four households having lived there for twenty years or more.

It's quiet, leafy and spatially defined. There are no footpaths through The Woods or pedestrian access to adjoining streets, and no pedestrian network behind the houses. The entrance to The Woods, a neck of about 40 metres, gives on to a space visible from several houses where children play and supervising adults often congregate. I asked residents whether they thought there was a sense of community in The Woods, before the incident. Most certainly did, and we will come back to their comments towards the end of this chapter, but it is interesting that the victim and his partner were unsure:

> We didn't really. We moved from London. We wanted a community feel, we wanted a reduced pace of the London-type hectic lifestyle. But we ended up driving around. We were driving around everywhere so not really getting to know the neighbourhood . . . We didn't really think we were part of it. (Derek)

The reaction

Derek told me what happened when he wrote the note:

> I wrote the letter, my wife reviewed and made some minor changes. We weren't sure where it (the vandalism) was coming from. I wanted to find out whether it was only us. It was just to confirm whether or not it had happened to other people, to be able to rule it out . . . The surprising thing was how that (the letter) created a reaction. There was a response from maybe half of the residents . . . people were offering all kinds of ideas and suggestions. For example, No. 8 said, did we want to leave his dog in the car?

A couple of residents came round in the evening for a chat, offering support, asking for more information, exploring what might be done. It seems that the tyres were being punctured with a tiny instrument, perhaps a dart, so that the damage was hard to identify and the tyres took some time to deflate. In due course a total of four others joined the meetings which became fairly regular: with Derek and his partner Cheryl, that made eight. With approximately 40 residents in The Woods (albeit some of them very young children) was there a reason why others weren't brought in? In fact, others were consulted for specific purposes, as we shall see, but the core group remained and in retrospect there were mixed views about that:

> I felt we could have involved more people. But I was happy being led by other people, I just came along to the meetings . . . I thought we could have talked to Mike and Jenny earlier than we did, we could have talked to everyone really.

> Maybe in a way we should have involved some others, but for one thing we didn't really need any more, and also we thought it best to keep it tight – the fewer people who knew we were on the case, the better.

Meanwhile, Derek and Cheryl were trying to attract the attention of the police, but this was an instance of relatively trivial anti-social behaviour compared to many of the incidents that they have to deal with:

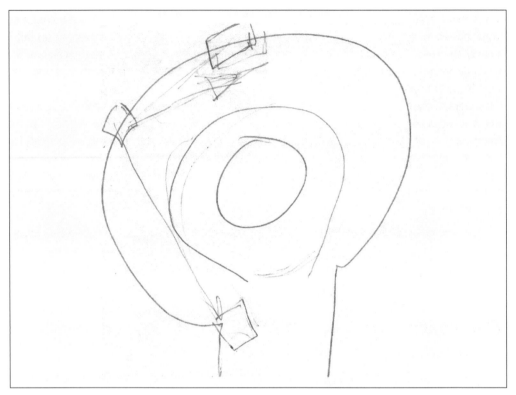

Figure 6.1   Cul-de-sac strategies. A hand-drawn map of the cul-de-sac, sketched during one of the evening meetings as residents pieced together what they knew and planned their response

> *We felt helpless going to the authorities. On one occasion, the police finally came round 24 hours after they were due to visit. Although it seemed important to us, it was not in their scale of priorities. We understood the scale of problems that they have to deal with, but at the same time we felt helpless.*

When the group got together they immediately agreed to set up a night vigil, coordinating two hour shifts and using text messages for information and handover. On the very first occasion on which they did this, one resident almost came face-to-face with the perpetrator, while others hid from view. It turned out that four residents watched him to within a few feet of the car. In each case either their view was slightly obscured at a critical moment, or they dipped out of sight because they felt visible to the line of his glance.

Shortly after he had left The Woods, around four o'clock in the morning, they gathered out in the street, assuming that because they'd witnessed no contact with the car and the tyres appeared undamaged, no vandalism had occurred. They were mistaken. Nothing else happened that night, but a few hours later, one tyre was found to be flat. The perpetrator had been fractionally out of view for one or two seconds as he'd passed the car, and the deed was done.

This was the sixth tyre to have been lost. The expense was not insignificant, and the inconvenience, for a family with both partners working, was not trivial. The sinister invisibility of the crime, in such an unlikely context, was disturbing:

It must have been distressing for them but they bore up pretty well I reckon, Derek was pretty calm. The kids, it can't have been easy, it went on for quite some time.

The support and commitment

The group worked out that there was a pattern to the incidents. They sought to share the workload, and watched on specific nights of the week:

People went out of their way to help. People were getting up in the night and taking risks, it could have been dangerous. We still think, there's still that bond there, as a result of the nasty incident. (Derek)

In total, in addition to the victim and his partner, there were five men and one young woman. From one of the houses, sometimes there were three people watching: whenever there was an alert, one would slip out the back door, round the side of the house, and observe in shadow from behind a bush. After a couple of weeks, routines were well practised, although the action had not been repeated. On one occasion, one of the other residents experimented with sitting in his car at the appointed time, uncomfortably crouched down but ready to bring up the headlights on target if needed.

It had a knock-on effect on the lives of people around here, to some extent I felt, I was a bit worried about that, people not having proper sleep, I was worried about the effect on their family life. (Derek)

One resident who was not active in the vigils remarked:

I was quite pleased that there were so many people who cared enough to do something, and I think they'd have cared whoever it was.

The participants themselves also felt pleased:

We reacted how I would have liked us to react. I was pleased and happy about that.

In the meetings that we had, it sometimes got very intense . . . I thought, the amount of effort that people are putting into it, it was really good. The getting up at four in the morning. It was just the willingness of everyone to do it.

The motivation and the explanation

How do we explain the commitment of this group of residents? My questions explored their motivations, and their comments suggest a mix of territorial defensiveness, awareness of reciprocity, and concern for the victim.

You do take it personally, it's a personal insult really.

My territory had been invaded. It was someone coming into my road.

It was just the right thing to do. It wasn't even peer pressure. It was because it was happening in my vicinity, in my area.

It wasn't just duty, it was empathy as well.

What motivated me was just this guy I knew and his family facing malice, something nasty, of course you get round and try to help.

If we were in that position, we'd have wanted . . . it would have been nice to have people doing that.

Most of the respondents felt, at least initially, that the vandalism was probably racially motivated, but none said that their response was a reaction to that.

Derek is the only black guy in The Woods. Is it a coincidence?

I think it happened probably because of the way the car was parked, but I'm sure his colour had a part to play.

One said he didn't believe it was racial, at any point, but purely down to the angle at which the car was sometimes parked, jutting out in the road slightly. While a few people said that they had *wondered* at the beginning if the perpetrator was one of their neighbours in The Woods, none seems to have held this as a firm view for any time at all.

After a few meetings and enquiries the group felt fairly confident that they knew who had been doing the damage, and they had an explanation for their suspect's presence on the street. They also narrowed down to within an hour the likely time at which the damage had occurred previously and was likely to happen again. In two ways, the group then extended its resources. First, they acquired two digital video cameras with tripods, and set these up in rooms overlooking the parked car. This necessitated a quick negotiation with one other resident, whose bedroom provided the ideal line of sight. I asked the resident how he felt about his role at that point: he said simply 'Yeah, fantastic, anything to help, anybody round here would have done the same.' Secondly, it transpired that there was a connection between the man who the group suspected, and a friend of one of the residents. Thus another family was brought into the flow of communication, in the search for better quality information.

As nothing happened for several weeks, the night vigils stopped but the cameras were set running for specific times at night. Occasional checks were made through the footage. After a couple of months the entire process was discontinued. No further damage to the tyres had occurred, the perpetrator was never apprehended and he almost certainly never knew how close he had been to exposure.

Cul-de-sac sociability

The sense of belonging associated with living in a cul-de-sac is unsurprising. The tension between privacy and neighbourliness, discussed in Chapter 4 above, is very clearly lived-out in this relatively concentrated environment. This is well described by a respondent in research carried out in Manchester by Savage and colleagues:

. . . as you can see, we're in a cul-de-sac and everybody keeps their own distance, it's quite an advantage I think that everybody watches everybody's house without being overly neighbourly so you've got that balance . . . I much prefer it as it is, I like to be friendly with people, I like people to speak and it's nice that we have got those people there if there's a problem, but I think it would be a nuisance having them constantly on the doorstep, and likewise if I was constantly on theirs.

(Respondent quoted by Savage et al. 2005: 83)

Not all culs-de-sac are circular of course, but where they are, there often seems to be a sense of social intent, and not just planning convenience, in the design. The visibility of the interactional space at the neck of The Woods is clearly an important factor in people's sense of belonging, a prerequisite for people to discover that others are present and possibly engage in social activity (Skjaeveland and Garling, 1997: 184).

> I suppose because it's a cul-de-sac you get much more of a sense of belonging in it. You can see everybody else's house. You can see everybody, that gives you much more of a sense of ownership.

> I don't know if the people we don't know much of (in The Woods) lead terrible private lives, it's none of my business . . . you don't know. If you live in a circle like this, we just look out for each other. It's only because there's a certain number of people you'd see. You'd acknowledge them even if you don't meet them, then you get to know, if relatives come to visit (a neighbour) you'd wave to them as well. They've got to have business here. That's probably what people miss in a community.

> There was always the feeling that if something happened people would do something about it. It (the incident) was sort of proof of that really. There's a sense that it's a 'safe' community and we've proved it.

In a small cul-de-sac, from the moment a new resident moves in and looks around them, it's fairly obvious who their neighbours are. A resident's presence is less subject to any general confusion either from a wider constituency or from those passing through. When they then step out, and happen to see someone, it's rude not to greet them with at least the minimum nod, wave or half-smile. In her long-term study of the Twin Rivers neighbourhood in New Jersey, Suzanne Keller wrote that closed cul-de-sac arrangements gave a sense of spatial, if not always social, cohesion.

> The visual awareness generated there made for a **gradual development of mutual recognition** followed by verbal greetings, and these led to whatever further social contacts seemed agreeable.

(Keller, 2003: 157, emphasis added.)

It's this basic level of mundane, accretive interaction that forms the foundation for concerted action should the need arise. The consistent low-level maintenance of neighbourly relationships provides the benefits outlined in Chapter 4, especially instrumental support. It is not necessarily stronger on a cul-de-sac. In their research into sociability, Brown and Werner concluded that:

> . . . living on a cul-de-sac probably does not influence people to become more sociable, but it can facilitate any nascent tendencies in that direction.

Their corollary is that:

> . . . living on a through street may not prevent people from interacting, but it can make it easy for people to avoid each other.

(Brown and Werner, 1985: 560)

Culs-de-sac and straight streets

The respondents were invited to compare their response to the tyre vandalism with the likely response from residents in a through street or a straight street. They did this by reflecting on comments made to them by outsiders (e.g. friends or work colleagues with whom they had discussed the episode) or on their own experience from places where they had lived previously:

Pretty much every place I've lived has been a straight street . . . For the immediate neighbours I suppose they'd have reacted, but I imagine it would have been more difficult in terms of practicalities. Enlisting their help would have been comparable, to an extent. But living in a circle, it was easier. On a straight street, with immediate neighbours, you could go to them, even if you didn't know them all that well.

There was no sense in which people were claiming the uncontested superiority of culs-de-sac. It was simply noted that, first, the practicalities of their operation were felt to be simpler given the circular design; and secondly, that it might be harder to establish a collective response if initial levels of interaction were low, which it was felt could well be the case:

I suppose if it was a small street like this it might have been the same.

Where I lived before on a straight street, I doubt if I'd actually have told anybody. I can't imagine that people would have gone to the lengths that we went to.

When I spoke to one of my friends, who lives on a straight road, she said 'well we don't talk to anyone, we wouldn't even have heard about it, we wouldn't know, it's down to the police . . .'

I suppose if you're on a street and one person lives at one end and another at the other, they're not gonna have those sort of opportunities. Whereas if you're at either end of this street, you're actually closer.

We should note here that the lack of through traffic on The Woods is critical for sociability, because the relative safety affords a sense of space. The entrance into The Woods is a ninety degree turn, so vehicles that do come in, do so slowly. They then cannot accelerate because within a short distance, the roadway divides around the spinney. As a consequence, the space at the dividing point is a relatively safe play and congregating space. The presence of families with children of similar ages, in the houses either side of this divide, clinches its use. The meaning of this space for the practice of neighbouring is probably comparable in significance to the circularity of the housing: Skjaeveland and Garling in their detailed analysis of interactional space in Bergen (1997) found that objective and perceived spaciousness are the most consistent predictors of neighbouring.

The cul-de-sac in urban design

In his extensive survey of street forms, Stephen Marshall reviews the 'grid pattern' versus 'tributary' (or loop and cul-de-sac) form of planning, and notes 'the lack of a consistent theoretical justification for grids over culs-de-sac'. (Marshall, 2005: 39) From the planners' point of view, the dilemma is presented like this:

Planners have known for decades that crescents and dead ends are a clever use of real estate. The streets themselves require up to 25 percent less land than an equivalent grid, and the layout ensures that most streets see only local traffic. The trade-off is that suburbs are notoriously difficult to traverse on foot. Getting from point A to point B – even if the distance is short as the crow flies – often involves a convoluted journey, so pedestrians become supplanted by cars.

(Carpenter and Feck, 2005)

Randall Arendt puts it more strongly:

Because they interrupt the pattern of connecting streets, thereby decreasing accessibility between adjacent neighborhoods (for residents, mail vehicles, rubbish trucks, school buses, etc.), culs-de-sac should be strongly discouraged. In fact, it would help stem the further erosion of interneighborhood accessibility if all future residential streets were simply required to connect with other streets, either existing or planned.

(Arendt, 1994)

Culs-de-sac sit uncomfortably at the centre of a theoretical dispute between what is known as new urbanism and the principles of 'designing out crime' or 'secured by design'. This is not the place for an extended review of this often fierce and intensely polarised debate, but we need to consider the key dichotomy because it illustrates for us some of the problems of civil relations at local level.

At the core of this debate are two disagreements: over whether more human activity encourages or discourages criminal behaviour, and whether the outsider is the key source of threat. New urbanists promote open and accessible environments partly because design has a role in promoting sociability and partly on the grounds that more human presence deters crime. By contrast, 'secured by design' principles include the claim that closure works better, because busier environments 'provide greater anonymity (and therefore opportunity) for most offenders, with their presence and behaviour generating less attention from others' (Knowles, 2002). Furthermore it is argued that fully closed culs-de-sac are more secure because the lack of alternative escape routes deters criminals. In some ways, this can become a debate about social and political priorities. Thus when Knowles writes that 'communal space directly contradicts the principle of creating defensible space' (ibid.) we are tempted to turn the phrase round – defensible space contradicts the principle of communal space – to show this as a challenge to society to make an either/or choice about the principle by which we live together: defensiveness or openness.

The arguments can get oversimplified if such nuances as different kinds of crime, mixed land use in surrounding areas, modes of travel, and patterns of pedestrian movement are not taken into account. But one focus of disagreement between the camps is the question of whether culs-de-sac should have footpaths punched through them to make them into pedestrian thoroughfares (Epstein, 2005). Town and O'Toole (2004) describe an example where this action was pursued with the result that:

> . . . a neighborhood that had been virtually crime-free saw its burglary rate rise to 14 times the national rate, with matching increases in overall crime, including arson, assault, and antisocial behavior.

From space syntax work on housing estates, Bill Hillier has built a systematic argument against enclosed spaces and exposed some of the flaws in the theories of defensible space. Significantly, space syntax suggests that the pattern of adult pedestrian movement in a street (a function of the spatial accessibility of the street) is one of the most efficient ways to control crime in housing estates. He notes that commonly with enclosed spaces, the 'natural' relationship between the presence of people on the one hand, and the spatial pattern of the environment on the other, tends to break down (Hillier, 1988: 77). Hillier's argument is compelling for several reasons, including the finding that, in many estates where sections are closed off, adults and children use the spaces in very different ways, suggesting an unhealthy separation which can lead to the fear of young groups by older people. However, observing people watch their kids while they're chatting out front in The Woods, it's difficult to see how you could get a much closer fit between the presence of these residents and the spatial design. The design encourages people to occupy their space, which they do, turning it from public space into semi-public or 'community' space.

It seems that a single cul-de-sac design on its own like this is not in question for its contribution to sociability among residents. Rather, the issue is whether or not it privileges cohesion over diversity

– contributing to a wider imbalance between homogeneity and heterogeneity as discussed in Chapter 4 above. One resident offered his mental map of The Woods as 'Fortress Woods', and several commented that anyone who comes into the cul-de-sac has to have a purpose for being there. So here, in our exploration of how neighbours' behaviour is influenced, we are taking a conceptual turning into an argument about exclusion by design.

Why should someone from an adjacent street not feel comfortable to walk their dog around here, or their children come and play here? They seldom do, it seems, because the design and the level of community presence send a clear message of cohesion based on territory. One resident told me:

> If a load of yobs came in and started playing in the middle of The Woods, you want to get rid of them, cos it's our street. That sounds a bit primeval. But this is our bit of the world, I like the peace and quiet and I don't want it spoiled.

Given the possibility that it is not the cul-de-sac in itself that stimulates neighbourliness, but the scale of the street, (Mayo, 1979; Brown and Werner, 1985) the arguments in favour of culs-de-sac themselves are somewhat weakened. If we redesigned some of our interconnecting linear streets in shorter sections on the scale of culs-de-sac, and inhabited them as community spaces not as through routes for traffic, many of the 'designing out crime' arguments might be answered. To some extent, such a change in planning culture would be facilitated by speaking of 'the neighbourhood' as something much smaller than planners and local authorities tend to do: a locality of several hundred units is unlikely ever to give the kind of basic level of sociability needed to counter the 'diminished need to be neighbourly' which was discussed in Chapter 4. We might also be addressing the question raised in Chapter 4 about promoting WIMBY ('welcome into my back yard') cultures rather than NIMBY cultures. The evidence from home zones, although not yet conclusive, is already encouraging (DfT, 2005).

Before, during and after

In this book we are concerned with behaviour and relationships at local level. This chapter has looked at a single instance of a crisis in a neighbourhood, and invites reflection on three phases: before, during and after.

What were neighbouring relationships like before the incident occurred?

I asked respondents whether they thought there was a sense of community in The Woods before the episode took place. Their comments suggest a comfortable level of mutual awareness without particular involvement in one another's lives:

> I don't stop and have conversations with people but I'll say hello and I'll smile at them.

> Yes. Not close community, but yes, indeed. If only because we know each other, we smile, we wave, there's safety there built-in.

> It's as you would expect, it's very good really.

> Of course, it's what you'd expect because of the layout, the place is designed exactly for that. Nothing to get excited about, just good neighbourly relations without people spending all the

time partying in each other's homes. Helping with chores, borrowing tools, Christmas cards, bringing in the wheelie-bins, that sort of thing.

I grew up in Nigeria, the neighbourhood then was very different. With the culture we had, anybody in the neighbourhood could discipline your kids. For example, if anyone sees a kid running in the road, others would watch out for them. Yes, to some extent it does happen here (in The Woods).

As soon as you turn into The Woods you feel you're home. I can't imagine it being any different really. You can be private here, you don't have to get involved, you don't have to talk to people. We don't have to live in each other's pockets, but if say Brenda had a problem, we'd be there.

One uncertainty remains. A telling comment hinted at the possibility that the approachability of the residents – surely a measure of the adequacy of their low-level sociability – was only just about adequate for the crisis in hand:

I almost felt embarrassed when the letter came round, the attacks were happening for weeks, I thought he should have felt he could have talked to us sooner.

We can consider this in relation to the fact that, although it was not mentioned, the initial reaching out of the family in adversity to their neighbours was by semi-formal letter, posted through their doors. While this was a logical practical choice of medium in the circumstances, it could be taken to imply a low level of confidence in any resident's ability or right to draw on the common goodwill that was there. This should give us pause, because it suggests that even in an environment that seems to have been highly conducive for neighbourly support, this family, having lived there for five years, only just had the confidence to make the tentative contact which stimulated such a positive response. This in turn suggests that in a car-dominated culture with a diminished need to be neighbourly, we take grave risks if we neglect long term informal ties with those around us. The point is reinforced by Sandra Wallman in her research in south London: she notes that the residents of Pearman Street were able to deal with a planning threat because of 'ties forged by years of continuous and viable neighbouring' (Wallman, 1998: 204).

How did neighbours respond?

The residents seem to have responded with immediacy and sought to coordinate their efforts:

I went straight round and talked to Cheryl about it. I hardly knew her then but I was appalled and wanted to give them reassurance that we'd try and help.

I was quite surprised. I thought he was on his own with this, but, everybody's getting together. This wouldn't happen anywhere else.

There was not always agreement in the meetings, but consensus was reached and they deferred to the victim (in whose house all the meetings took place) for approval of any suggestion:

I was quite proud that there was a band of us who were willing to make a stand, someone in our road had been attacked and there were a few of us got together to try and sort it out. The emphasis on 'us'. It was almost as if it was 'us' that was being attacked.

On the whole, we felt pleased with the way we responded in that we showed solidarity with our neighbour.

Also, we forget, but we had a lot of laughs in those meetings, it was very convivial – always a bottle of wine and it was a lot of fun, and we'd come away very determined and knowing how to work together on our plan.

There was a sense of 'fun' as well as 'duty'.

Did the episode bring about a change in behaviour and relationships?

We might expect that an episode of this intensity, with the kind of commitment that finds people working together in stealth in the dead of night, could have a lasting effect on their sense of mutuality and solidarity. Joong-Hwan Oh notes that crime victimisation 'tends to strengthen local social control among the proximate neighbors' (Oh, 2003: 503). All the residents I spoke to felt that the 'sense of community' had been strengthened, some more than others:

It has changed, greatly. We were very grateful to the residents. You have a vague sense that once the adversity is over, we will all lapse back into how we were before. But now when I do run into people, I just tend to stop and have a chat, which possibly we wouldn't have done before.

The incident brought us a lot closer to most of the neighbours.

Afterwards, well it's even better I'd say. It's easier to just go and knock on the door and ask this or that – especially as the warmer weather's coming, we'll all be out the front more and the kids'll be playing out there. So maybe, slightly more confidence, among us.

(Afterwards) It was easier to go and ask for something. I needed a pair of combats for a silly play at school, I just went over to Alan and asked . . .

We didn't have to have the meetings, but we did, and now I know that I can knock on certain doors. The closeness is definitely there, that wasn't there before, the bond is there. With summer coming I'm sure we'll find the reason to you know have a party. I can see that, that can't be taken away, I think it's there forever now.

By comparison with what many people suffer in terms of anti-social behaviour in their neighbourhoods, it would be easy to dismiss this episode as an exaggerated household hassle; and the residents' response as a mixture of territorial muscle-rippling and boys playing with toys. A demonstrative concern for damage to private property, the written appeal, and the easy access to resources with which to deal with the problem, could all be regarded as characterising routine middle-class stimulus-response behaviour. But that is not where the lessons of this case study are to be found.

It's more significant that the residents' accounts reveal a subtle variety of motivations and an emphatically co-operative reaction based on a mix of territorial and politically principled values. This case study has suggested that the collective response was possible because the soil of sociability was fertile; it was healthy and could support growth. The action of the residents was not just possible; it could probably have been predicted, because of the small-scale spatial design of the cul-de-sac and the latent sense of community. If there are slight doubts about the confidence that the victim and his family had, in their right to draw on this resource, in the end, as one participant put it:

Nothing major's changed. We just dealt with it at the time. But if something else like it erupted, we'd probably think, oh yeah we can deal with this.

Chapter 7

Respect: No Panacea for Injustices and Inequalities

Aydin Mehmet Ali

Introduction

'He cried and begged me to stop them. To stop the police from taking him away. My son my baby cried. And I said no, take him, take him.' She sobs, 'You see I had to. He doesn't listen to me. He swears and beats me up. He doesn't respect me. His father doesn't live with us and doesn't want him. Every time he goes to see him he beats him up and tells him he is no good. He blames me. I can't cope with him. So I told the police to take him away. Maybe they will be able to control him, to educate him, show him how to respect others. Maybe they will give him a chance in life to become a better person. As a woman on my own I can't do it.' She seeks assurance, 'Do you think they will do that? Do you think I've done the right thing?' and continues without waiting for the reply, 'Maybe they can. My poor child', and breaks down sobbing in desperation and confusion.

This was one of the numerous desperate phone calls I receive, some late into the night. While trying to overcome my shock of the implications for the 14–15-year-old boy's state of being and the effects of incarceration, the betrayal and rejection by his family he must feel, she tells me more. Her son did not respect her, was violent, beat her and his two younger sisters, was mixing with 'bad' boys, was into drugs, smoking cannabis, playing pool and gambling in the cafes, and getting mixed up in crime and fights. He was carrying a knife. Sooner or later he will kill someone or get killed or get involved in serious crimes, drug or gun trafficking. No one helped her. She hoped that if he was contained at this age and disciplined he might change. She was doing in for him. I was overwhelmed by the pain of her sacrifice on the one hand, and the desperation, loneliness and state of fear the young boy was going through on the other.

This woman was from Turkey, one of many living on their own in an area of north London with high levels of poverty and disadvantage. In line with national trends, divorce and separations have increased in the Turkish speaking communities where lone women are bringing up children with much of the stigma of shame and loss of respect in the communities attached to them. She had been in the UK over 15 years. She hits many of the government's buttons for policy development and initiatives: immigrant, political asylum seeker or refugee, lone parent, unemployed, living on a run-down housing estate, a woman, inarticulate in English, dependent on her children to communicate with the outside world, from the black and bilingual communities, socially excluded, with children at risk, a Muslim, and so on – her very existence a challenge to social cohesion and to an integrated society which she is probably unaware of: the target of top-down initiatives with a veneer of 'consultation' but of course someone who is considered hard to reach and to engage.

This chapter will look at some of the issues and concerns faced by black and bilingual young people and their communities, focusing more closely on the Turkish speaking communities. It will explore some of the recent socio-political changes in the UK which impact more negatively on their lives and their understandings of respect. It will consider reflections of respect in the extra-ordinary lives of people living in pockets of poverty.

Respect: some questions

If definitions of respect vary according to usage and context, are there gaps between the perceptions of policymakers, agents trying to implement those policies, and those targeted? Can respect be force-fed, can it be established by dictate or meaningfully quantified? Is it a neutral concept? And if neutral what impact does it have?

In a society whose common history is increasingly challenged with official and unofficial versions, there are disparities between interpretations and implementation. How can the spaces between communities from different ethnic groupings, first to fourth generation, with varying interpretations of even shared histories, different languages and religions, from different geographic backgrounds or shared inner cities, be spanned? Individuals face these challenges in addition to living through the internal dynamics of ethnic groupings, trying to make sense of them in relation to others' sharing the same landscape, and reaching consensus on concepts of 'respect'. How does respect manifest itself in the institutions that communities have to share: schools, streets, parks and neighbourhoods? What role does it play in bullying, gang fights outside school gates, opting to hang around with one's own ethnic group, excluding others?

Is tolerance a prerequisite of respect? Does respect necessarily follow as a result of understanding and tolerance? Do I have to respect female infanticide or infundibulation? Where is respect in white assumptions of the homogeneity of various ethnic groupings, while denying their own non-homogeneity? These assumptions are problematic and do not allow for differences within and alliances across groupings. Are concepts of democracy/liberal/good the exclusive prerogative of western cultures which push the 'other' into 'the opposite' and justify the demand for the 'other' to accommodate, change, compromise or integrate in order to become all those? The barrage of demands by the UK authorities for black and bilingual communities to satisfy particular criteria and become 'integrated' are unrealistic, false, and widen the gap of respect, especially among young people who may be the third or fourth generation of their family in this country. Knowledge of electrical voltage, the patron saint of Scotland or hoisting the England flag for the duration of the world cup are not reliable measures. And what of the importance of power relations in determining expectations and realities of who sets the agenda for respect and who and what is to be respected?

In Turkish there is a constant reminder chanted at school assemblies, to which lifelong adherence is expected. I am sure it has resonance amongst many cultures, faiths and language groups:

> *Büyüklerimi saymak küçüklerimi sevmek*
> *(Show respect to my elders, love to those younger)*

And yet as a young child I found it very confusing when teachers and members of my family beat me up, those who were supposed to love me in return for my respect. After years of arguments about my behaviour, which had a bearing on my respectability and that of my family and ethnic community, I chose to be disrespectful and decided that I would respect only those who earned my respect, not because of their age or status. It served me well in a career in education for over 33 years and even longer as an intellectual activist in gaining the respect of three year olds, young men or elders.

Who respects young people?

Our treatment of young people reflects a serious crisis in western societies. We have lost the plot with them and increasingly depend on coercion politics, or punitive and ineffective legislation to bail us out. Despite the rhetoric of participation, consultation, reaching out, involvement, reducing exclusion and talk of integration, black and bilingual young people and communities feel increasingly disempowered and alienated. The reality of failure stares back at us daily from newspapers and other media.

Knife and gun use is out of control, used to murder friends or other young people. Many young people live in a state of terror and in fear of potential violence. Recent survey analysis of young people's sense of victimisation and fear (Owen, 2006; Deakin, forthcoming 2006) found that almost half of all children surveyed, aged between nine and sixteen, fear being shot: even higher numbers (over 50 per cent) fear being followed or being attacked by a stranger. Forty-one per cent fear gangs of teenagers (Deakin, forthcoming 2006: 9). One consequence is that young people seek ways to protect themselves, and move around in gangs:

> We walk around in groups and they say we are a gang. If we are on our own we get attacked. No one helps us. When we go around with our own group no one messes with us. I don't want to but they made me fight every day when I first went to school. After I head-butted the Irish boy who was bullying me they left me alone.

> (14-year-old Kurdish boy in Enfield who arrived in the UK three years ago)

Arif, 18, who was a leader of a group at school, describes how he was excluded ten times in addition to the times he was truant in his last year. He left at Year 10. He felt angry with most of his teachers for demoralising, undermining and humiliating him, treating him like an idiot: 'So I had to prove myself. I was in every fight. I had a group of ten people. We stuck together, never betrayed each other.'

Amazing leadership skills, I think, as he tells me how he organised them. Their intelligence, organisational and communication skills, team work, grasp of logistics and protection of the more vulnerable is admirable: all desirable skills we teach young people. Arif could have been encouraged to become a positive role model but was left vulnerable and might have become prime Mafia material. 'I am not proud of what I've done, I don't want to boast', he says. He keeps glancing over his shoulder as he tells me some of the horrific things he has done like setting a boy on fire, hospitalising other young people, trapping and humiliating teachers. 'I don't want them to hear these things', he gestures towards the younger boys at the pool table; earlier we had all been talking about experiences of school, 'because they are young and impressionable. I don't want them to think that it's OK to do all these things and I don't want them to emulate me' (interview with Arif, north London, 2005).

We are shocked by the statistics: 29 per cent of secondary school children have carried a knife at some time; 80 per cent of children had experienced some sort of harassment that they found frightening; more than 25 per cent of all rapes recorded by the police are committed against children under 16 years of age; over 50,000 truant in one given day; 140,000 were given counselling by Childline in 2005 (Owen, 2006). Many parents share the fear and insist on taking and collecting their children to and from school. The movement and activities of young people may become restricted especially if they live on housing estates notorious for violence and drug abuse:

> The other day I couldn't open the door of my flat. A group of crack addicts had passed out against my door and no one was around to help me. I couldn't take the children to school as I

couldn't open the door and I was afraid. And another time, I watched through my window as a group of fifteen nine-ten year olds attacked and viciously beat up two fourteen year olds as they were walking on the estate. No one even shouted out of the window let alone intervened. If it was in Turkey that's what we would all have done. There is terror everywhere. It's got out of hand. And when my son started secondary school he was beaten up in the first week; he came home with cuts and bruises to his face. They told him it was the custom of the school! And it was a Turkish boy who beat him up. He later apologised and said he didn't realise my son was Turkish, but he shouldn't be beating up any child; the school should be preventing such barbaric behaviour.

(Fatma, mother of two children, Hackney, London, 2004)

It amazes me that we can dismiss and be so blasé about the real fears of young people. Why don't we respect them? Later in this chapter I reflect on some of the forces that impact on young people's understandings of respect.

The new socio-political context in the UK

Our understanding of how black and bilingual people in the UK experience respect has to be considered within the new socio-political context. Recent historical events and actions have impacted on long accepted norms in British society. Polarisation in the world arena and the alignment of the UK with the US government has sharpened the internal and external contradictions, shifting associated norms. Definitions of justice, democracy, legality, civil liberties, and personal belief amongst others have been shaken, creating vacuums and new juxtapositions.

11 September 2001 and 7 July 2005

The 11 September fall-out has had an immeasurable impact on the lives of the Muslim communities, amongst them the Turkish speaking communities in the west. Islam has been politicised and demonised and has become yet one more disadvantage to be added to the hierarchy of disadvantages facing the black and bilingual communities. Women with head-scarves were attacked on buses and in streets; children were bullied and beaten up in the playgrounds and streets, to the taunts of 'Osama, Osama'; mosques became targets of indiscriminate searches and disruption in pursuit of terrorists and propaganda; young women hid their names while serving in West End department stores to avoid abuse; windows of off-licences, supermarkets, shops, restaurants, cafes, hairdressers, jewellers, community organisations were smashed and those working in them attacked and terrorised. All Muslims became perceived as synonymous with terrorists or the unwanted 'other'. Even large sections of non-practicing Muslims and atheists in the Turkish speaking communities were forced into a new category, an identity not of their choice, which brought with it stereotypes and racist behaviour not encountered previously. The London bombings in July 2005, the subsequent security and anti-terrorism measures, and the rush to pass legislation have exacerbated this situation.

Iraq War

The lead-up to the war, and its conduct, has shaken a number of assumptions in British society and changed how Britain is perceived both in the countries of origin and the communities living in the UK. Its impact on young people in the UK is of great concern. The use of force without justification seems to be echoed in everyday bullying. While young people are daily subjected to images of bullying, killings, torture, degradation and victimisation on television and in the press, condemnation of bullying in schools and streets seems hypocritical. Concepts of democracy and citizenship education are brought into question if young people exercising their rights as citizens demonstrate alongside millions opposing the war on Iraq, only to witness their effort dismissed. The continued deceits about weapons of mass destruction and the illegal bombing of defenceless people have created an abyss in morality: while we demand young people don't lie to us, we lie to them. We are in danger of further brutalising young people, who we are no longer able to reach or reason with. Some of the young people involved in acts of violence, murder, gang fights, drugs, self-harm or criminal activities, no longer have moral boundaries or human or societal values against which they care to measure their actions.

Refugees and asylum seekers

The pressures on immigration legislation and emphasis on enforcement, coupled with racist headlines, compound the humiliation suffered by refugees and asylum seekers and their communities. Practically all families in the Turkish speaking communities have had members who have experienced the fear of authorities, constant uncertainty, marginalisation, and humiliation at the hands of immigration and other officials. Recent government strategies are felt to be deliberately creating and driving a wedge between the older, settled and 'more legitimate' communities and those more recent arrivals, characterised as 'bogus', 'economic refugees', 'spongers' – out to defraud the benefits system, health and education entitlements without legitimate reason for being in the UK. By contrast, we don't see any generalisation of disrespect to established society by association when, say, a white middle class man is convicted of financial fraud.

There are also attempts to drive a wedge between 'good Muslims' and 'bad Muslims.' Critics of the Iraq war are identified as the enemy within and support is sought from 'good Muslim' leaders and incorporated establishment blacks who adopt positions of 'spokesman' to isolate them. The attacks by the state on refugee and asylum seekers can be interpreted as legitimising racist violence and murders against those most vulnerable. In this interpretation, black and bilingual communities are further alienated, driving some underground. This would lead to sections of society withdrawing sympathy or concern for the plight of those escaping wars, rape, political and other persecution.

Civil liberties and citizens' rights

The agenda is being driven by the promotion of thinly disguised nationalism and the discourse of homogeneity of society. This includes laws targeting political asylum seekers and refugees, Islamophobia, and erosion of citizenship rights under the pretext of anti-terrorist legislation. It creates polarisation on religious, race and ethnic lines, and a state of fear (Kennedy, 2004; Swift, 2005). Inequalities based on race, ethnicity, language, religion and particular cultures which hitherto were a concern for the state, have been diluted and removed from its responsibility, relegating them to matters of individual concern despite the much publicised Race Relations Amendment Act 2000. Kennedy argues that fear-inducing rhetoric about international terrorism is used to create fundamental shifts in the UK justice system:

> The public are always sold the erosion of civil liberties on the basis that decent citizens have nothing to fear. And we, the citizens, can easily feel the current move is all about the 'other' – terrorists, paedophiles, anti-social yobs, Muslims, young blacks, the mentally ill. We always think

it is other people's liberty that is being traded, which somehow makes it all right. We do not realise that liberty is not divisible in this way. Anti-terror laws cannot be vacuum-packed; they seep into the policing culture and create new paradigms of state power . . . What is introduced today for terrorism almost invariably enters general usage shortly thereafter.

(Kennedy, 2004)

Integration

Debates on integration are not new. Over the last four decades, educational policies, strategies and actions have been developed reflecting the educational vision for black and bilingual communities. This moved from an 'assimilationist' vision in the 1960s, through 'anti-racist' in the 1980s, equalities and equal opportunities in the 1990s, to 'diversity' and 'legislationist' in the 2000s. 'Integration' was hotly debated and rejected in education in the 1970s. It is important to emphasise that the participation of black and bilingual communities was pivotal in changing the agenda at these different stages. The newly resurrected integration debates are but an extension of this debate. They are racist and expose a strategy of barely disguised nationalism.

The situation is compounded by poor access to good health care, transport, training, job and leisure opportunities; plus increased criminality, drug abuse, human trafficking and unemployment. This contributes to further polarisation, fragmentation and disengagement. Disproportional numbers of black and bilingual people living in inner cities face this multiplicity and hierarchy of disadvantage. Inner city poverty, economic, social, educational and political inequalities and the alienation of young people from existing structures and processes are serious. Collectively, they are hardly the raw material for 'integration' or respect but more like the fuel for riots and rebellions (Ramadan, 2005).

Issues and concerns in the Turkish speaking communities

In the remainder of this chapter I consider some of the issues and concerns that make understandings of respect so elusive and problematic for the Turkish speaking communities. These issues have reverberations for all black and bilingual communities. While my experiences are in the inner city settings in London and major cities in the rest of Europe where large numbers of Turkish speaking communities have settled, it's likely that some of the issues may be applicable to many white working class young people.

Invisibility and selective visibility

The Turkish speaking communities have become targets of negative selective visibility in the British media due to the criminal activities of the Turkish speaking mafia and criminal elements. Headlines both in the Turkish and English language media dwell on the involvement of Turkish speaking criminals in mafia killings and shootings, heroin trade, human trafficking, credit card fraud and prostitution amongst others (see for example Boggan et al., 2002; Cobain et al., 2006; Olay, 2005). This contributes to a sense of insecurity, instability, marginalisation and low esteem of young people who constantly receive negative images of their communities in the media. Young people either internalise the invisibility or try to compensate by acting out. There seems to be a lot of anger amongst Turkish speaking young people about invisibility at school and in general:

At school they are always doing things for the black boys. Nothing for us. Sometimes we act up. We do the things black boys do so they'll take notice of us. We show we are tough so no black boys can mess with us.

(Volkan, 16, Enfield secondary school pupil)

Racism

Racism continues to be a major issue for the Turkish speaking communities. However, it is only recently that the younger generations are able to name and challenge its impact on their lives, while the older generation still prefer not to talk about it. The approach in the 1980s reflected fear of problematising the Turkish speaking communities and their alignment with other black and bilingual communities. This has since changed, especially amongst Kurdish young people who are more forthcoming in acknowledging racism, partly due to the historical experiences, discrimination, brutalisation and oppression suffered in Turkey which has been passed on by members of their communities. Secondary teachers I have spoken to report unfair treatment especially of Turkish speaking young boys who are excluded from school for the kind of behaviour which school authorities tolerate among African-Caribbean or African boys. Turkish speaking young people also report this and complain of unfair treatment. One such case involved a bright student being excluded from school for refusing to take off a baseball cap: he argued that African-Caribbean boys were not asked to remove theirs. These are unacceptable excuses for excluding and frustrating Turkish speaking young people and disrupting their already fragile education. (Jan Steyaert discusses other peculiar tensions to do with headgear and ethnicity in Chapter 8).

Educational under-achievement

There has been long-standing educational under-achievement within the Turkish speaking communities. This is a continuing concern and indicators suggest that the position has not changed. I still stand by my description of this situation as educational genocide (Mehmet Ali, 2001). What has changed over the last 25 years is that, while limited fragmented work is going on in some schools, the Turkish speaking communities have sustained weekly high visibility debates and discussions through the Turkish language press, meetings, seminars, events and limited research. Statistical data for 2001–2005 (DfES, 2006) indicates that recent government initiatives targeting raising achievement levels such as AimHigher, Excellence in Cities, literacy and numeracy strategies have not had a significant impact on young people in Turkish speaking communities. This confirms that general approaches are insufficient to raise the achievement levels of such groups with severe and long-standing low achievement. Targeted, well thought out and resourced 'holistic' approaches are needed urgently to shift this position (Mehmet Ali, 2001).

Refugees and asylum seekers

The Turkish speaking communities still suffer insecurities, injustices and humiliations by people in authority which leave them vulnerable to abuse. There is a substantial percentage of people who are refugees and asylum seekers and may be at different stages of the process of 'normalising' their status. Many young people experience high mobility, having to move between temporary accommodation and different schools. The length of processing applications causes anxiety for applicants and young people in particular. At a focus group discussion at Edmonton Green, London, in 2003, a young woman of 18 talked about her family making an application when she was seven: she had been waiting for the Home Office to make a decision for 11 years. Recent developments suggest that as the legal and media attacks on political asylum seekers and refugees increase and entry into the UK is frustrated, in line with other communities, people from Turkish speaking communities are also becoming victims of the *Şebeke*, the people smuggling mafias and gangs.

Crime, mafia, gangs

It is only recently that Turkish speaking communities have begun to talk openly about these issues in the press and amongst themselves. Recent policing approaches have also contributed to a new recognition of the issue. In the past, threats of mafia retaliations of beatings and killings prevented open discussion. The interdependency and mutual benefit of people within the same communities who may feel under attack by legislation, racism and fear of authority may also have contributed to silence. Here we have an extreme form of the unwillingness to intervene discussed by Jacqueline Barnes and by Kevin Harris elsewhere in this volume.

Most basic needs such as finding a place to live, a school for young children, registering with a doctor, finding a job, making an application to regularise immigration or political asylum and refugee status, finding a lawyer and registering for benefits, would be dealt with by someone from within the Turkish speaking communities. Some may be part of extended families. Some may be involved in criminal, others in political activities. Most Turkish speaking men have gone through training in the use of firearms whether because of military service, previous involvement in armed left-wing groups or fighting in Kurdistan. The dissolution of the Balkans and USSR has also led to proliferation of arms in the UK and mafia and criminal collaboration from these countries. Criminal activities are big business and have implications for the relatively small Turkish speaking communities. Young men in particular may be vulnerable and unable to resist extended family pressure, either directly or indirectly, to get involved in such activities. They may be experiencing the conflict of living in a multicultural society, humiliated at school because of low achievement, bullying and racist taunts, suffering the humiliation of being a refugee or an asylum seeker, the prospect of low paid and dead-end jobs, and conflict at home. 'Easy money' and 'respect' acquired through the barrel of a gun, status and material gains – these may become irresistible. Some young people may be persuaded to do small, 'innocent' jobs, which do not hurt individuals, such as credit card fraud, in return for a favour done for the family in the past, such as sorting out their immigration status. The fact that family elders may lie to the authorities about their status and history in obtaining certain benefits (e.g. housing, health care, passports, refugee and political asylum status) also creates a crisis of morality and ethics amongst young people compounded by the wider issues they face in society and the general crisis of morality and values in the UK. Young people are made the conduits of lies and immorality as they are used as interpreters in dealing with schools, law and DSS offices, hospitals and immigration issues.

Gang fights and the use of knives are rife. While not reported in the media, the communities are aware that vicious fights leading to murder and serious bodily harm have been going on for the past six or eight years amongst Turkish speaking and African-Caribbean young people; Turkish speaking and Bengali; Turkish speaking and African; as well as within the Turkish speaking communities, between Turkish and Kurdish young people.[3] While some of this may be ascribed to political

---

[3] For an analysis of 'race' and identity in gangs, see Alexander (2000), pp. 94–104.

differences, most is a response to the hierarchy of disadvantage imposed upon black and bilingual young people in the inner cities. Turkish speaking young people have become prominent in killings and serious injury both as victims and perpetrators. They tell me that they feel unsafe more than ever before. As adults fail to protect young people as young citizens in schools or in the streets, they have been forced to develop strategies and means of protecting themselves. While moving around in groups may afford them protection from attacks, it may also stigmatise them as a gang both as perceived by authorities and other groups of young people. They report that the lack of success in dealing with bullying has been the major contributor to the increased gang activity. Inevitably they will find ways of protecting themselves if they feel that schools and society are not doing so. Unfortunately, this may lead to criminalisation, death and riots.

Family relations

While general issues of migration, insecurity, economic position, displacement and generation gap, amongst others, are important, the position of bilingual children in the family hierarchy needs to be highlighted. The continued dependence on the child for all outside links with authority creates a position of 'inverted authority' for the child and a confusion of respect. This is often resented by parents who feel their limited authority in a strange land is usurped. Similarly, the child may both revel in the authority over parents, and resent being forced prematurely into the responsible adult world, while experiencing expressions of anger from frustrated parents. Professionals who choose to deal with parental authority through children, undermine any remnants of authority the displaced parents may have left. I hear of various cases where children used as interpreters at parents' evenings translate concerns and weaknesses highlighted by the teacher as the child doing really well at school.

Health and self-respect

Our ability to feel and express respect depends to some extent on self-respect. In the experience of any ethnic grouping this easily becomes a major issue. For example, traditional notions of respect are played out in Turkish speaking communities where the impact of torture and trauma – not only on those who were subjected to it but also on their families – has yet to be dealt with openly. Macho Turkish speaking society with its hero worship and heritage of armed struggle, demands the proof of manhood in bearing torture, and very few torture victims have sought help in coming to terms with their ordeal. Many carried their unhealed mental scars into their societal and personal relations, unable to show weakness faced with the culture of hero worship ever present on the walls in practically every Turkish speaking community centre in London. Seeking help may be perceived as weakness, which among other things, is felt to imply disrespect to others who perished in the line of duty. There will be some painful experiences in demythologising heroes-heroines in the process of not forgetting but humanising them, in the interests of restoring a balanced culture of mutual and self-respect.

Depression and psychosomatic illnesses are prevalent amongst women in Turkish speaking communities: mental health, smoking and dependence on anti-depressants have been issues since the 1980s. Amongst young people a more recent concern has been self-mutilation and threats of suicide: unfortunately some have been carried out. Young women seem more prone to self-harm although it has also been reported amongst young men. Such desperate acts tend either to be dismissed or hidden by the family, since acknowledgement brings dishonour. Some young women may find the solution in either running away from home or asking to be taken into social services care, which in itself is perceived as dishonouring the extended family and communities. There is a suggestion that some deaths of young women, reported as suicide, may be honour killings, especially amongst Turkish speaking communities elsewhere in Europe.

HIV and AIDS are on the increase but continue to be taboo subjects due to the macho culture and association with gay life styles. The increased number of women infected by husbands may also help bring the issue into the open, but it serves to illustrate the connection between health, self-respect and respect.

Conclusion

The changed socio-political context in the UK inevitably challenges assumptions in the Respect agenda presented by the government. This discourse is a continuation of a series of initiatives on community cohesion and integration which in themselves are not neutral concepts. Many in the black and bilingual communities regard the Respect agenda as a diversion by a government which has failed to deliver on the serious issues faced by many, especially young people. The issues have never been about cultures and their differences, distance, proximity or respect, but about the injustices and inequalities that they experience. And it is not particularly a British phenomenon, as witnessed by the rebellions of young people in France in 2005 and 2006 (Sabatier, 2005). Without the commitment and resources to tackle such injustices and inequalities, from the infrastructure to the personal, the Respect agenda is destined to be ignored or ridiculed for exposing the hollowness and desperation of the ruling elites, which have lost the plot and are out of spin. Young people have a right as citizens to expect that their views will shape the initiatives that impact on their lives, from good schools and housing, to safe streets and parks, without fear of bullying from fellow pupils or teachers, without fear of racism. Next time young people riot or rebel, burn down inner cities or banlieues or murder each other, we should remember that it is a rage against injustices and inequalities. As for Turkish speaking young people, I am confident that they know they have more to offer British society than the kebab culture to which they are so readily assigned.

Chapter 8

Respect in the Lowlands and the UK: A Cultural Comparison of Policy and Practice

Jan Steyaert

Introduction

Ever since 9/11, Bali, Madrid and London, international terrorism has been high on everybody's agenda. The traditional focus of police forces shifts to the higher levels of the violence spectrum. It's intriguing to observe that this development seems to go hand in hand with an equally increased focus on the very lowest levels of the violence spectrum, where it's more about respect, anti-social behaviour and incivility than 'real' violence.

Is this development an example of a policy-hungry government taking us towards a 1984-type of society, or a next step in civilisation? This chapter tries to tease out some of the issues surrounding governmental involvement with respect by contrasting the UK development with those in 'the lowlands' (Flanders and the Netherlands). In both countries, respect also features on the public agenda and both policy and new social interventions are being developed and implemented. It should however be noted that the choice to describe these two countries, to contrast the UK developments described elsewhere in this book, is a convenience sample rather than the result of cross-European assessment of innovative practices or policies dealing with respect.

A thought experiment

Let us start with a thought experiment. When was the last time that you had problems with the behaviour of somebody else, that the way another person acted in the public domain annoyed you? That could be because of queue jumping, throwing litter on the street, making loud mobile phone calls on the train, dog shit that some dog owner didn't clean up, loud music, smoking in a restaurant, or any other kind of frequently occurring but potentially unpleasant behaviour. Secondly, try identifying the last time you took the trouble to address someone else about their behaviour towards you and other citizens, or when somebody else addressed you regarding your behaviour?

My assumption and personal experience is that the first question of this thought experiment is easy to answer and results in numerous recent memories of little irritations we felt as a result of somebody else's behaviour in the public realm. But at the same time the answer to the second question is less easy and results in fewer and older recollections. Does this mean that we have lost the skills or interest to address other citizens regarding the cost of their behaviour in the public domain on our own well-being? Has the framework for informal social control been eroded?

A number of factors could contribute to such development. For one, our activities and social networks are no longer tied to the neighbourhood. Over the past century, the average distance a person travels a day has increased tenfold, from 4 km to almost 40 km a day (Grübler, 1998; Urry, 2003). Moreover, much of that mobility no longer allows interaction (as in trains or by bicycle) but happens in our own private cocoon (cars).

Not only has mobility changed the nature of the interpersonal contacts we have, so has technology. Kevin Harris, in his opening chapter to this book, rightly mentions the growth of self service in shopping and entertainment. We no longer go to the bank office, but spend our Sunday afternoon working our way through e-banking. We no longer spend time in the bookshop, but use amazon.co.uk. The replacement of face-to-face contacts by face-to-screen contacts is of course a transition that started 50 years ago, once the number of televisions started equalling and surpassing the number of households. Putnam's (2000) seminal work on the decline of social capital identifies this as one of the key elements in changing interpersonal relations, although others argue changes in civic engagement are more related to changing content preferences than changing technology (Hooghe, 2002; Norris, 1996).

Both developments give us great freedom to be more selective in our social contacts and no longer limit our social network to neighbours. At the same time, they also imply that we see many more utterly unfamiliar people. There's a process towards polarisation of the familiarity of our interpersonal contacts. While half a century ago most citizens tended to meet more or less the same people over longer periods of time, given restricted mobility, this is now very different. Currently, that familiarity of the average interaction with fellow citizens has either increased (through selectivity in our social network, we are more picky about our strong social relations) or decreased (through spending more time in the 'anonymous public realm'). An increasing part of our time involves interacting with people who we have never met before, with whom our interaction is very limited and whom we may never meet again. Lacking a sense of social function for the public space, we continue to privatise it:

> Today, we experience an ease of motion unknown to any prior urban civilization . . . we take unrestricted motion of the individual to be an absolute right. The private motorcar is the logical instrument for exercising that right, and the effect on public space, especially the space of the urban street, is that the space becomes meaningless or even maddening unless it can be subordinated to free movement.

(Sennett, 1978: 14)

Another explanation for diminished informal social control might be the erosion of social hierarchy and increased informality. Again, that is a welcome change in society as it reflects equality between citizens and democratisation. But it comes with a rebound effect. 'Status problems are a logical consequence of informalisation. The clothing of status – the uniform – no longer automatically commands respect. Respect must be earned and that can imply struggle' (Schnabel, 2004: 58).

Continuing the thought experiment and answering the question about the last occasion that we confronted someone about their behaviour, I can personally only come up with memories of talking to some kids playing with matches, and unsuccessfully trying to persuade an obviously very drunk adult not to drive his car home. In both cases, there's an assumed presence of hierarchy (being adult, being sober). Can we develop new skills that allow us to build respect and exercise informal control without reinstating hierarchy in the public sphere?

We seem to have lost the skills, assuming we ever had them, to negotiate with fellow-citizens about behaviour in public space. The implication is that at the same time we both accept a wider range of behaviour and get irritated by some other behaviours. Rather than discuss and challenge uncivil behaviour, it seems we expect government to provide a framework to guarantee respect. We outsource our responsibility regarding respect.

This is not a development that's specific to the UK. In this chapter, I will outline how governments react to this outsourcing process. I describe the Flemish and Dutch situation, concluding with a consideration of the lessons that can be learned from comparing those with each other and the UK.

The Netherlands

In April 2006, the Dutch minister for integration and immigration, Rita Verdonk, accepted the first copy of a new book entitled *How we do this . . . in the Netherlands*. It attempts to summarise the everyday values and norms in the Netherlands, and is intended for use in integration courses (Snel and Van der Zaag, 2006). It notes for example that when somebody has their birthday, one also wishes the other members of that household a happy birthday (p78); or that making eye contact is important during a conversation; and that Dutch people are quite candid when it comes to telling somebody else that they are mistaken (p181). In addition it provides resources like the text and origins of the national anthem or the structure of the education system. This book provides a kind of manual for interaction with the Dutch and living in the Netherlands.

The respect agenda in the Netherlands is however much broader than can be covered by a printed 'manual'. Shortly after starting in his post, Minister-president Balkenende made reference to the Commission on human values in Norway[1] and announced a similar initiative for the Netherlands: 'the discussion about values and norms must return to the centre of the political and social arena'.[2] There is political consensus around the analysis that an assertive lifestyle and increased candidness has provided the ground for uncivil behaviour. While goals like self-development are legitimate and part of human progress, there has been insufficient recognition that not everybody has enough skills and capacities for self-development (this analysis is reflected in, for example, the work of Gabriël van den Brink). Government consequently needs to move beyond a socio-economic agenda and engage with ethics, values and norms.

The suggested commission didn't happen, but a broad debate on values and norms emerged, partly through established media like television and partly through new media (see, for example, www.16miljoenmensen.nl). Furthermore, the highly respected Scientific Council for Government Policy (Wetenschappelijke Raad voor Regeringsbeleid, WRR) started a project on norms and values in Dutch society and what government could and should do in this area (de Beer and Schuyt, 2004; Van den Brink, 2004; WRR, 2003).

The WRR suggests using a continuum of norm-trespassing behaviour, not fundamentally different from the one suggested by Kevin Harris in Chapter 1. The WRR's version starts with unpleasant behaviour and continues to uncivil behaviour, through unacceptable behaviour to end at illegal behaviour. Along this continuum, a transition happens from social informal norms to legal formal norms. There is also a transition from diversity to unity. What exactly constitutes unpleasant behaviour can differ from one person to another, even for the same person from one mood setting to another. Sometimes we might find loud conversations over mobile phones annoying, e.g. when we're trying to get some work done or have just found out we've been lied to; at other times such behaviour

---

[1] See their website at http://www.verdikommisjonen.no/english.htm
[2] Speech by Balkenende, 31 August 2002, available at http://www.minaz.nl/data/1030783766.pdf

doesn't bother us. With uncivil behaviour, there's already less diversity, for example fewer people would find it normal and pleasant for litter to be dropped rather than put in a garbage can. With illegal behaviour, there's near-unity, enforced by police and the legal system. The issue is to strike a healthy balance between diversity and unity. A permissive society allows for greater diversity, while a cultural-pessimist such as Dalrymple would rather see less of it, even where it relates to informal social norms (Dalrymple, 2005).

Based on research carried out by the Dutch Social and Cultural Planning Office (Sociaal en Cultureel Planbureau, SCP) since 1970, one can conclude that Dutch citizens have gained an increasingly coherent consensus about values and norms, also in the informal area. But they are increasingly pessimistic about the implementation of these values and norms in daily behaviour (WRR, 2003: Chapter 3). Expectations regarding behaviour in the public realm have become clearer and are given higher priority, which contradicts the belief that our values and norms have been weakened (Van den Brink, 2004). There is a process of increased normative awareness (*normatieve ophoging*) which results in high expectations that easily turn into frustrations. Contrary to expectations, 'large and increasing concerns about values and norms seem to go hand in hand with decreasing uncertainty about what those values and norms should be' (de Beer, 2004: 237).

Higher and better defined norms are one thing: developments in actual behaviour might well be different. Has behaviour worsened during the last decades? Are we now more anti-social participants in the public sphere than 50 or 100 years ago?

One problem is that the kind of low-level incivilities we're talking about here (spitting, queue jumping, not cleaning up dog shit . . .) remain well below the radar of research and don't show up in statistical surveys. That makes it problematic to make statements about this kind of behaviour occurring more or less regularly over time. Analysis of several years of the security monitor (one of the regular surveys in the Netherlands) does not allow us to identify clear trends in anti-social behaviour. In the absence of such data, one can nonetheless ask if increased attention for anti-social behaviour in the media and some highly watched programmes (e.g. the 'Tokkies' or 'probleemwijken') contribute to our increased sensitivity to incivilities (de Beer, 2004).

Whether our behaviour has worsened or expectations have increased, the result is an increased tension between behaviour and expectations, resulting in a call for government to act against the burden of incivilities. The WRR describes the role of government as reducing formal norm-trespassing behaviour, guaranteeing the values of an open society and democratic state as well as supporting public morality. It argues that the 'management' of social norms is not a task for government, but for citizens. Van den Brink uses the concept of 'civilization offensive' (*beschavingsoffensief*), by which he refers to the need for a massive initiative to bring morality back into social life and decrease the variety of both private and public norms and values (van den Brink, 2004). That call resulted, among other things, in a media campaign against people with short fuses and promoting tolerance.

Others see an important role for education, and call for a democratic-pedagogical offensive (*democratisch-pedagogisch offensief*) (De Winter, 2004). Socialisation processes are now geared too much towards the individual, and not enough towards the community. Engaging with the values and norms of a democratic society in the educational process is not a free choice of individuals, but something to which society (for which read: government, schools) must commit itself. Democracy does not naturally reproduce itself. Education for citizenship through schools should safeguard the structural elements of the current and the future democracy. Since early 2006, all schools in the Netherlands have been obliged to have activities around citizenship. How this is done varies between schools. Through projects like 'the peaceful school' (*de vreedzame school*),[3] pupils can already learn the importance of tolerance and conflict handling skills at primary school.

Street etiquette and mediation

There are many ways to work on strengthening respect. While some Dutch politicians would love to import the British innovation of anti-social behaviour orders (ASBOs), this has not yet happened. A more popular and regularly used intervention is working with so-called street- or city-etiquettes. This approach originally stems from Rotterdam (Diekstra, 2001, 2004), where work on behavioural rules for young citizens led to the question whether the city would not benefit from behavioural rules for all citizens, not just youth-at-risk. The core element of the street-etiquette is that citizens define the behavioural rules on how to act in the public realm themselves. This includes designing the rules, and also monitoring implementation. In such situations, the local authority is not extending its control into the fine details of daily life nor is it expanding the formal legal rules to a painstaking level of detail. Rather it supports citizens in their self-regulating capacities. This includes 'positioning the subject in the media, scanning the city for existing or emerging etiquettes and supporting citizens experimenting with etiquettes' (Diekstra, 2001: 103). This approach differs from the Rotterdam citizenship code that was launched early 2006. This code also deals with behaviour in the public realm (such as 'use Dutch as main language' and 'treat homosexual people as equal to heterosexual people') but was developed by the city council rather than citizens themselves.

Meanwhile, the experiences in Rotterdam resulted in city- and street-etiquette initiatives in other Dutch cities. There are now 'golden city rules' in Gouda, the guidelines in Maassluis, Ede has its *mEdeburgerschap* (fellow citizenship) and street-etiquette experiments in Amsterdam, Delft and Almere. This approach is not very different from the rules developed in the robotics class as described by Kevin Harris towards the end of Chapter 1. Or to the house rules students have and develop when new students enter college accommodation (who cleans the hall or stairway, do we cook and eat together once a week, who takes care of the garbage . . .?). But it is innovative in the sense that it happens on the level of a street or small neighbourhood, and the rules emerge bottom-up with the local authority only facilitating.

The other social intervention that emerged from the increased attention for incivility and call for respect is neighbourhood mediation. It's basically a problem solving intervention (whereas street etiquette is of a more preventive nature). Where problems between neighbours or citizens in the same public realm occur, independent trained mediators are available. Across the Netherlands, there are currently about 70 of these initiatives, involving 1,200 voluntary mediators. Key to their approach is re-establishing the dialogue between all citizens involved in a conflict, so they can solve the issue themselves. This avoids taking things up to courts, but also generates problem solving skills that can be useful for possible future conflicts.[4]

Flanders

The respect agenda in Flanders is much less outspoken compared to the UK or the Netherlands. Rather, one could describe it as a mosaic, with different little stones being in place but no clear design of the larger picture emerging yet. Four recent developments can be described as examples of these little stones.

---

[3] See http://www.devreedzameschool.nl/
[4] See http://www.hetccv.nl/ for more information on the method of neighbourhood mediation.

The most recent example is the committee on 'orientation on society'. The committee was initiated by Marino Keulen, Flemish minister of housing, media and sport. Their task was to describe what the Flemish values and norms are and which common basket of values and norms is necessary for living together in diversity. When they presented the results of their work, early May 2006, the committee's chair indicated that it was surprisingly easy to outline the essential values: freedom, equality, solidarity, respect and citizenship. These values are the basis on which norms are built. These come as legal norms (which can be enforced by law) and as social norms (which are related to specific groups to which people can belong).

While initially the work of this committee was to be used to develop courseware for the numerous training initiatives that welcome new immigrants, minister Marino Keulen has already used the report as the basis for a meeting with top-level representatives of the six major religions. After the local elections (autumn 2006), he proposes a larger debate around the committee's findings.

A second development that relates to respect comes from the same minister. When redesigning the law on social housing in 2005, two new regulations were inserted. One was that new tenants in social housing estates had to be able to speak Flemish, or be willing to learn the language within two years. Free courses are provided. The other regulation indicated that there was a 'probation period' of two years in each new social housing contract. Within that timeframe, people could lose their right to social housing if there were problems with anti-social behaviour or unpaid rent. Both regulations were argued for by referring to them as cornerstones for more respect and civil behaviour in social housing neighbourhoods. How could tenants establish some respect and civility towards other citizens and in the communication between tenants and housing associations if there was not at least a minimal level of a common language? One director of a housing association supported the regulation by indicating they had tenants speaking as many as 80 different languages with few people sharing the same language, let alone Flemish. That makes communication between tenants and between tenant and housing association a daunting task, leaving civil relations vulnerable to rapid erosion.

This development is extra sensitive because of Belgium's history. Language issues are sensitive in Flanders, being one part of the three-language nation of Belgium (French is spoken in the Walloon area, German in a small part in the east of the country). Only since the 1930s has higher education been provided in languages other than French. The hope to establish Flemish as an official language played an important part in both world wars and politics throughout the twentieth century. Given that Flanders is now economically stronger than the Walloons, imposing language requirements seems like taking revenge. Citizens from Walloon would have to learn Flemish in order to be able to apply for social housing in the Brussels area. The Walloon politicians are furious, while some Walloon academics defend the language requirement.

A third development involves a new infrastructure to support respect and to police incivilities through a transition of responsibilities from national law and courts to local authorities. A new law (initially from 1999, but only fully implemented in 2005) recognises the fact that justice courts were not structured to deal adequately with incivilities and anti-social behaviour. This resulted in the situation that local police could only register violations of national laws and depended on the justice courts to follow them up. In most cases, this didn't happen. This resulted in police not bothering very much about small unpleasant or anti-social situations. Since 1999, local authorities can outline their own 'codes of conduct in the public realm' for those situations which are not covered by national law. Since April 2005, national law no longer covers anti-social situations like noisy neighbours, graffiti or low-level vandalism. This gives local authorities the room to develop their own policy in this area. Moreover, local authorities can issue local fines, currently up to 250 euros. These so-called *'gemeentelijke administratieve sancties'* no longer have to pass through justice courts, which makes it a more efficient and reliable instrument to handle incivilities. Additionally, unlike 'real' fines, they can also be issued to young people, under the age of 16.

The first of these new fines was issued in August 2005, in Maaseik, to a woman wearing a burka. Some ten years earlier, a national regulation already indicated that all citizens should be recognisable in the public realm and no 'disguises' are allowed. In June 2006 the woman lost her appeal procedure in court. The argument for people being personally identifiable in public space, visible for face-to-face communication, trumped arguments about diversity and the individual freedom to express cultures. It is now expected that more local authorities will implement a local 'code of conduct' against burkas. A parallel in local practice, although not supported by national regulation, can be drawn with the banning of young people wearing 'hoodies' and baseball caps at the Bluewater shopping centre in Kent, England. This was followed up by discussion in the UK on the 'hoodie generation' and the opinions expressed by Deputy Prime Minister John Prescott and Archbishop John Sentamu (BBC News, 2006a).

It is not only local governments that struggle with respect and 'symbolic clothing' in public spaces, but also employers and trade unions at the workplace. In early summer 2006, the multinational Group 4 Securicor sacked a long-time employee (a receptionist) in Antwerp, just after she started wearing a head scarf. A year earlier, that same employee had received a bonus as a result of her good work. The employer now argues it requests strict neutrality from its employees. The trade union has already announced it is exploring taking this to the labour court.

The discussion on burkas and other signs of religion and culture is of course highly sensitive. It relates to diversity and global citizenship, and also to the question of how these religious/ethnic symbols relate to modern values like gender equality and emancipation. There seem to be fewer problems in accepting Jewish men wearing skull caps (kippahs) than Islamic girls wearing head scarves, or westerners wearing jewellery with the Catholic cross as a symbol. Is that because we identify head scarves with oppression of women, because the Islamic culture is more distant from our western culture than the Jewish culture, or the result of power and status positions? Should we expand the discussion to include tattoos, which could also be said to be symbols of a certain lifestyle?

In Flanders, the use of the new framework is however more extensive than the specific situation referred to. Some of the bigger Flemish cities have taken up the new opportunities to develop a policy to reduce incivilities and strengthen respect. Noteworthy examples are Mechelen (where young people acting in an anti-social way are taken to police headquarters, from where their parents can pick them up again after a warning about their parental responsibilities); Leuven (a small university city, where incivilities related to student parties have become less tolerated); and Antwerp (for example with a very successful campaign against dog shit on pavements and in the parks). Other cities, like Gent or Brussels, have so far taken little action.

A final little stone in the Flemish mosaic of respect relates to a public debate, emerging early in 2006, after a judge ruled that youngsters could no longer make use of a youth centre in the village of Lauwe, after complaints by neighbours. There had been earlier cases of neighbours complaining about infrastructure for children, for instance centres for after school child care. The complaints mostly focused on the burden of noise and dangerous traffic situations around the time children were brought or recollected. In other cases, people complained about too many cyclists going too fast through their neighbourhood, resulting in a local speed limit of 30 kph.

But no earlier case raised the amount of reaction and discussion Lauwe did. The youth centre is the property of the local authority and a venue where activities during school holidays and youth parties during the year are organised. It is in the middle of a neighbourhood where houses dominate the scene, and not near industry or other noise/traffic producing infrastructure. Once the judge ruled that the centre could no longer be used during school holidays, a lot of people and institutions protested about anti-social citizens and the decline of tolerance and respect. They included the Children's Commissioner, the minister for youth and a whole range of youth organisations such as the boy scouts. A protest march against closure of the youth centre attracted about 10,000 participants. All expressed shock at how easily people step into the NIMBY attitude: 'not in my backyard'. In one case, a neighbour even complained about the noise of a child day care centre which her own daughter previously attended. Public space is typically used by different citizens for different purposes and that calls for tolerance. The examples are seen as attempts from private citizens to colonise public space and make it an extension of their private space.

However, there's also another side to this story. In Lauwe, we're not talking about a small-scale youth centre but an accommodation that draws around 250 people each day, attracting young people from other villages outside Lauwe. It wasn't the youth centre as such that led to the complaint from some neighbours, but the scale of it. Also, these neighbours had been attempting for years to communicate with the local authority about noise reduction opportunities but were stone-walled. Other situations similar to Lauwe have more recently demonstrated that open communication and some minor changes (stop the noisy activities by 22.00 hours, replace noisy metal football goals with less-noisy goals . . .) can provide a more constructive platform for tolerance. Respect is not a one-way street or a blank cheque but the result of dialogue and reciprocity.

Concluding remarks

Interest from media and politicians in how to safeguard respect in society is not restricted to the UK, but is found in the Netherlands, Flanders and other parts of Western Europe. That is somehow noteworthy, as there are no indications from survey data that there is an increase in anti-social behaviour. Although most of this behaviour is too small to pop up on the radar of social surveys, what's available in terms of data suggests that we are less tolerant of diversity of behaviour, rather than there being an increase in incivility. From that perspective, a heightened interest in respect is a further cultivation of society, rather than a defence against the erosion of our culture. Not less challenging, but a more optimistic agenda.

Also, there's a similarity between the three countries in that citizens (and media!) call on government and authorities to organise respect. While Jane Jacobs (1961) noted the importance of informal control for public safety ('eyes on the street'), there seems to be an expectation among citizens of more 'official presence', more professionals and civil servants monitoring behaviour in the public realm.

'Negotiation' about what's acceptable behaviour and what's less acceptable is nothing special, but has always taken place. There are marvellous historical examples in Norbert Elias' major work on *The Civilizing Process*, on subjects like eating with a knife and fork, spitting, or blowing one's nose (Elias, 1978–1982). The historical rules we have established in these areas (no spitting, use a handkerchief) are not the same for people from all cultural backgrounds, causing diversity in norms and behaviour. There is consequently a 'permanent negotiation'.

But negotiations are also expanding into new parts of the public realm, following innovations and changes. Examples include netiquette, codes of conduct developed for behaviour in cyberspace; and the rules of conduct for mountain biking (ride on open trails only, don't leave trash).[5] Values and norms are a 'moving target'. It is not surprising that a society that is more diverse in age and ethnic background needs to do some maintenance. It's only surprising that it took so long before there was any explicit attention paid to values and norms.

Within that context of maintenance work on our values and norms, it is surprising that in the three countries, UK, Netherlands and Flanders, most attention goes to our behaviour as pedestrians in the public realm, to interpersonal meetings. From surveys, we know that behaviour in traffic is the origin of most irritation; it is respect in traffic that's high on the agenda of citizens. In physical terms as well, in square metres, traffic makes for an increasing part of the public realm. Here, we have outsourced some aspects of respect to the physical infrastructure, with sleeping policemen, speed cameras and roundabouts forcing us to respect others in traffic, at the risk of damaging our car. Whatever progress has been made here, does not result in a decrease of traffic irritations in surveys. The focus policy-makers have on respect still seems to be off centre, looking too much into a direction the citizen isn't looking.

---

[5] See http://en.wikipedia.org/wiki/Netiquette, and http://www.abc-of-mountainbiking.com/mountain-biking-etiquette/

Chapter 9

Formalising the Informal? Policy and Local Social Relations

Kevin Harris

Introduction

When people open their front doors to go out, they should not do so in fear of violence or abuse from their neighbours or strangers. Nor should they have to fear the consequences of the conflicts of others, or their vehicles or animals. Citizenship implies a shared 'ownership' over and responsibility for the space surrounding the dwelling, i.e. the neighbourhood. We have cause to use that space for various reasons: the instrumental imperatives of everyday life, the basic need for social interaction, the impulse to be moving. Our sense of citizenship will be profoundly affected by the encounters that take place there.

Jane Jacobs believed that the cultivation of trust in an urban neighbourhood cannot be institutionalised (Jacobs, 1961: 67). But it is a legitimate goal of policy to seek to strengthen civil relations where they are perceived to be so weak as to jeopardise social order. This is of importance for a democratic society because democracy is about relationships: it won't work if too many relationships are dysfunctional. What then is the role for policy in seeking to influence civil relations at local level?

Respect in the neighbourhood depends not on formal edict from government, but on certain conditions at local level, most of which are themselves susceptible to policy influence either directly or indirectly. Local social norms assume particular meaning when they can be linked to the norms of the wider society (Janowitz, 1967: 206). Where there is less consistency of norms across society, the greater the problems for policy are likely to become.

What happens in neighbourhoods, informally between passing residents who nod, glance or exchange a few words, is both trivial and massively important. Our intention in this book has been to reassert the connection between such fundamental social interaction and civil renewal, between informal sociability and a healthy society. My view is that the quality of civil relations is a valid topic for policy attention; that it is an important measure of a civilised society; that its understanding needs to be far broader than is encompassed by current government policy; and that the role for policy is largely indirect. As Ray Pahl has put it, 'the important goal is to provide the social framework in which a culture of mutual respect may take root and flourish' (Pahl, 2006: 184). In this chapter I discuss some of the ecological conditions of life in neighbourhoods that merit policy attention.

Poverty and difference

I begin with two general reflections. First, there is a fundamental concern of social policy which must underpin all others: reducing the level of *poverty* and associated social exclusion. Put simply, the quality of social relations is jeopardised by income inequalities. As David Halpern notes:

The evidence is strong that the stretching of the socioeconomic distance between people tends to undermine the common ground on which social capital is built.

(Halpern, 2005: 291)

There is a wealth of material as the basis for reflection here, including two collections of resources: the extensive research brought together by Jeanne Brooks-Gunn and her colleagues (1997) under the aegis of the Russell Sage Foundation, covering a range of interdisciplinary research in the USA; and in the UK, the work established by the Social Exclusion Unit and supported by various research centres such as CASE, the Centre for the Analysis of Social Exclusion. It's important to reiterate here the point that in low-income areas, neighbourhood relations are subject to significant stresses not apparent elsewhere:

Even when personal ties are strong in areas of concentrated disadvantage, daily experiences with distrust, fear of strangers, uncertainty, and economic dependency are likely to reduce expectations for taking effective collective action.

(Sampson et al., 1999, p637)

Secondly, policy and practice relating to neighbourhoods has to take account of individual differences in relation to proposed measures. This has an impact at the most local level, of course: a given service may not appeal to some people who have difficulty with groups; another may not work with people for whom family relationships are problematic. The point is that not only is there no 'one-size-fits-all' solution to the promotion of community cohesion, civil relations, parenting, acceptable behaviour or whatever; but also that if policies fail to take account of individual differences in factors such as personality, attitudes, mental health, and early life experiences, they could struggle to engage the most vulnerable residents and those who may benefit most from becoming more connected to others locally (Barnes et al., 2006).

We have tried to make a case for the significance of neighbourhoods as an essential context for developing mutual respect among citizens. For positive civil relations to flourish at local level, neighbourhoods have to be consistently inhabited. This is the foundation of 'community presence'. Failure to be visible as residents, as occupiers of the territory, favours those who thrive on disorder, and its effects can be disastrous. Presence means that a neighbourhood is visibly occupied, its places and spaces are used and valued, and local people expect visitors to respect them.

To establish or restore community presence requires a level of collective *confidence*. Confidence is apparent where local people are ready and willing to articulate their concerns and needs and how they feel about their locality, *themselves* – including expressing pride in it and celebrating their strengths. For residents to express that confidence, official agencies have to allow them space and attention.

Five principles for local life

The importance of informal relations has been a recurring theme throughout this book. It lies at the core of our argument. The case study reported in Chapter 6 hints at the possibility that even in an environment highly conducive to informal interaction between neighbours, a family that had been in the neighbourhood for five years seems to have been only just sufficiently confident to contact others in time of need. In less conducive contexts – meaning most other neighbourhoods – there will probably be less likelihood of maintaining a level of collective efficacy and a sense of responsibility which all residents feel they have the right to draw on. Policy has to explore ways of supporting informality at the same time as ensuring that formal systems are there in support and where appropriate. In a later section of this chapter I discuss this relationship in more depth. In what follows, I suggest five principles which government at local and national level needs to take into account, if local social relations are to provide a foundation for reliable civil relations more broadly. I suggest that where these principles are followed, respect will look after itself.

Promote neighbourhood stability

Policy should seek to minimise the sense of disorder, unpredictability and instability at local level. As noted in Chapter 4, from his extensive research in Baltimore Ralph Taylor (1996) emphasises the principle of neighbourhood stability. He argues that it has particular impact both on sense of attachment and on community participation, and is therefore key to neighbourhood viability not just for organised collective responses, but also for behavioural and emotional (i.e. individual) responses to disorder. The key components of stability are an ordered local environment, which I cover below, and geographic mobility or transience. I will add here a few comments to the points raised in Chapter 4, drawing out the theme of belonging.

A report from a Cabinet Office seminar on geographic mobility in 2002 shows that policy makers have already been discussing issues like the extent to which residents should be able to influence who moves into an area, and the situation in some localities where inhabitants are expected to conform to social norms as part of the conditions of entry (PIU, 2002). The Home Office funded research reported by Liz Richardson in Chapter 3 adds to the feeling that this is a set of sensitive issues with no clear solutions likely to meet with universal consent (see also Flint and Nixon, 2006). Efforts to protect local homes for local people, in popular rural locations like the Peak District and parts of Wales – where agricultural employees, for instance, can easily get priced out of the homebuyers' market – suggest increasing recognition that solutions need to be found to such problems of belonging.[1] These issues highlight the need for policy to find a balance between 'rights' for free choice (within a distorted housing market) and the need for stability and a sense of belonging which is not closed. They suggest that closer and perhaps more radical policy attention could be paid to the way the housing market influences these themes.

Meanwhile, Sarah Holloway's (forthcoming 2006) research into the debate surrounding the burning of a mock gypsy caravan in Sussex in 2003, as part of a traditional village bonfire event, illustrates how the autonomous lifestyle of the white rural idyll (including an attitude which regards local traditions as unquestionably inviolable) can be fiercely protected. The ambiguous figure of the gypsy-traveller – part romanticised, part threatening, neither neighbour nor guest – may be fuzzy, but it throws into sharp focus the way in which *belonging* becomes defined and defended as *lifestyle*, exposing the dark side of neighbourhood stability and cohesion.

Elaine Wedlock (2006) has illustrated a distinction between sense of community and sense of belonging, demonstrating that the former is the more important predictor of lower levels of crime. The difference between them is explained in the way that, for example, people can experience a sense of community without having lived in a place for very long. This suggests that it would be possible to have an area with high turnover, a strong sense of community, and low levels of crime. Possible but, one suspects, unlikely. Given the current interest in mixed tenure (Allen et al., 2005;

[1] Also we should acknowledge the accumulation of comparable global issues. See for instance Kibreab (1999).

Bennett and Morris, 2006; JRF, 2006) for sustainable communities, we continue to need research that explores the tipping point at which neighbourhoods with high levels of transience become unstable.

Maintain an orderly local environment which is walkable

While we can distinguish informal social control conceptually from the sense of order in the neighbourhood, it's as well to remember that what residents may be experiencing is a challenging mix of uncertain norms with 'observable signs and cues that social control is weak' (Ross et al., 2001: 571). In my own work on the Havelock estate in west London I have been struck by the extent to which people sense a crisis of community presence and direct their energies to the *visible* disorder which authorities may have failed to address (Harris, 2006: 6). Residents sense invisible negatives like weak local social capital epitomised by low levels of community participation and a glowering drugs threat. One resident, who had lost the sight in one eye through a mugging incident on an ill-lit path, responded by spending hours in the evenings cataloguing the street lights that were out of order. That is an illustration of the action of people who want to ensure that their neighbourhood has a platform of respect.

Philip Connolly (Chapter 5) has dealt at length with the need for our built and green environment to be conducive to social interaction. The principles he discusses raise issues about the relative power of the car lobby. Governmental reluctance to confront this lobby is explicable in political terms. But the problem is not just one that influences sociability at local level; it is of course a major global problem of sustainability. It follows that policy has more than sufficient cause to urgently explore and pursue innovative ways of reducing the use of cars. As a key negative influence on local civil relations (Freeman, 2001) which also happens to be contributing to massive environmental and health problems, the lack of effort being invested in the reduction of car use by comparison with, say, anti-social behaviour could become problematic.[2]

The success of home zone initiatives needs to be publicised and the movement injected with far more urgent momentum. Traffic calming schemes have long-since proven their worth. One of the early schemes in this country – Borehamwood town centre in Hertfordshire – was established as long ago as 1989, and yet the principles still seem to be regarded as exceptional. Even on a main street, the reduced speed differential increases the likelihood of eye contact between driver and pedestrian. The gentle ambiguity of the ramped informal crossings contributes to this new notion of pedestrian and driver being on comparable terms. This is in dramatic contrast to the traffic signals loathed by both parties, and serves to illustrate the limitations of formal systems.

One of the barriers to the adoption of home zones has to do with the unnatural accounting of public spending: these initiatives are said to cost between £200,000 and £300,000 per street (JRF, 2001), perhaps a daunting figure. But I am not aware of any study which has yet sought to quantify the value of potential savings (projected or actual) that these schemes offer in terms of reduced vandalism, police time and resources, improved physical health, reduced loneliness and depression, increased sociability among children, immediately available play opportunities, minimised stress from danger, less pollution, and higher levels of community involvement. The lack of systematic evaluation in the Department for Transport's first report was a missed opportunity (DfT, 2005).

---

[2] Contradictions between transport and environmental policies are not encouraging. Reports that the government regards rail fare increases as 'a good commercial solution to the problem of overcrowding' do not suggest that it takes seriously the need to reduce car use (Webster 2006).

Promote informal social networks

Policy has to find ways of taking the vitality of local informal social networks into account. Local networks become weakened through policies that promote or condone car travel (e.g. school selection policies, under-taxation of fuel consumption, under-investment in public transport, endorsement of out-of-town shopping centres etc), that make neighbourhoods dangerous or unpleasant to inhabit, or that design-out opportunities for encounter. Addressing such negative effects would be a start. In Chapter 5 Philip Connolly has provided a simple example by pointing out how in the past, standards for street lighting penalised residents in neighbourhoods with low car ownership.

But Nash and Christie want us to go further:

> Public policy should **actively support** the development of a rich and diverse range of social ties at the local level.
>
> (Nash and Christie, 2003: 39, emphasis added)

How can policy strengthen local social relations? We return to the importance of a variety of places and spaces within the neighbourhood that are flexible and that provide or reflect ownership or identity. It is not just the *use* of local facilities, but the interpersonal contacts that grow up around their use, that contributes to community cohesion (Janowitz, 1967: 197). There are real challenges here but it's apparent that government is beginning to recognise their importance. In their 2005 paper on *Support for Parents*, the Treasury hinted that in preparing for the 2007 Comprehensive Spending Review they will consider 'how the government can best support the development of community networks and local engagement' (Treasury, 2005: 38).

The Joseph Rowntree Foundation has begun exploring the importance of informal networks. Thus for example, they have part-funded research in which Seaman et al. note the importance of 'safety enhancing informal networks' (2005: 86). Their policy recommendation is for 'initiatives to facilitate and support the development of the parental networks utilised to gain the knowledge required for keeping children safe'.[3] A conclusion to be drawn from Barnes's chapter in this volume is that the trend to perceive children as 'possessions' (as women were in the past, and still are in some cultures) could be addressed by an approach that promotes shared responsibility for children's behaviour and their development among all the residents and institutions in a neighbourhood: less parenting orders but more child and family support, and stronger informal networks.

At the very least, locally applicable policies should be risk-assessed for the extent to which they might promote or damage informal social networks. This proposition may seem insufficiently rigorous to gain credibility. If changes are proposed to a local street network, say, or to local amenities, who is to say what will be the impact on local networks, and how would they justify their decision? The first rejoinder is obvious: these are exactly the kinds of point that people can't make in the conventional consultation context, because the language is not regarded as legitimate. The first thing policy needs to do is to help legitimise the language of informality.

In this respect it's enlightening to reflect on the way Ivan Illich, 30 years ago, noted how people can become dependent on having their knowledge produced for them. This 'cognitive disorder', as he called it:

---

[3] This needs to be related to Deakin's (forthcoming 2006) call for 'sensitive, low-key safety advice to children about victimisation by people known to them'.

... rests on the illusion that the knowledge of the individual citizen is of less value than the 'knowledge' of science. The former is the opinion of individuals. It is merely subjective and is excluded from policies. The latter is 'objective' – defined by science and promulgated by expert spokesmen. This objective knowledge is viewed as a commodity which can be refined, constantly improved, accumulated and fed into a process, now called 'decision-making'. This new mythology of governance by the manipulation of knowledge-stock inevitably erodes reliance on government by people.

(Illich, 1975: 100–1)

The second rejoinder is simply that we need to address the strength of informal social networks as a matter of urgency and we will have to develop a methodology as we go. Had we done so decades ago, much of the damage that we are now trying to confront might have been avoided. Mechanistic solutions are not necessarily called for: in cases like changes to a street network or to local amenities, the statutory requirement for community involvement in planning (ODPM, 2004) could easily be used, and should be. The third response is that a social network analysis of the effect of home zones would get us some way down this path and is long overdue. It's surprising but symptomatic that as far as I am aware none has yet even been planned.

One area of heralded potential for strengthening local social networks is the development of online connections at neighbourhood level. This is a field in which there has been much promise but relatively little demonstration. Keith Hampton, who pioneered systematic work in this area in Toronto, found that:

Online forums provided a visibility to participation that encouraged individual contributions, overcame high thresholds to participation, supported the appearance of group solidarity, and prevented the loss of individual involvement.

(Hampton, 2003: 426)

Given the current policy concern for collective responses to anti-social behaviour within neighbourhoods, the point about group solidarity in particular would seem to merit further systematic research and development. At the very least, the value of the local Ringmaster communication systems set up by neighbourhood watch committees[4] should be assessed and the options for extending them could be evaluated.

The issue of communication networks – technology-based or not – returns us to the points made in Chapter 4 about the information role of informal social relations. It seems a trite cliché to say that information is the lifeblood of a neighbourhood (as it is for organisations of course): but where information does not flow freely into, within and from a locality, that will affect social relations and local social life could quickly atrophy (Harris, 1999). Because informal social networks are so invisible in policy, they are vulnerable to other measures that may not be sensitive to their health. From his work on community newspapers in Chicago, Morris Janowitz concluded:

Social cohesion, whether it be in an army or in a local community means, in effect, the existence of a communications system by means of which individuals are oriented towards group action.

(Janowitz, 1967: 220)

---

[4] See http://www.crimereduction.gov.uk/neighbourhoodwatch/nwatch09.htm

Make sure there are formal opportunities for community engagement

This fourth principle is about what we might call engaged formality. Since 1997 the government has placed increasing emphasis on community engagement and volunteering. Recent policy has tended to focus on community involvement as if alone it will restore 'safer and stronger communities', with almost no attention paid to informal social networks. The drive to increase formal volunteering is part of the same unconvincing syndrome. For example, as Flint and Nixon have noted, there may be a trend for housing entitlement to include notions of civility that encompass proactive volunteering. This is of concern because it shifts the boundaries from 'an individualised desistance from prohibited activity towards public acts of citizenship in the arena of community' (Flint and Nixon, 2006: 950). Is it appropriate to be promoting measures that penalise civil but inactive citizens?

If one assumption in the call for active citizenship is that increased involvement in formal organisations will help to reduce levels of incivility, irrespective of informal connections between residents, it needs clarifying. Boyd is critical of policies oriented towards strengthening involvement in formal voluntary groups, noting that 'civility may exist in the absence of formal groups and not all groups are conducive to the virtue of civility' (2006: 875). Mayo's research, among several studies that have looked at this issue in passing, shows that:

> *If a person tends to know a greater percentage of persons on the street block, he or she does not necessarily tend to participate more or less in the neighbourhood.*

(Mayo, 1979: 394)

Other research provides insights that may help here. Joong-Hwan Oh (2003) notes that perceived disorder strengthens participation in neighbourhood organisations. But he found negative correlations between community participation and social cohesion, trust and informal social control. While both informal social relations and participation in formal organisations generate social capital, Green and Brock (2005) indicate that they provide a notably different set of benefits: communities that are safer and stronger will have both. Approximately nine million adults who are not in paid work or full-time education do not participate in any social, political, cultural, or community organisations.[5] According to Docherty et al. (2001) the key to engaging them is in the creation of opportunity structures that build confidence in the efficacy of participation. Gilchrist (2004b) in particular has sought to assert the complementarity of both community organisations and informal social networks for community development. Perhaps the angle discovered by Lewicka will be the most promising: she found that social ties within the neighbourhood can mediate between sense of attachment and civic participation:

> *It is not enough then to be fond of a place – a locally based social network is necessary to help convert emotion into action.*

(Lewicka, 2005: 392)

As a Home Office study on community engagement in policing points out, the policy principle here is not new:

> *Anglo-Saxon codes of law placed certain obligations on the community. For example, the laws of Athelstan directed that a thief who fled 'shall be pursued to his death by all men who are willing to carry out the king's wishes'.*

(Myhill, 2005: 3)

---

[5] http://www.poverty.org.uk/indicators/index.htm (accessed 8 June 2006).

It's not clear whether the flight and the pursuit were assumed to take place after justice had been dispensed or before. A few hundred years on, hopefully we've got that bit clear and we're now trying to bring some influence over governance closer to local level. As the localisation agenda gathers momentum, it will be important to explore the connection between neighbouring and engagement with governance. Unsurprisingly, the suspicion is occasionally voiced that residents are being invited to take on responsibilities off-loaded by the state (Herbert, 2005: 851). Low levels of neighbouring do not necessarily mean disengagement from democratic processes, but in many residential areas they suggest an impoverishment of the public sphere. The balance between cohesion and heterogeneity, discussed in Chapter 4, can be critical here. Neighbourhoods with strong internal ties may be precisely those where there is the greatest suspicion of the wider civic society and its governance processes. By the same token, neighbourhoods where place-based relationships are less in evidence can have relatively high levels of participation in governance. Again, the commentary on gated communities has often raised concerns about the fracture between local governance and contributions to shared municipal responsibilities in the surrounding areas.

Maintain formal policing, an official presence, and an accessible justice system

The perceived decline in respect and civility may be down to the weakening of what is sometimes called the parochial order; it might be attributed to insufficient collective efficacy, or to the phenomenon of networked individualism (Wellman, 2001). In some cases it may be down to inadequate formal policing; or to some combination of these and other factors. This final principle is about what we might call detached formality. In no sense have I been arguing against the role of formal policing and a dependable, respected system of justice. As Liz Richardson clarifies in Chapter 3, the availability and visibility of agencies that perform this role is fundamental. And Jacqueline Barnes in her chapter makes the point that 'informal control and formal systems each work more effectively when both are in place'. The formal role has its own spectrum, as is demonstrated by the recent success of various kinds of 'semi-official presence' such as neighbourhood wardens and community support police officers.

The research carried out by Atkinson and Flint (2004) in Edinburgh and Glasgow illustrated the importance for residents of disadvantaged areas of a reliable formal response from the police and other authorities, from beyond the neighbourhood. Where a culture of non-cooperation between residents and authorities has developed, there are significant well-recognised barriers which take time to break down. We may rightly wish to think of detached formal policing and justice as a last resort – and Ellickson's (1991) research encourages us to do so – but it has to be in place and effective whenever other, less formal measures, are not robust enough to take the strain of anti-social behaviour and crime.

At the same time, the issue of what I have called 'civic absence' (Chapter 1) has to be addressed. The presence of housing officers, youth workers, health workers, neighbourhood wardens, librarians, street cleaners and other public representatives remind us that we inhabit a public realm in which we have a stake. It seems sensible that whatever the preferred degree of formal presence by way of support, (a) there should be *some*, and it should be taken seriously with dependable response times, (b) it cannot be the primary mechanism for promoting civil relations, and (c) local people should have some input to and say in its governance.

The formal and the informal: more law and less order?

Much of the policy debate about the perceived decline of social capital has directed attention to the strengthening of *trust*, in ways that can be measured (Putnam, 2000; Halpern, 2005). This thinking largely overlooks the emphasis that Barbara Misztal places on 'an optimal balance between the informality and formality of interactional practices', and yet as she argues:

> The fine-tuning of informality and formality is central to the creation of social trust, which is constitutive of civil society.

> (Misztal, 2000: 238)

For Misztal, as our social context becomes increasingly uncertain and unpredictable, we need to create conditions for cooperation and integration which requires both formal structural preconditions, and the familiarity of informal relations (p7).

The tension between formal and informal modes is neatly represented by Elizabeth Burney in her book about anti-social behaviour policy. She points out that there is a conflict between formal policing agents who encourage victims of repeated incidents to keep diaries or otherwise to document their experiences, and mediation experts who point out that doing so builds up a 'sense of victimhood' and too easily becomes a weapon (Burney, 2005: 139, 155).[6] If we stand on the policy side of this issue, we can see the advantages of formal records; standing on the side of the citizen, we may be able to see value in their absence.

How do we reconcile such tensions? Philip Abrams could be very negative about the fluidity of the relationship between formal and informal neighbourhood care. The value of both is evident, but the question for Abrams was: 'How does one organise to promote lack of organisation?' (Bulmer, 1986: 206). And that remains the issue for policy. Formal systems are characterised by inertia, they need constantly to be refreshed; whereas social relationships in neighbourhoods are organic, requiring a healthy ecology that reflects informality and also requiring that most of the time formality keeps its distance. In contemporary social policy we can see government committed to encouraging more take up of power at the local level, through community empowerment networks, local area agreements, neighbourhood governance and so on; but it has yet to commit to what should be a parallel theme of recognition for informal interaction. Perhaps we are on the verge of a subtle policy refinement here, as government explores ways of encouraging civility within a formal framework. (Such optimism receives occasional setbacks, as with the confrontational government announcement of a 'Respect Squad' from which 'Mission Squads' will be selected and will emerge to do battle with locals behaving anti-socially.)[7] Nash and Christie certainly have their doubts:

> . . . little has been done to address the distortions introduced by targets and rigid performance indicators tied to inputs and outputs. The way forward is to reduce the Whitehall indicator set radically.

> (Nash and Christie, 2003: 78)

Of course, there are areas of public interaction where the interface between formal regulation and informal codes is clearly set out, as in *The Highway Code*, even though for many of us the boundaries may be blurred. Rule 125 for example encourages us to 'try to be understanding if other drivers cause

---

[6] The use of diaries seems to be reasserted by the Respect Task Force in a recent paper on 'Strengthening communities': see http://www.respect.gov.uk/assets/docs/Strength%20coms.pdf, p5.

[7] See http://www.respect.gov.uk/whats-being-done/squad/index.html, accessed 29 June 2006.

problems; they may be inexperienced or not know the area well'.[8] This is obviously not a legal requirement: you can't be taken to court for not trying to understand another driver's behaviour. Nonetheless:

> *Although failure to comply with the other rules of the Code will not, in itself, cause a person to be prosecuted,* The Highway Code *may be used in evidence in any court proceedings under Traffic Acts to establish liability.*

In this way policy seeks to exert influence over behaviour in public places by augmenting legal stipulations with exhortations of one kind or another: advertising campaigns such as those against smoking or speeding perform the same function. Where possible, increasingly, current policy looks to contractualise relations, which is all part of 'the contemporary politics of behaviour' (Flint and Nixon, 2006: 949). What we seem to be witnessing in the area of anti-social behaviour is a bold expansion of this kind of policy approach, using a mixture of aggressive legal enforcement and enforced 'support' such as parenting classes. There is little or no recognition of the role of informal support systems within this framework. Norms of behaviour are being asserted from the top down without acknowledgement that they need to be mutually accepted and owned at local level.

When faced with challenges on the sort of scale that results from the protracted neglect of social relations, perhaps there is a tendency to over-estimate the need for formal systems and to under-estimate the role of informal systems. We tend to be acutely aware of the dark side of social capital and the negative effects of gossip, which give informality a bad name; and perhaps policy makers reach too hastily for regulation, rather than looking for ways of nurturing more positive informal social networks. Buonfino and Mulgan, reviewing broad social changes in recent decades in the UK, claim that:

> *Again and again policy makers either failed to notice, or chose to ignore, the webs of informal mutual support that are decisive in helping people get by, to live, learn, or be healthy.*

(2006: 4)

Drawing attention to what they see as a 'quiet crisis of connections' they note that most governments invariably 'rely too much on mechanistic tools' (p12). In terms of the restoration of respect and standards of civil behaviour – the civil renewal agenda – as I have suggested, this is a mistake to be avoided. Robert Ellickson puts it most tellingly:

> *. . . lawmakers who are unappreciative of the social conditions that foster informal cooperation are likely to create a world in which there is both more law and less order.*

(Ellickson, 1991: 286)

Concluding remarks

In Chapter 1 I drew attention to the contrasts between the pre-history of the Respect agenda, and much of the reality of disrespect and incivility in society. The rhetoric of citizenship is at odds, as John Pitts puts it, 'with a culture which prizes individualism above collective endeavour and rewards egotism disproportionately' (Pitts, 2003: 151). Will Davies has characterised this as a (possibly irreconcilable?) tension between the communitarian appeal for respect and 'community', and the consumer demand for flexibility and self expression:

---

[8] See http://www.highwaycode.gov.uk

Undesirable behaviour is to be defied by the will of the community and technology of the State, while individuals demand more choice for themselves and their families. Government's role swings constantly between enforcer and provider, seeking new forms of restraint for one segment of society, while feverishly removing restraints from another.

(Davies, 2006: 69)

This tension is being played out in an ill-defined realm which we call the public. We are constantly questioning our understanding of freedom because, when people are bothered by street drinkers or a huddling gang from which someone spits as you walk past, it threatens 'the moral integrity of relations in public spaces' (Dixon et al., 2006: 204). Once we move from the fuzzy uncertainty of public space into 'community' space – the estate, the cul-de-sac, the back-street – our assumptions come slightly more into focus. As residents we are likely to be more ready to assert our right to be there unthreatened, and more prepared to consider measures that limit the freedoms of others, in the interests of protecting the stability that matters to us.

Most of the time, the quality of social relations in neighbourhoods is not going to be a concern of policy. Where the metabolism of community functions more or less smoothly, policy makers can leave neighbourhoods alone. If neighbourhoods appear not to be functioning as we'd like, we should regard the impulse to regulate, contractualise and formalise with scepticism. In the present context, it is not entirely unrealistic to ask how long it will be before the notion of indicators of respect, or even of neighbourliness, begin to feature as part of local government 'modernisation'. To what extent would it be acceptable, say, to publish 'league tables' of neighbourly behaviour across a city? Why should we not be able to *promote* neighbourliness without measuring it? As the policy microscope focuses down, it is as well to have thought through what it is we are getting into here.

There is certainly a great deal of popular appreciation for the attention being paid by government to the nasty reality of anti-social behaviour at local level, and for the belated official acknowledgement of the extent to which it blights people's lives. There is also undoubtedly a lot of criticism, including some within this volume, of what is seen as a partial, clumsy and heavy-handed policy approach. Of course, these are early days: the kinds of social trend that have been identified as symptoms of the perceived crisis are unlikely to respond immediately to treatment. But our emphasis on the importance of local social relations constitutes in our view a valid criticism of policy: until policy demonstrates an appreciation of the fundamental importance of informal social relations in neighbourhoods, and absorbs a broader-based recognition of the nature of respect, the civil renewal and respect agendas are unlikely to gain the momentum or impact intended.

I return then to the nature of civil renewal in a democratic society. There is a profound and enduring connection between neighbouring, civility and a broader understanding of democratic participation. The notion of civility contains a sense of continuity and of minimising the sense of disruption – a sense of order and unhurried consensus. We expect a society that is civil to have a democratic culture that has pertinence for all citizens and reflects an unspoken principle of the respectful recognition of others as its basis.

References

6, P. (2003) Can Government Influence Our Friendships? The Range and Limits of Tools For Trying to Shape Solidarities. In Phillipson, C. et al. (Eds.) *Social Networks and Social Exclusion: Sociological and Policy Issues*. Aldershot: Ashgate.

Adams, J. (2005) Streets and the Culture of Risk Aversion. In *What Are We Scared of? The Value of Risk in Designing Public Space*. London: Cabe Space.

ADT (2006) *Anti-Social Behaviour across Europe: An Overview of Research Commissioned by ADT Europe*. Sunbury: ADT Europe, http://adt.co.uk/cc4471AD-Great-Britain.pdf. (Accessed 14 June 2006)

Age Concern (1997) *Driven Indoors: Walking Conditions for Older People*. London: Age Concern and Pedestrians Association.

Airey, L. (2003) 'Nae as Nice a Scheme as it Used to Be': Lay Accounts of Neighbourhood Incivilities and Well-Being. *Health and Place*, 9: 129–37.

Alexander, C.E. (2000) *The Asian Gang: Ethnicity, Identity, Masculinity*. Oxford: Berg.

Alford, V. (1996) Crime and Spaces in the Inner City. *Urban Design Studies*, 2: 53, 45–76.

Allen, C. et al. (2005) *Mixed Tenure Twenty Years on: Nothing out of the Ordinary*. London: Chartered Institute of Housing.

Anderson, E. (2000) *Code of the Street: Decency, Violence, and the Moral Life of the Inner City*. London: Norton.

Aneshensel, C.S. and Sucoff, C.A. (1996) The Neighbourhood Context of Adolescent Mental Health. *Journal of Health and Social Behavior*, 37: 293–310.

Angel, S. (1968) *Discouraging Crime through City Planning*. Working Paper 75. Berkeley CA: University of California.

Appleyard, D. et al. (1981) *Livable Streets*. Berkeley: University of California Press.

Arendt, R. (1994) How to Create a Subdivision with Character. *Planning*, 60: 5.

Atkinson, R. and Flint, J. (2004) Order Born of Chaos? The Capacity for Informal Social Control in Disempowered and 'Disorganised' Neighbourhoods. *Policy and Politics*, 32: 3, 333–50.

Audit Commission (2005) *Contents of Reward Incentive Scheme Pack*. London: Audit Commission.

Aynsley-Green, A. (2006) Treat Children with Respect and You'll Get it Straight Back. The *Guardian*, 19 January: 30.

Bannister, J. et al. (2006) Respectable or Respectful? Incivility and the City. *Urban Studies*, 43: 5, 919–37.

Barnes, J. and Baylis, G. (2004) *Place and Parenting: A Study of Four Communities: the Relevance of Community Characteristics and Residents' Perceptions of Their Neighbourhoods for Parenting and Child Behaviour in Four Contrasting Locations*. London: Institute for the Study of Children, Families and Social Issues, University of London.

Barnes, J. and Cheng, H. (2006) Do Parental Neighbourhood Perceptions Contribute to Child Behaviour Problems? A Study of Disadvantaged Children. *Vulnerable Children and Youth Studies*, I: 1, 2–14.

Barnes, J. et al. (2006) *Children and Families in Communities: Theory, Research, Policy and Practice.* Chichester: Wiley.

Barton, H. et al. (2003) *Shaping Neighbourhoods: A Guide for Health, Sustainability and Vitality.* London: Spon Press.

Bastow, S. et al. (Forthcoming) The Role of Individual Incentives within Strategies Promoting Civil Renewal. In Brannan, T. et al. (Eds.) *Re-Energising Citizenship: Strategies for Civil Renewal.* Basingstoke: Macmillan.

Bauman, Z. (2000) *Liquid Modernity.* Cambridge: Polity.

BBC News (2005) Boy, 15, Wins Curfew Legal Battle, http://news.bbc.co.uk/1/hi/england/london/4699095.stm. (Accessed 20 July 2005)

BBC News (2006a) Archbishop Woos Hoodie Generation, http://news.bbc.co.uk/1/hi/england/bradford/4962624.stm. (Accessed 2 May 2006)

BBC News (2006b) Boy Stabbed to Death Near School, http://news.bbc.co.uk/1/hi/england/london/4995800.stm. (Accessed 18 May 2006)

Bennett, J. and Morris, J. (2006) *Gateway People.* London: IPPR.

Berg, M. and Medrich, E. (1980) Children in Four Neighbourhoods: The Physical Environment and Its Effect on Play and Play Pattern. *Environment and Behaviour,* 12: 3, 320–48.

Berry, H.E. et al. (1990) A Longitudinal Analysis of Neighboring in Rapidly Changing Rural Places. *Journal of Rural Studies,* 6: 2, 175–86.

Blears, H. (2003) *Communities in Control.* London: Fabian Society.

Blokland, T. (2003) *Urban Bonds: Social Relationships in an Inner City Neighbourhood.* Cambridge: Polity.

Blunkett, D. (2003a) *Civil Renewal: A New Agenda.* London: Home Office.

Blunkett, D. (2003b) *Active Citizens, Strong Communities: Progressing Civil Renewal.* London: Home Office http://www.togetherwecan.info/acc/active_citizens_strong_communities.html (Accessed 17 May)

Boddy, T. (1992) Underground and Overhead: Building the Analogous City. In Sorkin, M. (Ed.) *Variations on a Theme Park: the New American City and the End of Public Space.* New York: Hill and Wang.

Boggan, S. et al. (2002) War on the Godfathers. *Evening Standard.* 21 November.

Boyd, R. (2006) The Value of Civility? *Urban Studies,* 43: 5–6, 863–78.

Brewer, J. D. et al. (1998) Informal Social Control and Crime Management in Belfast. *British Journal of Sociology,* 49: 4, 570–85.

Brooks-Gunn, J. et al. (Eds.) (1997) *Neighborhood Poverty: Volume I: Context and Consequences for Children.* New York: Russell Sage Foundation.

Brooks-Gunn, J. et al. (Eds.) (1997) *Neighborhood Poverty: Volume II: Policy Implications in Studying Neighborhoods.* New York: Russell Sage Foundation.

Brown, B. and Werner, C. (1985) Social Cohesiveness, Territoriality, and Holiday Decorations: The Influence of Cul-De-Sacs. *Environment and Behavior,* 17: 5, 539–65.

Bulmer, M. (1986) *Neighbours: the Work of Philip Abrams.* Cambridge: Cambridge University Press.

Buonfino, A. and Mulgan, G. (2006) Porcupines in Winter: An Introduction. In Buonfino, A. and Mulgan, G. (Eds.) *Porcupines in Winter: the Pleasures and Pains of Living Together in Modern Britain.* London: Young Foundation.

Burney, E. (2005) *Making People Behave: Anti-Social Behaviour, Politics and Policy.* Cullompton: Willan.

Bursik, R.J. and Webb, J. (1982) Community Change and Patterns of Delinquency. *American Journal of Sociology*, 88, 24–42.

CABE (2005) *What It's Like Living There: the Views of Residents on the Design of New Housing*. London: Commission for Architecture and the Built Environment.

Calhoun, C. (1998) Community without Propinquity Revisited: Communications Technology and the Transformation of the Urban Public Sphere. *Sociological Inquiry*, 68: 3, 373–97.

Campbell, K. and Lee, B. (1992) Sources of Personal Neighbor Networks: Social Integration, Need, or Time? *Social Forces*, 70: 4, 1077–100.

Carpenter, T. and Feck, S. (2005) Neighbourhood Fusion. *Canadian Geographic*, July-August. http://www.canadiangeographic.ca/magazine/ja05/alacarte.asp. (Accessed 6 June 2006)

Christensen, M. et al. (2002) Space, Culture and Meetings in a Local Community in East Jutland: An Anthropological Analysis of the Architectural and Social Conditions of the 'Cross-Cultural Meeting' in Dwelling, Neighbourhood and Village. In Mortensen, P.D. and Ovesen, H. (Eds.) *Fields of Urban Research*. Copenhagen: Royal Danish Academy of Fine Arts, School of Architecture, www.karch.dk/udgivelser/publikationer/content/88/christensen_uk.pdf. (Accessed 1 June 2006)

Chung, H.L. and Steinberg, L. (2006) Relations between Neighborhood Factors, Parenting Behaviors, Peer Deviance, and Delinquency among Serious Juvenile Offenders. *Developmental Psychology*, 42: 2, 319–31.

Churchman, A. (1980) Children in Urban Environments: the Israeli Experience. In Michelson, W. and Michelson, E. (Eds.) *Managing Urban Space in the Interests of Children*. Ottawa: MAB Committee.

Churchman, A. and Ginsberg, Y. (1989) The Image and Experience of High-Rise Housing in Israel. *Journal of Environmental Psychology*, 4: 1, 27–41.

Clinton, H.R. (1996) *It Takes A Village: and Other Lessons Children Teach Us*. New York: Simon & Schuster.

Cobain, I. et al. (2006) These Men Flooded the UK With Heroin. Now, the Story of Their Strange Deal With Customs. *The Guardian*, 28 March, 8–9.

Cohen, A.P. (1985) *The Symbolic Construction of Community*. London: Ellis Horwood.

Cohen, L.E. and Felson, M. (1979) Social Change and Crime Rate Trends: A Routine Activity Approach. *American Sociological Review*, 44, 588–608.

Coleman, J.S. (1993) The Rational Reconstruction of Society: 1992 Presidential Address. *American Sociological Review*, 58: 1–15.

Connolly, P. (2004) Reclaim the Streets. *Regeneration and Renewal*, 27 February, 21–2.

Coulthard, M. et al. (2002) *People's Perceptions of Their Neighbourhood and Community Involvement: Results from the Social Capital Module of the General Household Survey 2000*. London: Stationery Office.

Coulton, D. et al. (1996) Measuring Neighborhood Context for Young Children in an Urban Area. *American Journal of Community Psychology*, 24: 5–32.

Cowan, R. and Lewis, P. (2006) Screams of Dying Special Constable Stabbed to Death Outside Home After Confronting Thieves. *Guardian*, 13 May, http://www.guardian.co.uk/crime/article/0,,1773949,00.html

Crenson, M. (1983) *Neighbourhood Politics*. Cambridge: Harvard UP.

Crime Concern and Social Research Associates (1999) *Personal Security Issues in Pedestrian Journeys*. London: Department for the Environment Transport and the Regions.

Crow, G. and Allan, G. (1994) *Community Life: An Introduction to Local Social Relations*. Hemel Hempstead: Harvester Wheatsheaf.

Crow, G. et al. (2002) Neither Busybodies Nor Nobodies: Managing Proximity and Distance in Neighbourly Relations. *Sociology*, 36: 1, 127–45.

Cuff, D. (2005) Enduring Proximity: The Figure of the Neighbor in Suburban America. *Postmodern Culture* 15: 2, January.

Curtice J. et al. (2005) *Public Attitudes and Environmental Justice in Scotland: A Report for the Scottish Executive on Research to Inform the Development and Evaluation of Environmental Justice Policy.* Edinburgh: Scottish Executive Social Research, http://www.scotland.gov.uk/resource/doc/77843/0018790.pdf. (Accessed 15 June 2006)

Dalrymple, T. (2005) *Our Culture, What's Left of It: The Mandarins and the Masses.* Chicago: Ivan R. Dee.

Davies, W. (2006) Beyond Communitarianism and Consumerism. *Renewal*, 14: 1.

DCLG (2006). *Moving on: Reconnecting Frequent Movers.* London: Department for Communities and Local Government.

De Beer, P. (2004) Normvervaging in Nederland: perceptie of realiteit. *Sociologische Gids*, 51: 236–47.

De Beer, P. and Schuyt, K. (2004) *Bijdragen aan normen en waarden*, Amsterdam: Amsterdam University Press.

De Winter, M. (2004) *Opvoeding, onderwijs en jeugdbeleid in het algemeen belang, de noodzaak van een democratisch-pedagogisch offensief*, den Haag: WRR.

Deakin, J. (2006) Dangerous People, Dangerous Places: The Nature and Location of Young People's Victimisation and Fear. *Children and Society*, Forthcoming.

DETR (2000) *By Design: Urban Design in the Planning System: Towards Better Practice.* London: DETR/Commission for Architecture and the Built Environment.

Dewey, A.E. (2004) One-Child Policy in China. Testimony before the House International Relations Committee, Washington DC, December 14, 2004, http://www.state.gov/g/prm/rls/39823.htm. (Accessed 22 May, 2006)

DfES (2006) *Ethnicity and Education: The Evidence On Minority Ethnic Pupils Aged 5–16.* London: DfES.

DfT (2004) *National Travel Survey: 2003 Final Results.* London: Department for Transport, http://www.dft.gov.uk/stellent/groups/dft_transstats/documents/page/dft_transstats_031840.pdf (Accessed 17 June 2006)

DfT (2005) *Home Zones: Challenging the Future of Our Streets.* London: Department for Transport.

Diekstra, R. (2001) Stadsetiquette: aansprekend gedrag in de publieke ruimte. In Hortulanus, R. (Ed.) *Jong geleerd, oud gedaan.* Amsterdam: Elsevier.

Diekstra, R. (2004) Stadsetiquette: over waarden, normen en collectieve zelfredzaamheid van burgers. In De Beer, P. and Schuyt, K. (Eds.) *Bijdragen aan normen en waarden.* Amsterdam: Amsterdam University Press.

Dixon, J. et al. (2006) Locating Impropriety: Street Drinking, Moral Order, and the Ideological Dilemma of Public Space. *Political Psychology*, 27: 2, 187–206.

Docherty, I. et al. (2001) Civic Culture, Community and Citizen Participation in Contrasting Neighbourhoods. *Urban Studies*, 38: 12, 2225–50.

DoE (1994) *Circular 5/94 Planning and Crime*, Section 14. London: DoE.

Donovan, N. et al. (2002) *Geographic Mobility.* London: Cabinet Office. http://www.strategy.gov.uk/downloads/su/gmseminar/gm_analytical.pdf. (Accessed 9 June 2006)

Dovey, K. (1999) *Framing Places: Mediating Power in Built Form.* London: Routledge.

DPTAC (2002) *Attitudes of Disabled People Towards Public Transport*. London: Disabled Persons Transport Advisory Committee.

Eck, J. (1995) A General Model of the Geography of Illicit Retail Marketplaces. In Weisburd, D. and Eck, J. (Eds.) *Crime and Place*. Crime Prevention Studies Vol 4. New York: Crime Justice Press.

Eck, J. (1997) Preventing Crime at Places. In Sherman, L. et al. (Eds.) *Preventing Crime: What Works, What Doesn't and What's Promising: A Report to the United States Congress*. Washington DC: US National Institute of Justice.

Edwards, R. et al. (2003) *Families and Social Capital: Exploring the Issues*. London: London South Bank University, Families and Social Capital ESRC Research Group. http://www.lsbu.ac.uk/families/workingpapers/familieswp1.pdf. (Accessed 9 June 2006)

Elias, N. (1978–1982) *The Civilizing Process*. Oxford: Blackwell.

Ellickson, R.C. (1991) *Order Without Law: How Neighbors Settle Disputes*. Cambridge, MA: Harvard University Press.

Epstein, L. (2005) The Path to Pedestrianization. *Planning*, 71: 5, 23.

Evans, K. (1997) 'It's All Right Round Here If You're A Local': Community in the Inner City. In Hoggett, P. (Ed.) *Contested Communities: Experiences, Struggles, Policies*. Bristol: Policy Press.

Felson, M. (1998) *Crime in Everyday Life*. Thousand Oaks, CA: Pine Forge Press.

Flint, J. and Nixon, J. (2006) Governing Neighbours: Anti-Social Behaviour Orders and New Forms of Regulating Conduct in the UK. *Urban Studies*, 43: 5–6, 939–55.

Ford, L. (2000) *The Spaces Between Buildings*. Baltimore: Johns Hopkins University Press.

Forrester, D. et al. (1988) *The Kirkholt Burglary Prevention Project, Rochdale*. Crime Prevention Unit Paper 13, London: Home Office.

Foster, J. (1997) Challenging Perceptions: Community and Neighbourliness on a Difficult-to-Let Estate. In Jewson, N. and Macgregor, S. (Eds.) *Transforming Cities: Contested Governance and New Spatial Divisions*. London: Routledge.

Franklin, T. (2002) Oral Evidence to House of Commons Health Select Committee, http://www.parliament.the-stationery-office.co.uk/pa/cm200203/cmselect/cmhealth/uc755-vi/uc75502.htm . (Accessed 30 May 2006)

Frazer, E. (2002) Local Social Relations: Public, Club and Common Goods. In Nash, V. (Ed.) *Reclaiming Community*. London: IPPR.

Freeman, L. (2001) The Effects of Sprawl on Neighborhood Social Ties: an Explanatory Analysis. *Journal of the American Planning Association*, 67: 1, 69–77.

Friedland, L.A. (2001) Communication, Community, and Democracy: Toward a Theory of the Communicatively Integrated Community. *Communication Research*, 28: 4, 358–91.

Friedrichs, J. and Blasius, J. (2003) Social Norms in Distressed Neighbourhoods: Testing the Wilson Hypothesis. *Housing Studies*, 18: 6, 807–26.

Furedi, F. (2006) It's Time That We All 'Interfered' More. *Daily Telegraph*, 4 June, http://www.telegraph.co.uk/opinion/main.jhtml?xml=/opinion/2006/06/04/Do0409.xml&ssheet=/opinion/2006/06/04/ixop.html. (Accessed 8 June 2006)

Furstenberg, F.F. (1993) How Families Manage Risk and Opportunity in Dangerous Neighborhoods. In Wilson, W.J. (Ed.) *Sociology and the Public Agenda*. Newbury Park, CA: Sage.

Garbarino, J. and Sherman, D. (1980) High-Risk Neighborhoods and High-Risk Families: The Human Ecology of Child Maltreatment. *Child Development*, 51: 1, 188–98.

Garland, D. (2001) *The Culture of Control*. Oxford: Oxford University Press.

Geis, K. and Ross, C. (1998) A New Look at Urban Alienation: The Effect of Neighborhood Disorder on Perceived Powerlessness. *Social Psychology Quarterly*, 61: 3, 232–46.

Geller, E.S. (1980) Application of Behaviour Analysis to Litter Control. In Glenwick, D. and Jason, L. (Eds.) *Behavioral Community Psychology: Progress and Prospects*. New York: Prager.

Ghate, D. and Hazel, N. (2002) *Parenting in Poor Environments: Stress, Support and Coping*. London: Jessica Kingsley.

Giacopassi, D. and Forde, D. (2000) Broken Windows, Crumpled Fenders and Crime. *Journal of Criminal Justice*, 28: 5, 397–405.

Gilchrist, A. (2000) Design for Living: The Challenge of Sustainable Communities. In Barton, H. (Ed.) *Sustainable Communities: the Potential for Eco-Neighbourhoods*. London: Earthscan.

Gilchrist, A. (2004a) *Community Cohesion and Community Development: Bridges or Barricades?* London: Community Development Foundation.

Gilchrist, A. (2004b) *The Well-Connected Community*. Bristol: Policy Press.

Goffman, E. (1963) *Behavior in Public Places: Notes on the Social Organization of Gatherings*. New York: Free Press.

Graham, S. and Marvin, S. (2001) *Splintering Urbanism: Networked Infrastructures, Technological Mobilities and the Urban Condition*. London: Routledge.

Green, M.C. and Brock, T.C. (2005) Organizational Membership versus Informal Interaction: Contributions to Skills and Perceptions that Build Social Capital. *Political Psychology*, 26: 1, 1–25.

Greenbaum, P. and Greenbaum, S. (1981) Territorial Personalization: Group Identity and Social Interaction in a Slavic-American Neighbourhood. *Environment and Behavior*, 13: 574–89. Cited by Unger and Wandersman (1985)

Grübler, A. (1998) *Technology and Global Change*, Cambridge: Cambridge University Press.

Guest, A. and Wierzbicki, S. (1999) Social Ties at the Neighborhood Level: Two Decades of GSS Evidence. *Urban Affairs Review*, 35: 1, 92–111.

Hackler, J. et al. (1974) The Willingness to Intervene: Differing Community Characteristics. *Social Problems*, 21: 3, 328–44.

Halpern, D. (2005) *Social Capital*. Cambridge: Polity.

Hamilton, K. et al. (1991) *Women and Transport: Bus Deregulation in West Yorkshire*. Bradford: University of Bradford.

Hampton, K.N. (2002) Place-Based and IT Mediated 'Community'. *Planning Theory and Practice*, 3: 2, 228–31.

Hampton, K.N. (2003) Grieving for a Lost Network: Collective Action in a Wired Suburb. *The Information Society*, 19: 5, 417–28.

Harcourt, B. and Ludwig, J. (2006) Broken Windows: New Evidence from New York City and a Five City Social Experiment. *University of Chicago Law Review*.

Harris, K. (1999) The Online Life of Communities: Nurturing Community Activity in the Information Society. In Pantry, S. (Ed.) *Building Community Information Networks*. London: Library Association.

Harris, K. (2003) 'Keep Your Distance': Remote Communication, Face-To-Face, and the Nature of Community. *Journal of Community Work and Development*, 1: 4, 5–28.

Harris, K. (2006) *Common Knowledge: Community Development and Communication on a Housing Estate*. London: Proboscis. http://proboscis.org.uk/publications/snapshots_commonknowledge.pdf. (Accessed 6 June 2006)

Harris, K. and Gale, T. (2004) *Looking Out for Each Other: The Manchester Neighbourliness Review*. London: Community Development Foundation.

Herbert, S. (2005) The Trapdoor of Community. *Annals of the Association of American Geographers*, 95: 4, 850–8.

Hilder, P. (2005) *Seeing the Wood for the Trees: the Evolving Landscape for Neighbourhood Arrangements*. London: Young Foundation. http://www.youngfoundation.org.uk/wp-content/1neighbourhoodarrangementsseeingwoodfortrees_03.pdf. (Accessed 13 May 2006)

Hillier, B. (1988) Against Enclosure. In Teymur, N. et al. (Eds.) *Rehumanizing Housing*. London: Butterworths.

Hillman, M. (Ed.) (1993) *Children, Transport and the Quality of Life*. London: Policy Studies Institute.

Hillman, M. et al. (1990) *One False Move: A Study of Children's Independent Mobility*. London: Institute for Policy Studies.

Hoffnung, G. (2002) *Hoffnung: A Last Encore*, BBC Spoken Word (Audio CD).

Holloway, S.L. (Forthcoming 2006) Burning Issues: Whiteness, Rurality and the Politics of Difference. *Geoforum*.

Home Office (2003) *Respect and Responsibility: Taking a Stand against Anti-Social Behaviour*. London: Home Office.

Hooghe, M. (2002) Watching Television and Civic Engagement: Disentangling the Effects of Time, Programs, and Stations. *Harvard International Journal of Press and Politics* 7: 220–40.

http//publications.teachernet.gov.uk/OrderingDownload/DFES-0208-2006.pdf. (Accessed 17 July 2006)

Huttenmoser, M. (2005) Presentation to Childstreet Conference, Delft, 2005. http://www.urban.nl/childstreet2005/downloads/paper-ute-marco-cf.pdf. (Accessed 13 June 2006)

Huttenmoser, M. and Degen-Zimmerman, D. (1995) Living Space for Children. Unpublished Translation of *Lebensraume Fur Kinder*. Zurich: Maria Meierhofer-Institut Fur Das Kind.

IHT (2000) *Guidelines for Providing for Journeys on Foot*. London: IHT.

Illich, I. (1975) *Tools for Conviviality*. Glasgow: Fontana.

Jacobs, J. (1961) *The Death and Life of Great American Cities*. London: Pimlico.

Jain, S.S.L. (2002) Urban Errands: the Means of Mobility. *Journal of Consumer Culture*, 2: 3, 385–404.

Jamieson, L. (2000) Migration, Place and Class: Youth in a Rural Area. *Sociological Review*, 48: 2, 203–23.

Janowitz, M. (1967) *The Community Press in an Urban Setting: the Social Elements of Urbanism*. 2nd edn. Chicago: University of Chicago Press.

Jensen, G.F. (2003) Social Disorganisation Theory. In Wright, R.A. (Ed.) *Encyclopedia of Criminology*. Chicago: Fitzroy Dearborn.

Jiao, A.Y. (2004) Integration of Formal and Informal Social Control in China. In Broadhurst, R.G. (Ed.) *Crime and Its Control in the People's Republic of China: Symposia Proceedings of the University of Hong Kong Center for Criminology*. Hong Kong: Center for Criminology, University of Hong Kong.

JRF (2001) Planning and Designing Home Zones. *Findings*, D41: http://www.jrf.org.uk/knowledge/findings/socialpolicy/d41.asp. (Accessed 6 June 2006)

JRF (2006) Mixed Communities: Success and Sustainability. *Findings*, 0176: http://www.jrf.org.uk/knowledge/findings/foundations/0176.asp. (Accessed 6 June 2006)

Keller, S. (2003) *Community: Pursuing the Dream, Living the Reality*. Princeton: Princeton University Press.

Kennedy, H. (2004) For Blair There is No Such Thing as Legal Principle. The *Guardian*, 27 November: 22.

Kenworthy, J. and Newman, P. (1989) *The Cities and Automobile Dependence: an International Sourcebook*. Aldershot: Gower. Quoted in Jenks,M. et al. (Eds.) (1996) *The Compact City*, London: Spon.

Kershaw, C. et al. (2000) *The 2000 British Crime Survey: England and Wales*. London: Home Office, http://www.homeoffice.gov.uk/rds/pdfs/hosb1800.pdf. (Accessed 13 June 2006)

Kibreab, G. (1999) Revisiting the Debate on People, Place, Identity and Displacement. *Journal of Refugee Studies*, 12: 4, 384–410.

Kinsey, R. et al. (1986) *Losing the Fight against Crime*. London: Blackwells.

Knowles, P. (2002) *Designing Out Crime: The Cost of Policing New Urbanism*. Operation Scorpion. http://www.operationscorpion.org.uk/design_out_crime/design_main.htm. (Accessed 6 June 2006)

Kromkowski, J. (1976) *Neighborhood Deterioration and Juvenile Crime*. South Bend, IN: South Bend Urban Observatory. Cited by Garbarino and Sherman 1980: 195.

Kuo, F.E. and Sullivan, W.C. (2001) Environment and Crime in the Inner City: Does Vegetation Reduce Crime? *Environment and Behaviour*, 343–67.

Levine, M. et al. (2002) *Promoting Intervention Against Violent Crime: A Social Identity Approach*. ESRC, http://www1.rhbnc.ac.hk/sociopolitical-violence-science/vrp/findings/rflevine.pdf. (Accessed 17 June 2006)

Lewicka, M. (2005) Ways to Make People Active: The Role of Place Attachment, Cultural Capital, and Neighborhood Ties. *Journal of Environmental Psychology*, 25: 4, 381–95.

Leyden, K. (2003) Social Capital and the Built Environment: The Importance of Walkable Neighborhoods. *American Journal of Public Health*, 93: 9, 1546–51.

Liddle, A.M. and Bottoms, A.E. (1991) *Implementing Circular 8/84: A Retrospective Assessment of the Five Towns Crime Prevention Initiative*. Cambridge: Institute of Criminology, University of Cambridge.

Locke, J.L. (1998) *The De-Voicing of Society: Why We Don't Talk to Each Other Anymore*. New York: Simon and Schuster.

Lucas, K. et al. (2004) *Prioritising Local Environmental Concerns: Where There's a Will There's a Way*. York: Joseph Rowntree Foundation.

Luckhurst, T. (2005) Keep Out of Our Gardens. The *Times*, 2 June, http://www.timesonline.co.uk/newspaper/0,,173-1637130,00.html. (Accessed 6 June 2006)

Lupton, M., Hale, J. and Sprigings, N. (2003) *Incentives and Beyond? The Transferability of the Irwell Valley Gold Service to Other Social Landlords*.London: ODPM.

Lupton, R. and Power, A. (2002) Social Exclusion and Neighbourhoods. In Hills, J. et al. (Eds.) *Understanding Social Exclusion*. Oxford: OUP.

Madge, N. (2006) *Children These Days*. Bristol: Policy Press.

Mann, P. (1954) The Concept of Neighborliness. *American Journal of Sociology*, 60 2, 163–8.

Marshall, S. (2005) *Streets and Patterns*. Abingdon: Spon.

Martin, N. and Alleyne, R. (2006) Kiyan Was Killed Stopping A Fight. *Daily Telegraph*, 20 May.

Massey, D. (1994) *Space, Place and Gender*. Cambridge: Polity.

Mayo, J.M. (1979) Effects of Street Forms on Suburban Neighboring Behavior. *Environment and Behavior*, 11: 3, 375–97.

McPherson, M. et al. (2001) Birds of A Feather: Homophily in Social Networks. *Annual Review of Sociology*, 27: 415–44.

Mehmet Ali, A. (2001) *Turkish Speaking Communities and Education: No Delight*. London: Fatal.

Misztal, B.A. (2000) *Informality: Social Theory and Contemporary Practice*. London: Routledge.

MORI (2006) *British Views on Respect*. London: Ipsos MORI.

Myhill, A. (2005) *Community Engagement in Policing: Lessons from the Literature*. London: Home Office.

Nash, J.K. and. Bowen, G.L (1999) Perceived Crime and Informal Social Control in the Neighbourhood as a Context for Adolescent Behaviour: A Risk and Resilience Perspective. *Social Work Research*, 23: 171–86.

Nash, V. and Christie, I. (2003) *Making Sense of Community*. London: IPPR.

Neumann, M. (2006) Maximum Respect. *Catalyst*, 3, http://www.catalystmagazine.org/default.aspx.locid-0hgnew0e5.reflocid-0hg01b001006003.lang-en.htm. (Accessed 19 May 2006)

Newman, O. (1972) *Defensible Space: Crime Prevention through Urban Design*. New York: Macmillan.

Nixon, J., et al. (2003) *Tackling Anti-Social Behaviour in Mixed Tenure Areas*. London: Office of the Deputy Prime Minister.

Noble, M. et al. (2000) *Indices of Multiple Deprivation 1999 Review. Final Consultation. Report for Formal Consultation. Stage 1. Domains and Indicators*. University of Oxford: Social Disadvantage Research Group.

Norris, P. (1996) Does Television Erode Social Capital? A Reply to Putnam. *Political Science and Politics*, 29: 474–80.

ODPM (2004) *Planning Policy Statement 12: Local Development Frameworks*. London: ODPM.

ODPM (2006) *A Respect Standard for Housing Management*. London: ODPM.

Oh, J-H. (2003) Assessing the Social Bonds of Elderly Neighbors: The Roles of Length of Residence, Crime Victimization, and Perceived Disorder. *Sociological Inquiry*, 73: 4, 490–510.

Olay (2005) Eroin kaçakchgimn yuzde 90'l Turklerin elinde (90% of heroin smuggling is controlled by Turks). *Olay newspaper*. 1 February.

Oldenburg, R. (1989) *The Great Good Place: Cafes, Coffee Shops, Bookstores, Bars, Hair Salons, and Other Hangouts at the Heart of a Community*. New York: Marlowe.

Owen, J. (2006) The Teenage Terror List. *Independent on Sunday*, 12 March: 8.

Pahl, R. (2006) On Respect: the Social Strains of Social Change. In Buonfino, A. and Mulgan, G. (Eds.) *Porcupines in Winter: The Pleasures and Pains of Living Together in Modern Britain*. London: Young Foundation.

Pahl, R. and Spencer, L. (2003) Personal Communities: Not Simply Families of 'Fate' or 'Choice'. Working Papers, Institute for Social and Economic Research, University of Essex, http://www.iser.essex.ac.uk/pubs/workpaps/pdf/2003-04.pdf. (Accessed 6 June 2006)

Painter, K. and Farrington, D.P. (1997) The Crime Reducing Effect of Improving Street Lighting: the Dudley Project. In Clarke, R. (Ed.) *Situational Crime Prevention: Successful Case Studies*, 2nd edn, New York: Harrow and Heston.

Parr, H. et al. (2004) Social Geographies of Rural Mental Health: Experiencing Inclusions and Exclusions. *Transactions of the Institute of British Geographers*, 29: 401–19.

Pascoe, T. (1993) *Domestic Burglary: The Burglar's View*. Watford: Building Research Establishment.

PAT8 (2000) *Report of Policy Action Team 8: Anti-Social Behaviour*. London: Social Exclusion Unit.

Pavia, W. and Smith, L. (2006) Cadet Killed on Train was Role Model for Friends. *Times*, 30 May. http://www.timesonline.co.uk/article/0,,2-2202262,00.html. (Accessed 8 June 2006)

Perkins, D. and Taylor, R. (1996) Ecological Assessments of Community Disorder: Their Relationship to Fear of Crime and Theoretical Implications. *American Journal of Community Psychology*, 24, 63–107.

Phillips, T. and Smith, P. (2003) Everyday Incivility: Towards a Benchmark. *Sociological Review*, 51: 1, 85–108.

Phillips, T. and Smith, P. (2006) Rethinking Urban Incivility Research: Strangers, Bodies and Circulations. *Urban Studies*, 43: 5–6, 879–901.

Phillipson, C. et al. (1999) Older People's Experiences of Community Life: Patterns of Neighbouring in Three Urban Areas. *Sociological Review*, 47: 4, 715–43.

Pitts, J. (2003) *The New Politics of Youth Crime: Discipline or Solidarity?* Lyme Regis: Russell House Publishing.

PIU (2002) *Geographic Mobility: Strategic Thinkers Seminars*. London: Cabinet Office, Performance and Information Unit, http://www.strategy.gov.uk/downloads/su/gmseminar/gm_summary.pdf. (Accessed 9 June 2006)

Plickert, G. et al. (2006) It's Not Who You Know, It's How You Know Them: Who Exchanges What With Whom? In *Social Capital on the Ground*, Forthcoming, Oxford: Blackwell. http://www.chass.utoronto.ca/~wellman/netlab/publications/_frames.html. (Accessed 6 June 2006)

Poyner, B. (2005) *Crime-Free Housing in the 21st Century*. Cullompton: Willan.

Putnam, R.D. (2000) *Bowling Alone: the Collapse and Revival of American Community*. New York: Simon & Schuster.

Ramadan, T. (2005) Fear will Only Fuel the Riots. The *Guardian*, 12 November: 32.

Respect Task Force (2006) *Respect Action Plan*. London: Home Office.

Rogers, C. and Sawyer, J. (1998) *Play in the Lives of Children*. Washington DC: National Association for the Education of Young Children.

Ross, C.E. and Mirowsky, J. (2001) Neighborhood Disadvantage, Disorder, and Health. *Journal of Health and Social Behaviour,* 42: 258–76.

Ross, C.E. et al. (2001) Powerlessness and the Amplification of Threat: Neighborhood Disadvantage, Disorder, and Mistrust. *American Sociological Review*, 66: 568–91.

Sabatier, P. (2005) This is Blind Rage Against Injustice and Inequality. *Independent on Sunday*. 6 November: 47.

Saelens, B. et al. (2005) Residents' Perceptions of Walkability Attributes in Objectively Different Neighbourhoods: A Pilot Study. *Health and Place*, 11: 227–36.

Sampson, R.J. (1992) Family Management and Child Development: Insights From Social Disorganization Theory. In Mccord, J. (Ed.) *Facts, Frameworks and Forecasts: Advances in Criminological Theory*, Vol 3, New Brunswick, NJ: Transaction Press.

Sampson, R.J. (1999) What Community Supplies. In Ferguson, R.F. and Dickens, W.T. (Eds.) *Urban Problems and Community Development*. Washington, Dc: Brookings Institution Press.

Sampson, R.J. (2004) Neighborhood and Community: Collective Efficacy and Community Safety. *New Economy*, 11, 106–13.

Sampson, R.J. and Groves, W. (1989) Community Structure and Crime: Testing Social-Disorganization Theory. *American Journal of Sociology*, 94: 4, 774–802.

Sampson, R.J. and Laub, J. (1990) Crime and Deviance over the Lifecourse: The Salience of Adult Social Bonds. *American Sociological Review*, 55: 609–27.

Sampson, R.J. and Morenoff, J. (2006) Durable Inequality: Spatial Dynamics, Social Processes, and the Persistence of Poverty in Chicago Neighborhoods. In Bowles, S. et al. (Eds.) *Poverty Traps*. Princeton: Princeton University Press.

Sampson, R.J. et al. (1997) Neighborhoods and Violent Crime: A Multilevel Study of Collective Efficacy. *Science*, 277: 918–24.

Sampson, R.J. et al. (1999) Beyond Social Capital: Spatial Dynamics of Collective Efficacy for Children. *American Sociological Review*, 64: 633–60.

Sanderson, D. (2006) 'Yobs' Clash Lands Woman in Jail. *Times*, 1 May: 15.

Savage, M. et al. (2005) *Globalization and Belonging*. London: Sage.

Schnabel, P. (2004) Het zestiende Sociaal en Cultureel Rapport kijkt zestien jaar vooruit. In Schnabel, P. and Bronneman, R. (Eds.) *In het zicht van de toekomst, sociaal en cultureel rapport 2004.* Den Haag: SCP.

Seaman, P. et al. (2005) *Parenting and Children's Resilience in Disadvantaged Communities.* London: NCB.

Sennett, R. (1978) *The Fall of Public Man: On the Social Psychology of Capitalism.* New York: Vintage.

Sennett, R. (1994) *Flesh and Stone: The Body and the City in Western Civilization.* New York: Norton.

Sennett, R. (2003) *Respect: The Formation of Character in A World of Inequality.* London: Penguin.

SEU (2004) *Tackling Social Exclusion: Taking Stock and Looking to the Future.* London: SEU/ODPM.

Shafer, K.M. et al. (2006) *The Impact of Neighbor Interaction: Examining the Role of Social Trust, Pro-Social Behavior and Networks on Perceived Disorder.* Paper to Annual Meeting of the American Sociological Association, August 2006.

Shapland, J. and Vagg, J. (1998) *Policing by the Public.* London: Routledge.

Shaw, C. and Mckay, H. (1931) *Social Factors in Juvenile Delinquency.* Washington DC: Government Printing Office.

Simmons, M. (1997) *Landscapes of Poverty: Aspects of Rural England in the Late 1990s.* London: Lemos and Crane.

Skelton, T. (2000) 'Nothing to Do, Nowhere to Go?' Teenage Girls and 'Public' Space in the Rhondda Valleys, South Wales. In Holloway, S.L. and Valentine, G. (Eds.) *Children's Geographies: Playing, Living, Learning.* London: Routledge.

Skjaeveland, O. and Garling, T. (1997) Effects of Interactional Space on Neighbouring. *Journal of Environmental Psychology,* 17: 181–98.

Skogan, W. (1990) *Disorder and Decline: Crime and the Spiral of Decay in American Neighborhoods.* New York: Free Press.

Smith, M. (2001) *Transnational Urbanism: Locating Globalization.* Oxford: Blackwell.

Snel, K. and Van der Zaag, J. (2006) *Hoe hoort het eigenlijk . . . in Nederland?* Haarlem: Becht.

Sousa, L. and Eusebio, C. (2005) When Multi-Problem Poor Individuals' Values Meet Practitioners' Values! *Journal of Community and Applied Social Psychology,* 15: 5, 353–67.

Suttles, G. (1972) *The Social Construction of Communities.* London: University of Chicago Press.

Swift, R. (2005) State of Fear: The Global Attack on Rights. *New Internationalist,* March.

Taylor, M. (2002) Community and Social Exclusion. In Nash, V. (Ed.) *Reclaiming Community.* London: IPPR.

Taylor, R.B. (1996) Neighborhood Responses to Disorder and Local Attachments: The Systemic Model of Attachment, Social Disorganization, and Neighborhood Use Value. *Sociological Forum,* 11: 1, 41–74.

Taylor, R.B. (1999) *Crime, Grime, Fear and Decline: A Longitudinal Look.* Washington DC: National Institute of Justice, http://www.ncjrs.gov/pdffiles1/177603.pdf. (Accessed 13 June 2006)

Temkin, K. and Rohe, W. (1998) Social Capital and Neighborhood Stability: An Empirical Investigation. *Housing Policy Debate,* 9: 1, 61–88.

Thomas, W.I. and Znaniecki, F.W. (1918) *The Polish Peasant in Europe and America.* Boston: Gorham.

Town, S. and O'Toole, R. (2004) How 'New Urbanist' Planners Sacrifice Safety in the Name of 'Openness' and 'Accessibility'. Operation Scorpion. http://www.operationscorpion.org.uk/design_out_crime/crime_urbanism.htm. (Accessed 6 June 2006)

Tranter, P.J. and Doyle, J.W. (1996) Reclaiming the Residential Street as Play Space. *International Play Journal,* 4, 81–97.

Treasury (2005) *Support for Parents: the Best Start for Children*. London: HM Treasury; DfES.

Truss, L. (2005) *Talk to the Hand: The Utter Bloody Rudeness of Everyday Life (Or Six Good Reasons to Stay at Home and Bolt the Door)*. London: Profile.

Tucker, F. and Matthews, H. (2001) 'They Don't Like Girls Hanging Around There': Conflicts Over Recreational Space in Rural Northamptonshire. *Area*, 33: 2, 161–8.

Unger, D. and Wandersman, A. (1985) The Importance of Neighbors: The Social, Cognitive and Affective Components of Neighboring. *American Journal of Community Psychology*, 13: 2, 139–69.

Urry, J. (2003) Social Networks, Travel and Talk. *British Journal of Sociology*, 54: 155–75.

Van Alstyne, M. and Brynjolfsson, E. (1997) *Electronic Communities: Global Village or Cyberbalkans?* Cambridge Ma: Mit Sloan School, www.mit.edu/people/marshall/papers/cyberbalkans.pdf. (Accessed 6 June 2006)

Van den Brink, G. (2004) *Schets van een beschavingsoffensief: over normen, normaliteit en normalisatie in Nederland*. Amsterdam: Amsterdam University Press.

Waiton, S. (2001) *Scared of the Kids? Curfews, Crime and the Regulation of Young People*. Sheffield: Sheffield Hallam University Press.

Wallman, S. (1998) New Identities and the Local Factor: or When is Home in Town A Good Move? In Rapport, N. and Dawson, A. (Eds.) *Migrants of Identity: Perceptions of Home in a World of Movement*. Oxford: Berg.

Ward, M. (2006) How to Live in A Tower Block: An Insider's Guide to Tower Block Living. Unpublished Paper.

Warner, B. and Wilcox Rountree, P. (1997) Local Social Ties in a Community and Crime Model: Questioning the Systemic Nature of Informal Social Control. *Social Problems*, 44: 4, 520–36.

Watson, D. (1994) *Putting Back the Pride: Case Study of A Power-Sharing Approach to Tenant Participation*. Liverpool: Association of Community Technical Aid Centres.

Webster, B. (2006) Train Fares Double in Secret Deal by Ministers. The *Times*, 29 June, http://www.timesonline.co.uk/article/0,,2-2248275,00.html. (Accessed 29 June)

Webster, C. (2003) The Nature of the Neighbourhood. *Urban Studies*, 40: 13: 2591–612.

Wedlock, E. (2006) *Crime and Cohesive Communities*. London: Home Office, http://www.homeoffice.gov.uk/rds.

Wellman, B. (2001) Physical Place and Cyber Place: The Rise of Networked Individualism. *International Journal of Urban and Regional Research*, 25: 2, 227–52.

Wellman, B. and Frank, K. (2001) Network Capital in a Multi-Level World: Getting Support From Personal Communities. In Lin, N. et al. (Eds.) *Social Capital: Theory and Research*. Chicago: Aldine Degruyter.

Werkerle, G.R. and Whitzman, C. (1995) *Safe Cities: Guidelines for Planning, Design and Management*. New York: Van Nostrand Reinhold.

Wheway, R. and Milward, A. (1997) *Child's Play: Facilitating Play on Housing Estates*. London: Chartered Institute of Housing and Joseph Rowntree Foundation.

Wikstrom, P-O. and Dolmen, L. (2001) Urbanisation, Neighbourhood Social Integration, Informal Social Control, Minor Social Disorder, Victimisation and Fear of Crime. *International Review of Victimology*, 8: 121–40.

Wilcox, P. et al. (2004) Busy Places and Broken Windows: Toward Defining the Role of Physical Structure and Process in Community Crime Models. *Sociological Quarterly*, 45: 2, 185–207.

Williams, C. and Windebank, J. (2000) Rebuilding Social Capital in Deprived Urban Neighbourhoods. *Town and Country Planning*, (December): 351–3.

Wilson, J.Q. and Kelling, G.L. (1982) Broken Windows: the Police and Neighbourhood Safety. *Atlantic Monthly*, March: 29–38.

Wilson, W.J. (1987) *The Truly Disadvantaged*. Chicago: University of Chicago Press.

Winterman, D. (2006) Doing the Decent Thing. *BBC News Magazine*, 31 May. http://news.bbc.co.uk/1/low/magazine/5029260.stm. (Accessed 8 June 2006)

Wise, J. (1982) Gentle Deterrents to Vandalism. *Psychology Today*, 16, September: 31–38.

Wood, M. (2004) *Perceptions and Experiences of Antisocial Behaviour*. London: Home Office.

Wood, M. and Gwyther, G. (2002) The Poverty of Social Capital. Unpublished Paper, University of Western Sydney.

Wood, P. (2003) *Diversity: The Invention of a Concept*. San Francisco: Encounter.

Worpole, K. (2003) *No Particular Place to Go? Children, Young People and Public Space*. Birmingham: Groundwork UK.

Worrall, J. (2002) *Does 'Broken Window' Law Enforcement Reduce Serious Crime?* Sacramento, CA: California Institute for County Government. http://www.cicg.org/publications/cicg_brief_aug_2002.pdf

WRR (2003) *Waarden, Normen En De Last Van Het Gedrag*. Amsterdam: Amsterdam University Press.

Young, M. and Lemos, G. (1997) *The Communities we Have Lost and Can Regain*. London: Lemos and Crane.

Young, M. and Willmott, P. (1957) *Family and Kinship in East London*. London: Routledge.

Zimbardo, P.G. (1973) A Field Experiment in Auto-Shaping. In Ward, C. (Ed.) *Vandalism*, London: Architectural Press.

Index